reading Roddy Doyle

Sanford Sternlicht, *Series Editor*

Roddy Doyle

Photograph by Amelia Stein

reading Roddy Doyle

CARAMINE WHITE

 Syracuse University Press

First Edition 2001
01   02   03   04   05   06   6   5   4   3   2   1

The paper used in this publication meets the minimum requirements of American National Standard for Information Sciences—Permanence of Paper for Printed Library Materials, ANSI Z39.48–1984.∞™

Library of Congress Cataloging-in-Publication Data
White, Caramine.
    Reading Roddy Doyle / Caramine White.—1st ed.
      p. cm.—(Irish studies)
  Includes an interview with Roddy Doyle.
  Includes bibliographical references and index.
  ISBN 0-8156-2887-0 (alk. paper)—ISBN 0-8156-0686-9 (pbk. : alk. paper)
    1. Doyle, Roddy, 1958—Criticism and interpretation. 2. Doyle, Roddy,
1958—Interviews. 3. Ireland—In literature. 4. Dublin (Ireland)—In literature. I. Title. II. Irish studies (Syracuse, N.Y.)
PR6054.O95 Z93 2001
823'.914—dc21   00-046206

Manufactured in the United States of America

To Chuck

I loving vous

CARAMINE WHITE received her bachelor's degree in Latin and psychology from Duke University in 1988. After serving for several years in the United States Navy, she completed her master's degree in English at Old Dominion University. She received the Hayes-Taylor Fellowship from the University of North Carolina at Greensboro, which enabled her to pursue her doctorate in English. She completed her doctorate in 1996 and is currently teaching at Guilford Technical Community College in Greensboro.

Contents

Acknowledgments   ix

Chronology   xi

1. Introduction   1

2. Biography   25

3. *The Commitments*   42

4. *The Snapper*   62

5. *The Van*   83

6. *Paddy Clarke Ha Ha Ha*   98

7. *The Woman Who Walked into Doors*   116

8. Conclusion   142

Appendix A: An Interview with Roddy Doyle   149

Appendix B: *A Star Called Henry*   184

References   187

Index   191

Acknowledgments

I owe a great debt to many people who helped and encouraged me throughout this project. My sincerest gratitude goes to Dr. Keith Cushman, whose tireless editing and advice improved this work tremendously. I also must thank Roddy Doyle for being so accessible, helpful, and generous. Caroline White and John Sutton, both of whom work with Mr. Doyle, also were instrumental by providing research material and information. Hugh and Ann Morgan, Dena and Michael Flood, John and Carla Morgan, and Jerry and Tom Richardson made me fall in love with the Irish people by showing me true hospitality. My mother, Caramine Holcomb, provided constant love and encouragement, even though she had to listen to my incessant groans of despair. The wisdom of Drs. Lucy and Frederick Herman, who initially convinced me to pursue a doctoral degree, always put my concerns in perspective. Debbie Nahser's never-failing support throughout every stage of this undertaking was invaluable. Rev. Paul Teich was always available with his intercessory prayers and spiritual guidance. Tim Dineen and Kevin Smokler helped me unlock the mysteries of the library. Finally, but most important, I thank my husband, the always honorable Chuck White, without whose support I would never have been able to finish (or even start) this project.

Chronology

8 May 1958	Doyle born in Kilbarrack, a suburb of Dublin.
1971–76	Attends St. Fintan's Christian Brothers School in Sutton, a suburb of Dublin.
1976–79	Attends University College, Dublin; earns a B.A. in geography and English.
1979–80	Attends University College, Dublin; earns an Honor Diploma in Education.
1980	Begins teaching English and geography at Greendale Community School in Kilbarrack.
1981–85	Works on *Your Granny Is a Hunger Striker*.
January-June 1986	Writes *The Commitments*.
June 1986	Starts *Brownbread*. With John Sutton, founds King Farouk Publishing to publish *The Commitments*.
November 1986	Starts *The Snapper*. Supports and volunteers for divorce referendum, which fails.
Late March 1987	*The Commitments* published by King Farouk.
16 September 1987	*Brownbread*, produced by The Passion Machine and directed by Paul Mercier, premieres at SFX Theatre in Dublin.

18 November 1987	*Brownbread* moves to the larger Olympia Theatre. Doyle meets Belinda Moller while doing advertising for *The Commitments*.
1988	*The Commitments* published in England by William Heinemann Ltd.
1989	*War* published in Great Britain by The Passion Machine Ltd.
July 1989	*The Commitments* published in the U.S. by Vintage Contemporaries.
7 September 1989	*War*, produced by The Passion Machine and directed by Paul Mercier, premieres at SFX Theatre in Dublin.
October 1989	*War* transferred to the larger Olympia Theatre.
November 1989	Doyle starts writing *The Van*. Marries Belinda Moller.
1990	Follows editor Dan Franklin from Heinemann to Secker & Warburg Ltd. *The Snapper* published in Great Britain by Secker & Warburg.
1991	*The Van* published in Great Britain by Secker & Warburg; short-listed for Booker Prize.
February 1991	Doyle's first son, Rory, born.
21 July 1991	Film of *The Commitments*, released by 20th Century Fox, premieres at Cannes Film Festival.
1992	*The Snapper* published by Penguin and *The Van* published by Viking Penguin in the U.S. *Brownbread and War* and *The Barrytown Trilogy* published in Great Britain by Secker & Warburg. Doyle's son Jack born.
May 1993	Film of *The Snapper*, released by Miramax, premieres at Cannes Film Festival; airs on BBC. *Paddy Clarke Ha Ha Ha* published in Great Britain by Secker & Warburg.
4 June 1993	Doyle retires from teaching.

August 1993	General release of *The Snapper* film.
22 October 1993	Doyle wins Booker Prize for *Paddy Clarke Ha Ha Ha*.
1993	*The Van* published in the U.S. by Penguin.
1994	*Brownbread and War* published in the U.S. by Penguin.
January 1994	*Paddy Clarke* published in the U.S. by Viking Penguin.
May 1994	*The Family* airs on BBC.
1995	*The Barrytown Trilogy* published by Viking Penguin in the U.S.
November 1995	Doyle becomes deeply involved in divorce referendum, which passes by a narrow margin.
1996	Follows publisher Dan Franklin to Jonathan Cape Publishers. Film of *The Van*, produced by Doyle's own Deadly Films, released by Fox Searchlight.
April 1996	*The Woman Who Walked into Doors* published in the United Kingdom by Jonathan Cape.
May 1996	*The Woman Who Walked into Doors* released in the U.S. by Viking Penguin.
Summer 1998	Doyle's daughter Kate born.
August 1999	*A Star Called Henry* released by Viking Penguin.

reading Roddy Doyle

CHAPTER ONE

Introduction

Roddy Doyle is one of the brightest stars on the Irish literary scene today. His first six novels have all been well received, both critically and popularly. The literati have praised him: in his most signal accomplishment, Doyle won Britain's prestigious Booker Prize in 1993 for his fourth book, *Paddy Clarke Ha Ha Ha*—after *The Van*, his third novel, was short-listed for the prize in 1991. More generally, although he has on occasion been "condescended to as merely entertaining, just popular and funny" (Shepherd 1994, 164), the reviews of his work have been consistently good. He has been called "the laureate to a generation of thirty-somethings now ready to reconsider that experience [of growing up in Irish housing projects in the 1960s]. . . . Doubtless, *Paddy Clarke* will soon be included on school syllabuses, as Salinger and Twain before it" (Kiberd 1994, 24). And Doyle keeps getting better: "Each novel bears distinct resemblance to but is arguably better than its predecessor" (Shepherd 1994, 163).

Doyle is also a commercial success. His first two novels have been turned into popular movies, and a film version of the third was completed in 1996. *Paddy Clarke* has become the biggest seller of all the Booker Prize winners and has been translated into at least nineteen languages. Although his next two novels, *The Woman Who Walked into Doors* and *A Star Called Henry*, have not won any awards thus far, they have been well received critically and have sold enormously well. His most recent four novels have also been made into books-on-tape. In acknowledgment of his popularity, in 1993 the BBC gave Doyle carte blanche to write something for television; he created *The Family*, a four-part miniseries about a family in turmoil, which was widely viewed and discussed by its Irish audience. Moreover, the author does not stand aloof: Doyle's earringed and bespectacled visage is seen on numerous Irish magazine covers, and he periodically makes the international talk show circuit. Stephen Frears, the director of the movie versions of *The Snapper* and *The Van*, says of Doyle, "He's the only Irish writer I know of who's actually read by the kids he writes about in Dublin. You don't see them walking around with *Ulysses*" (Christon 1994, 5). In addition to his novels, Doyle has also written two plays: *Brownbread*, written and produced in 1987, a farcical comedy about three unemployed working-class youths who kidnap a bishop; and *War* (1989), a disturbingly dark comedy that counterpoints scenes in a pub (in which characters fiercely compete against each other in quizzes) and scenes of unhappy family life at the protagonist's home (see Doyle 1992). Both enjoyed local success and gave Doyle the reputation of being the most commercially successful playwright in Dublin since Sean O'Casey. Considering his popularity today, it seems almost absurd that he initially had to publish *The Commitments*, his first novel, at his own expense.

One key to the popularity of Doyle's novels can be found in their accessibility. He wants his work to be entertaining and readable: "Firstly, from my point of view, it's very important that they [his novels] be entertaining. We can talk then about what we mean by entertaining. I don't mean that it has to be escapist, though there's nothing wrong with escapism. A set of essays . . . is going to be entertaining, but not in the same way as *The Snapper*, but both have to be entertaining or no one will read them" (Fay 1993, 6).* Doyle himself reads widely: "I don't see why I can't read Salman Rushdie's new work and Elmore Leonard's new work. I don't see any real difference, except that one's more self-consciously literary than the other. They're both good literature. . . . So I've never liked the division between the high and the low, between the literary and the popular." Doyle's own books are lively, realistic, engaging, and hilarious, featuring characters with

---

* Quotations from published interviews with Doyle are cited under the name of the interviewer. Any unattributed quotations from Doyle are drawn from the author's 1996 interview with him at his publisher's office in Dublin, a transcript of which is included as Appendix A of this volume.

whom one can sympathize. Instead of the "thematic lumber which bolsters your average Booker winner" (Shone 1993, 48), Doyle provides for us simple, immediate themes couched in simple, immediate forms. He purposely avoids the multisyllabic vocabulary that appears in many canonized texts: "There's a school of writing which, though it may be unfair to summarize this way, has a lot to do with writers showing us how big their brains are. Like Anthony Burgess, who wants to show us that he has the biggest vocabulary in the world. . . . The type of writing I prefer is simple, straightforward and serves the characters. I like writers like Elmore Leonard, Anne Tyler, Raymond Carver and Richard Ford, where you tend to forget you're reading" (Christon 1994, F9). Doyle succeeds in achieving an unobtrusive literary style by using common, everyday language, which includes a great deal of profanity and slang, little description of any sort, and almost no authorial commentary—as he puts it, a "reflection of working-class life" (Fay 1993, 6).

Because Doyle's work is so popular and accessible, the inevitable debate over his value as a serious writer rages: "Why were the literary establishment so divided over Doyle? Elevated by some commentators as a social guru of enormous significance, other critics have objected to the unrelenting bad language which dominated the first three novels. Some questioned the authenticity of the life he described" (Battersby 1993, 10). Doyle has been accused "of playing up a professional Irishness for England and holding the Irish up to ridicule" (Bradshaw 1994, 129); according to one critic, "he simply serves up the foibles and patois of the working-classes for the patronising approval of the literary types" (Nolan 1991,). Moreover, Doyle's craft has been disputed: "There's an over-reliance on incessant wise-cracking, funny incidents, and teed-up punchlines" (McFarlane 1991). Predictably, many people object to his profanity and refuse to read his work because of the frequent use of vulgar language: "[E]arthiness is a great tool to flush prudes, but too many sexual and scatological references can send the situation down into wearisome schoolboy vulgarity and a tool becomes a crutch" (ibid.). Doyle says he has been criticized for "the bad language in my books—that I've given a bad image of the country" (Turbide 1993, 50). His lack of descriptive writing has also received criticism: "No significant effort is expended on physical description of character or locale. . . . There were unkind thoughts that this department was being left to some cinematographer fellow in California with dark specs and a ponytail" (McFarlane 1991).

Stephen Frears counters: "Roddy's a deceptive writer. On the surface the work seems simple, but it's really very sophisticated, and very funny. He creates an entire world" (Christon 1994, F9). Doyle himself commented in 1996 that his works

> were on the list for books to be taught in schools, but they're off the list now because the Minister of Education decided they weren't literary. It's utter drivel . . . the idea that they are less literary because they use the vernacular—I don't agree. The decision to use the vernacular is a literary decision. The decision to use the word "fuck" is a literary decision. It's a decision of rhythm . . . to use images from television instead of books, to use advertising jingles and such—it's a literary decision.

In this book, part of my aim will be to demonstrate that Doyle is indeed a serious artist. His novels are not simply entertaining, as a Brendan O'Carroll book is; although Doyle might cringe at my saying so, his works have literary merit and worth.

Doyle's first three novels—the Barrytown trilogy—are concerned with one family, the Rabbittes, who live in a fictional present-day working-class Dublin suburb, Barrytown. Each novel focuses on a different family member. *The Commitments* spotlights Jimmy Rabbitte Jr. and chronicles the rise and fall of the band he manages; very little mention is made of other family members. In *The Snapper,* we read about the unplanned pregnancy of Jimmy's sister Sharon, as the result of an acquaintance rape. The Rabbitte family, especially the father, Jimmy Sr., figures much more prominently in this novel, as we witness the chaotic but loving family dynamics. The last book in the trilogy, *The Van,* centers on Jimmy Sr., who has lost his job and with it a lot of his joie de vivre. After months of unemployment, Jimmy and his best friend Bimbo purchase a chipper van (a van equipped with grills and deep-fryers for cooking hamburgers, fried fish, sausages, and french-fried potatoes); the tensions resulting from—oddly enough—the success of the business severely test their relationship, and we see how fragile even the most secure friendships can be.

Each novel has a simple plot within a tangible, event-based frame: "Each narrative is propelled by the creation of something new—a soul band, a baby and a chip van respectively—which for a short time alters everyone's life. Along the way something always happens which acts as a test of people's true feelings; usually a threat of break-down, of resentment swelling to the bursting point" (O'Hagan 1993, 17). *The Commitments* opens with the inception of the band and closes with its demise; *The Snapper* begins soon after the discovery of the pregnancy, flashes back to the actual conception, and ends with the delivery of a healthy baby girl. To be sure, *The Van* is a little different: Jimmy Sr. has been unemployed for some time at the novel's beginning, and about a hundred pages pass before the partnership between Jimmy and Bimbo is formed; the novel starts to move forward only when the chipper van business begins. The novel culminates with the end of the partnership—and perhaps of the friendship. Within the general framework, each novel traces the rise and fall of various events in the protagonists' lives; indeed, *The Snapper* traces the actual rise and fall of Sharon's stomach. Although tangential events occur in the novels—Jimmy Sr.'s epiphany when he realizes the pain that his childlike behavior has inflicted upon his family in *The Snapper*, or Darren and Jimmy Jr.'s various female entanglements in *The Van*—these serve not as subplots but as added texture to the main story line. In general, the Barrytown trilogy, while not merely comic novels (they are in fact more complex than a first reading may lead one to believe), are not as serious as Doyle's later works. Each story contains some situations that are improbable, if not inappropriately farcical; the characters are not as fully developed as his later characters; and the novels, especially the first two, simplify reality by providing easy comic resolutions to difficult problems.

Doyle's fourth novel, *Paddy Clarke Ha Ha Ha*, although set in Barrytown, is a departure from the Barrytown trilogy and its Rabbittes—"There are no more Rabbittes," said Doyle. "I've eaten them" (Christon 1994, F9). *Paddy Clarke* is set in 1968 and is narrated by a ten-year-old boy—Doyle's own age in 1968. The novel is told from Paddy's perspective; the narrative importance of each other character is determined by their importance to Paddy. For example, we see a great deal of Paddy's mother, whom he adores, but very little of his younger sisters, as boys of his age and temperament do not usually spend much time with baby sisters. Perhaps unwittingly reflecting Doyle's success in conveying a young child's world, critics have faulted the novel for having no structure, or for having its only structure "tacked on" two-thirds of the way through:

> About halfway through the novel I began to yearn not so much for structure as for movement. I felt that Mr. Doyle had gone a vignette too far and that the book was in danger of stasis. I missed the sense of narrative machinery pushing toward a denouement. Moreover, if a non-narrative novel was his objective, what, then is the purpose of the marriage breakup? It is as though he too suddenly regretted the absence of story and decide he'd better supply one fast. (Flanagan 1994, 21)

However, the novel does have a genuine framework: it chronicles the dissolution of a marriage through the eyes of a young boy. We are introduced to Paddy somewhere in his tenth year, and we learn about his friends, his school, his games, his family. His family situation becomes more prominent as his parents begin to fight bitterly, and his parents' separation ends the book. In fact, the novel begins with the commencement of the parents' unhappiness; we do not perceive this unhappiness until later in the novel simply because Paddy himself does not see it until then. The familiar event-based frame is in place, except that instead of a rise and fall, the book shows a gradual fall: *Paddy Clarke* has no "pivotal moment" (O'Hagan 1993, 17) in the manner of the trilogy novels.

Doyle's fifth novel, *The Woman Who Walked Into Doors*, again uses a first-person narrator. This novel is not set specifically in Barrytown but in an anonymous urban location that might be part of almost any European city; the television miniseries *The Family*, which was written before the novel and out of which the novel grew, was set in the Dublin suburb Ballymun. Paula Spencer, an alcoholic mother of four, had been beaten severely by her monstrous husband Charlo for eighteen years before she mustered the courage to kick him out; the novel constitutes her explanation of her life with

Charlo, who is killed during a robbery attempt shortly after their separation. Combining Paula's memories with details of her present, the novel's
structure is not linear (as are Doyle's previous books) but spiral, with Paula
repeatedly returning to several key memories in an attempt to discern
where her life took its awful turn; as Doyle recalls, "I was aware, in the editing stages, of various books—*Black Water*, by Joyce Carol Oates, for example. It's a very short book, but it keeps going back to one episode. One
episode is the book. I wanted to do that as well. I wanted Paula to go back
to the first time she was hit, and I go back to that four or five times." In the
novel, Paula repeatedly thinks about the first time that she was hit and
about the circumstances leading up to Charlo's death.

In *A Star Called Henry*, published in 1999, Doyle again uses a first-person
narrator but sets the character, Henry, in Ireland's bloody past. The novel
opens in the early 1900s and follows the rise and fall of Henry's career as an
Irish revolutionary. As the novel ends with a twenty-year-old Henry saying,
"I'd start again" (Doyle 1999, 342), we can hope for further installments.
(*Henry* appeared during the preparation of my book, so any discussion of
the novel will be incomplete and is therefore best avoided. A brief overview
of the novel is included in an appendix.)

Although all of Doyle's novels are distinct and could never be connected as mere sequels, they do share common elements. His characters'
speech is one of the most often noted aspects of his works. Doyle has been
able to "prevent Yeats, Joyce, or Beckett from taking over [his] mind and
drowning out [his] voice" (Donoghue 1994, 3) because he does not see
himself as part of any great Irish literary tradition. Although he admires
Flann O'Brien, his favorite novelists—Anne Tyler, John Irving, E. L. Doctorow, Elmore Leonard, and George V. Higgins—are American. He claims
that Joyce has had no conscious influence on him whatsoever: "Well, I've
read [Joyce], so who's to say whether it's not in the back of your mind. But
if the influence is there, it's working subconsciously. . . . So certainly I was
aware of some influences, but I was unaware of Joyce."

Despite his claims to the contrary, Doyle's fascination with language
hearkens back to a long Irish "oral tradition of songs, laments, lays and bal-
lads" (Deane 1994, 17). Under British rule, especially harsh under
Cromwell, Gaelic civilization was reduced to "an immiserated peasant cul-

ture"; by the late eighteenth century, the Irish language had "receded to an unprecedented degree" as English became the official language of Ireland (21). In order to survive politically, the Irish had to deny their original tongue and to speak English. The language someone spoke, aside from what he or she actually said, became a political statement. Forced to communicate in a foreign language, the Irish learned to manipulate English to make it more palatable. As the number of people writing Irish fell, the Gaelic oral tradition remained alive through the efforts of storytellers and poets. (Brian Friel's *Translations* addresses this English subjugation of Gaelic language.) The spoken language became the conveyor of Gaelic culture. Doyle, with his obvious delight in the sounds of languages, reminds us of "this formidable tradition of truthtelling . . . brought to perfection in Ireland" (Lane 1994, 92).

Doyle's exceptional ability to transcribe exactly the idiomatic language of the working-class Dubliner has brought him considerable attention:

> Eliot once pointed out that 'an artisan who can talk English beautifully while about his work or in a public bar, may compose a letter painfully written in a dead language bearing some resemblance to a newspaper leader.' The language of most contemporary fiction is, by these standards, close to death, so we might as well rejoice when we meet the living thing. Roddy Doyle is that rare species: the artisan who comes home from the public house and makes art from what he heard there. (Lane 1994, 94)

Doyle himself says that by transcribing actual speech patterns, both those of his students and those of frequenters of the local pubs, he can give the reader a better sense of his characters:

> I've always wanted to bring the books down closer and closer to the characters—to get myself, the narrator, out of it as much as I can. And one of the ways to do this is to use the language that the characters actually speak, to use the vernacular, and not ignoring the grammar, the formality of it, to bend it, to twist it, so you get a sense that you are hearing it, not reading it. That you are listening to the characters. You get in really close to the characters. I think it's a stronger achievement, in the context of my books . . . because it gets you smack in the middle of it.

To be sure, his use both of profanity—so omnipresent in his works as to be called "a metalanguage" (Fitzgerald 1991, 16)—and of current slang has been faulted as being too obscure for the average non-Irish reader: "There are problems of local reference. . . . [O]pacity on the page is harder to cope with" (Donoghue 1994, 6). Doyle does not compromise the integrity of his work by heeding these criticisms: "If I start thinking about people, then there's a small line between people and market and you start thinking, 'Well, will they understand this snatch of dialogue in Wyoming?' " Like Synge with his Aran Islanders or O'Casey with his slum-dwelling Dubliners, Doyle has the gift of transcribing precisely (and enjoyably) a vernacular dialect. He gives literary voice to Barrytown.

Especially in Doyle's first three novels, understanding the characters' speech is crucial because there is so little description or authorial commentary. The novels at times read like screenplays, and in fact, huge chunks were lifted from the novels for the films. Doyle dislikes overly descriptive writing:

> I deliberately didn't want descriptions, because I think they interfere. Around the time when I wrote *The Commitments*, I read *The Sicilian* by Mario Puzo. The story was interrupted so often with unnecessary descriptions of the mountains the Sicilians were climbing over to escape the police, and ridiculous descriptions of physical characteristics. People with "generous lips" and things like that. All I could think that meant was that he had some kind of speech impediment and he sprayed people. I deliberately just let the words do the talking and it didn't seem necessary to describe places. (Eaton 1990, 1)

Similarly, Doyle also excludes authorial commentary from his work: "I love reading Charles Dickens—but if someone had pared him down and taken away the 'Now gentle reader' and all that and just left the story, I think it would be much more effective" (Heller 1993, 4). Doyle wants vivid characters and allows the characters to speak for themselves. The dialogue that emerges when the characters open their mouths is indicated not by quotation marks but by dashes (which annoyed critic Noel McFarlane so much that he nicknamed the author "Dasher Doyle"), and speakers change so often that voices seem to rush out from the page. Surprisingly, little confusion arises as to the identity of the speaker, and the dialogue is easy to follow.

Doyle's next two novels, written in the first person, do not contain as much dialogue but still avoid authorial presence. Paula and Paddy are telling us their stories, and while these novels do contain more descriptive writing, the language and perspective are those of the main character, either a ten-year-old boy or a thirty-nine-year-old uneducated woman. There are no "generous lips" in Doyle's work, regardless of the narrator.

Like the character's speech, the place in which they live is drawn from life. Although fictionalized (and with a name inspired by a Steely Dan song), Barrytown—the Dublin suburb that is the setting for the first four novels—is based on Doyle's native Kilbarrack: "It's not my life, but it's my geography" (Turbide 1993, 50).

Although there is little actual physical description of the suburb in his novels, Barrytown has a definite sense of place and community. According to Eudora Welty, place is central to the evocation of character: "Paradoxically, the more narrowly we examine a fictional character, the greater he is likely to loom up. We must first see him set to scale in his proper world to know his size. Place has most control over character: by confining character, it defines it" (1957, 11). Doyle, however, reverses Welty by defining place through character: The people *are* the place; they do not just live there. The community is comprised of individuals relating to other individuals, reacting to one another, speaking to one another: "Speech is the expression of individuality, not in isolation but in communication" (O'Toole 1991). Barrytown's inhabitants are so vibrant and alive that Barrytown itself looms up in our minds and becomes a character.

Toni Morrison, discussing the differing significance of place in black and white American writers, describes the "urban village" as a city neighborhood that "offered a nexus of community values and social purposes." She observes that historically, white writers have viewed a character's alienation from his city and subsequent retreat to the country as a heroic undertaking. Black authors (and characters), however, have not claimed cities as their own, because cities were the venue of whites; nor have they thought of the country, the place of slave labor and lynching, as a retreat. Therefore, the local community—the urban village—has been most important for these writers; alienation from the urban village, while a triumph for the white hero, may be an "outrage" for blacks (O'Toole 1991). Barrytown can be considered such an urban village; it is "more like a neighbourhood urban community such as Harlem than an Irish country village or a classical city like Joyce's or O'Casey's Dublin" (ibid.). Victory comes to its residents when they assimilate themselves into the culture of and affirm the values of their neighborhood. For instance, Sharon is not ostracized merely for being pregnant—a number of other Barrytown girls have been in the same situation, and the community has grown to accept unwed motherhood. Rather, she is ostracized because the father of the unborn child is not a young boyfriend but an older married man, a state of affairs that is not acceptable in Barrytown. Sharon's worst moments in the novel come when she has been spiritually cast out of the community's bosom. Similarly, Paddy's worst moments come when he is ostracized and given the silent treatment by his classmates because his parents have separated, another state of affairs not deemed acceptable at that time (and itself a form of severed community). Jimmy Sr. hates being out of work partly because his loss of income prevents him from spending time with his friends in the pub, the place from which he is able to derive his sense of belonging. Barrytowners need a sense of community to be successful characters.

Although Barrytown may be based on a real suburb, Barrytowners are not based on real individuals. Doyle says he has "never based a character on someone I know. . . . I would never do that. . . . I've never really needed to. . . . [I]t's not a particularly bright thing to do—to invade other's privacy, no matter how interesting that privacy is." Perhaps paradoxically, however, at the same time as he asserts that his characters are entirely fictional, Doyle views his job as simply "to describe things and people as they really are" (Turbide 1993, 50). "I just write the things. . . . [T]hey are based on reality. . . . [I]t's real life; granted it's speeded up and larger than life. . . . I'm looking at a part of Ireland, a part of Dublin, at an odd angle. I'm showing the part that's not in the Bord Failte catalogue" (Battersby 1993, 10).

Because Doyle is "depicting a reality," he does not judge his characters: "I'm not a priest or a moralist." Instead, confident of humanity's basic goodness, he allows them to judge themselves and each other and to behave according to their own consciences. Doyle treats his characters with respect. Although he is removed from them, his "forgiveness of just about everything and everyone" is the overwhelming characteristic of his relationship with his creations. In this, he is similar to Chekhov, "the good doctor who bore his characters' ridiculous affectations and self-dramatized torments with grace and bemusement, because he knew that everyone's body eventually breaks down in pain and dies, and that the enemy of life isn't death, it's futility" (Christon 1994, F9).

The Barrytowners' lives include much behavior that an author easily could judge. The characters do, after all, watch too much television, get intoxicated frequently, chatter about inane topics, have little soulful interaction, and have drunken sex. They live entirely in their own insular present, with no sense of Ireland's tormented history: there is no mention of English rule, no mention of the 1916 Easter Uprising, no mention of Catholic oppression; similarly, there is no mention of the present "troubles" in Northern Ireland, no mention of the Irish Republican Army (IRA), no mention of the numerous scandals involving the Catholic Church. Rather, the Barrytowners' sole concern is Barrytown:

> Reality is never presented as a private experience, something to be mulled over or worried about; it is always a social situation to be negotiated at the top of one's voice. Matters of concern to the rest of Ireland—the IRA, the Ulster Volunteer Force, murders in the North, Ireland's dealings with the European Community, financial scandals in high places—are of little interest to Barrytown. The world beyond Jimmy Rabbitte's house at 118 Chestnut Avenue, Dublin 21, has mainly televisual presence: life exists to end up on TV. . . . Modern Ireland, its history and political life, is also a matter of indifference in Barrytown.

Doyle's characters are concerned only with what is going on in their immediate lives. These characters' "sole context is whatever is enforced by dialogue and a short communal memory. The present tense is the only one, and it is fulfilled by speech" (Donoghue 1994, 4). The characters are reacting to so many immediate stimuli that they do not have the time or inclination to ponder world problems.

Some critics, such as Noel McFarlane, find this insularity improbable: "I recall not one passing reference to politics of any sort throughout. This would be rare in a faithful depiction of working-class people and very rare for unemployed people: in fact, it's rare for Irish people generally. Is Roddy Doyle over-reacting by under-reacting to the usual stylistic crudities of preachy propaganda, carried out by hands as heavy as Limerick hams?" (McFarlane 1991). However, McFarlane's comments miss the point: In the novels under discussion (the first three, especially *The Van*), it is realistic that the characters Doyle has created would have very little interest in politics at the particular time in their lives during which we see them. Jimmy Jr. is young, out of work, interested in girls and in music; although he tries to increase his peers' awareness by introducing them to soul music, he would have very little interest in who gets elected to what locally. He simply does not have the time for issues that do not affect him directly; and when he does get involved, his ideas are much larger than local politics. Sharon is a woman who has just been raped and is pregnant for the first time; she obviously has other things to ponder than Irish history. Jimmy Sr.—contrary to McFarlane's assertion—does discuss current topics such as child abuse when we see him with his friends, but when he starts working in the van, he also has no time to chatter about the political situation. Many people do not care about situations which do not directly affect them—witness extreme voter apathy in America. The political situation in Ireland, even the "Troubles" in Belfast—which, as Doyle says, cause Dubliners to "close down psychologically. . . . Belfast becomes a place very far away"—do not directly affect the Rabbitte family or their friends.

Moreover, the fact that the characters do not discuss politics does not mean that Doyle's books are not political. Doyle himself states it clearly: "It's the difference between politics with a little 'p' or a big 'P.' But a book about a woman in a violent marriage is a political book. A book about two unemployed men is a political book. This *Family* series brought domestic violence to a forefront, to the top of the political agenda, with a small 'p,' for a few months." Thus, McFarlane—who would like Doyle to tone down his use of profanity because, although true to life, profanity is distracting and unpleasant—takes a narrow view in suggesting that the omission of tedious political discussion misrepresents reality. Rather, Doyle's books are political, but his characters are not politicians. Simply because we do not witness political debates does not mean the characters do not, or have not, or will not engage in them at some point.

Another conspicuous absence in this book is religion. In novels about the Irish, one would assume that there would be some mention of Mass, prayer, or the Virgin. In Doyle, however, there is no mention of any religious life at all—or should I say, no mention that is not profane: Jimmy Sr.'s favorite exclamation is "Jaysis!". Modernity has removed these Dubliners from absolute fidelity to binding social and religious tradition:

> [One of] the most striking features of Barrytown in the years denoted . . . is the decline in the influence of the Catholic Church on the working-class families. . . . In Doyle's novels set in recent years, priests do not appear. Few parishioners go to Mass. The founder of Christianity is frequently invoked, but only as a residual expletive, Jaysis. Paddy Clarke thinks the best story he ever heard was the one about Father Damian and the lepers on Molokai . . . but . . . it was only a game. . . . [T]here is no sense of sin in Barrytown. No one feels guilt or shame. Or even misgiving. (Donoghue 1994, 4)

The novels contain no scenes in which any of the Rabbittes go to church. All, even the one-year-old Gina, regularly blaspheme. Jimmy once says that he is so hungry he could eat a "leg o' the lamb of God." At the beginning of *The Snapper*, although the Rabbitte parents discuss telling the younger members of the family that what Sharon did was "wrong," they never do say anything moralistic to the children, nor do they call her actions sinful. Abortion is not an option for Sharon, but this seems to derive more from habit than from any religious conviction. To be sure, *Paddy Clarke* does include more references to religion, but in Paddy's eyes, religion is more an amusement than a source of salvation.

Perhaps religion is absent in Barrytown because its position in Ireland has declined. Although churchgoing is still higher in Ireland than in most

European countries, the rate is dropping, "and reports from some priests in working-class Dublin parishes estimate that only 10% of their parishioners go to Mass every Sunday. It is also important to note that amongst those who attend church regularly there is an increasing number who do not accept the Church's definition of sin" (Kearney 1988, 84–85). Significantly, the Catholic Church in Ireland has been involved in numerous scandals in recent years. In 1992, the highly influential bishop of Galway, Eamonn Casey, who had been found guilty of drunk driving, was discovered to have an American mistress and a grown son. He sneaked out of the country with $115,000 of church funds. (Doyle says of him, "I've thought Casey was a prick since I was about eight . . . and all these years later, I've been proven right" [Fay 1996, 18].) There have been numerous other disgraces, including a priest found dead in a gay sauna in Dublin, priests accused of sexual assault and pedophilia, and recently discovered atrocities perpetrated on children by the nuns at the Golden Bridge Orphanage. The Church has also lost ground on its primary issues, namely, abortion, homosexuality, contraception, and divorce: although abortion is still illegal in Ireland, four thousand women a year emigrate to England for that purpose; in 1993, laws were changed to legalize homosexuality; also in 1993, contraceptives, previously obtainable only with a doctor's prescription, could be sold from vending machines; and in 1996, a referendum narrowly passed to allow divorces. Of course, religion is still very prominent in Ireland as a whole—the Church controls most of the education, and masses are still crowded with "people young and old . . . locked in concentrated prayer" (Toibin 1995, 53); but in the lives of the young, uneducated, and unemployed—Doyle's characters—religion is practically nonexistent.

Doyle considers the absence of religion in his novels to be a depiction of reality. Because of the aforementioned scandals and the resulting cynicism (which he shares), people do not display the respect and awe for the Church that characterize Ireland's religious history:

> That's the way it is. . . . I wanted to get away from the clichéd view of Ireland. An English critic of *The Snapper* said, "Where was the priest? This is a pregnant girl." And I wanted to say, "Fuck you pal—what do you know? You live in London." Priests in working-class parts of Dublin are peripheral

figures—few people know who they are at all, and they're not particularly welcome when they knock on the door. It's a new picture of Ireland. . . . [R]eligion is still there, but it's more of a surface thing. On a Sunday, you'll still see crowds and crowds going to Mass, but it's not the deep devotion. . . . They'll be chatting in the back of the church. . . . So there's no religion, partly because of my imaginative lack, and also because that's the reality.

Although Doyle is an atheist who loudly decries the Church, Doyle's characters do not share his vehement dislike of organized religion. For them, religion is an inconvenience, a weak presence. These characters do not have the original thinking or the philosophical stamina to flout openly the teachings and practices that have been inculcated in their society for thousands of years; rather, they ignore, or conveniently forget, those religious teachings.

Although Doyle himself does not judge his novels' lack of religion, the dearth of in-depth political discussion, or the frequency of drunken toots, other readers do. Some consider this insensibility to outside events, this aimlessness of purpose, this habit of reacting instead of acting, as signs that Doyle's characters lead meaningless lives. Doyle, although slow to anger, gets upset when the significance of his characters' lives is questioned:

> What's meaningless about that? That's not meaningless. So why don't they talk about politics? Talking about politics is as about as meaningless as talking about sex or talking about football. . . . It's just conversation—it's filling gaps. So their lives are not meaningless but are filled with meaning. Their conversation is not deep—so what, . . . whose is? In a lot of conversations, it's what they don't say that is more interesting than what they do say. I don't think they lead meaningless lives at all. . . . [Sharon]'s going through a stage in her life. When I was that age . . . and was earning money, one of the things I'd buy with that money is alcohol, and not because I had the burning need for alcohol, but for the sheer pleasure of being with a group of friends and talking all night and getting pleasantly drunk. Getting drunk is incidental, but it was just the whole thing. I don't see any problem with young people getting drunk.

Doyle believes that living one's life meaningfully is different for everyone. People must make meaning in their lives with the tools they have available.

In contrast to the reduced role he accords politics and religion, for Doyle a sense of family or community is essential. He frequently mentions his own family in his interviews, and four of his six novels are dedicated to family members. His characters, all uneducated, nevertheless have some type of supportive family, which provides them with an order (often rather chaotic). In the trilogy novels, the collective family is the mainstay for each individual member: "Families may break up . . . but no other social institution in Barrytown has replaced the family. Not even the pub, the likeliest contender" (Donoghue 1994, 3). In *The Commitments*, even the band—although so important to Jimmy Jr. as the vehicle through which he attempts to achieve greatness—is nevertheless a false family; when it dissolves, Jimmy Jr. will be able to return to his real family, who will give him the basis from which to try something else, even to start another band. Sharon's pregnancy is, admittedly, initially made more difficult when Jimmy Sr. becomes resentful, but in the end it is her family that enables her to survive her ordeal; Sharon's situation could have become tragic without her family. In *The Van*, Jimmy Sr., forced to choose between going to the pub with his unemployment check or to his home, unhesitatingly chooses his home: "But there you were; he'd a family to feed and that" (Doyle 1991, 35). Jimmy Sr. is last seen in his wife Veronica's arms; he has lost his best friend, Bimbo, and his wife is all he has left—and she comforts him. Overall, "Despite the unemployment, poverty, alcohol abuse and limited social mobility that beleaguer them, [the Rabbittes] embody their own brand of family values" (Turbide 1993, 50).

Doyle's next two novels address the topic of family support differently than does the Barrytown trilogy, His later characters, while they have their family's support, must use this support to learn independence. The dissolution of Paddy's family causes his troubles—his world is destroyed when his family breaks up. After his father leaves home, Paddy loses his friends, his place at school, his spark. However, Paddy still has his mother and siblings and will still see his father, and we sense that he'll survive; Doyle himself says, "But I imagine, if I project forward, that Paddy will be all right" (Flanagan 1994, 21). In order to be "all right," however, Paddy must use what family support is available to learn to be independent enough to handle his strained family situation. In other words, the Clarke family must provide enough support to enable Paddy to endure the problems that the Clarke family has caused. In *The Woman Who Walked into Doors*, Paula Spencer's relationship with her family is even more ambivalent. Although her father's coldness contributes to her marriage to the charming but brutal Charlo, her love for her children and the support of her sisters help resurrect her. Unlike Sharon, Paula cannot collapse into the arms of a lovingly supportive family; she must use the strength derived from her maternal and sisterly feelings to eke out an independent existence. Again, she must use her family's backing to bear the nightmares it created.

One of the ways in which Doyle shows family supporting the individual is through humor. Indeed, despite the potential tragedy of his plots, a good deal of Doyle's work is uproarious comedy (this is especially true of the first two novels). His works can be hilarious, laugh-out-loud funny, and all of Doyle's successful characters have a keen sense of the incongruous. Moreover, Doyle is able to use humor and comedy in a way that does not dissolve his characters' lives into farce but rather makes their situations endurable without (in the words of one theorist of comedy) "rendering absurd any part of the complex opinion on which seriousness rests" (Olson 1968, 109). How does he accomplish this?

In understanding Doyle, it is important to keep in mind that comedy and humor are not interchangeable terms. Comedy is a literary form, "basically the action of a sympathetic figure meeting and overcoming every obstacle, thus becoming heroic" (Grawe 1983, 14), exploring and engaging the everyday occurrences that "are part of the audience's normal experience, rather than . . . cosmic higher values" (Bowen 1989, 28). "Comedy as seen from a formal perspective is the representation of life patterned to demonstrate or to assert a faith in human survival, often including or emphasizing how that survival is possible or under what conditions that survival takes place" (Grawe 1983, 17). Comedy is a representation not of an individual action or event but of life as a whole; comedy does not deal in facts but in faith. Comedies celebrate "the survival, endurance or immortality of human life or identity . . . of fertility, rebirth and eternal life." To be sure, this survival comes at the expense of one of humanity's most deeply held ideas, that of a stable and unambiguous sense of self: "The more carefully one defines one's identity, the more likely the definition is to turn into a cliché. The more protective one is toward the self, the more likely one is to pity oneself. Negligence about identity is likely to be much more liberating; the self is free to become whatever it will become." The comic sense of self is, if not an oxymoron, a fluid, ever-changing and adapting conception. If one's identity is never rigidly defined, one's identity cannot be shattered. The comic vision allows one to take what life offers and to incorporate it into one's daily existence. More broadly, the comic vision is "hostile to the univocal mind. It rejects the neat, mechanical, perfectly balanced orders generated by logic and embraces the organic, irregular orders" (Lewis 1989, 68, 124, 31).

Humor is different from comedy, and indeed there is no "unequivocal relationship between comedy as a literary form and funniness . . . even though in practice many if not most comedies are also—at least in part— funny" (Palmer 1994, 112). Humor arises from a perceived incongruity, a "pairing of ideas, images or events that are not ordinarily joined and do not seem to make sense together." Laughter, or at least a smile, is produced when the incongruity is resolved. Of course, not all incongruities produce laughter, and "the difference between suicide and a self-effacing joke, between tragedy and [humor], lies in how we deal with the incongruous"; humor is, obviously, "a playful, not a serious, response to the incongruous." Humor is therefore both powerful and risky, and humorists must make value judgments about what is appropriate material for their jokes. By deeming something "joke material" they are trying to mold our attitudes about a subject and make us join in the laughter. Humor is "a force in controlling our responses to unexpected and dangerous happenings, a way of shaping the responses and attitudes of others and a tool in intergroup and intragroup dynamics" (Lewis 1989, 8, 18, 11, 13).

The artist must have a particular way of seeing the world to use comedy and humor successfully:

[Y]ou find yourself looking at a very wide range of situations all of which are characterized by a painful discrepancy between deserts and consequences—that is, you are studying injustice and finding it everywhere. Now the question becomes how can you make or savor [humor] in a world like *this?* Every true comedian deals with that question; each works out his own answer. None pretends that injustice is either rare or evanescent; in one way or another all accept injustice as the price of life and are willing to try to pay the price. Paradoxical as it may seem, one effect of the comic vision is to keep its possessor deeply aware of the reality of injustice. You make or savor [humor] in a world like this precisely because it is a world like this. (Galligan 1994, 152)

It is easy to see how this philosophical outlook applies to Doyle's novels, as he uses both humor and the comic form to direct our responses to his work. Obviously, Doyle's novels are funny. His characters possess the enviable quality of being able to find the humor in anything, even situations in which the average person would weep. This laughter facilitates the audience's acceptance of the comedic form in the tragic circumstances of which Doyle writes. His characters' misfortunes, like many of our own *real* misfortunes, are products of injustice: Jimmy Sr. is laid off because he is old and because there are too many younger men who want to work; Sharon is raped; Paula is threatened with murder if she tries to leave Charlo. Although some extraordinary people could avoid these misfortunes, ordinary people, with their ordinary training, cannot—and these are Doyle's characters, born into situations where education is not expected, unemployment and living on the dole are the norm, getting drunk is the usual way to handle life's ups and downs, and a show of weakness is ridiculed. Doyle's Dublin contains child abuse, theft, drunkenness, adultery, all of which seem ever-present conditions of life. While the horrifyingly bleak backgrounds to his novels illustrate Doyle's realistically grim view of the world, his treatment of these calamities illustrates the unlimited possibilities he sees for human beings. The backgrounds to Doyle's novels are serious, but all contain some glimmer of hope. In *The Snapper,* he is able to turn a story of rape, betrayal, and anguish into a novel about family support, togetherness, and triumph. Even in *Paddy Clarke* and *The Van,* Doyle's two darkest novels, the family still remains supportive.

The implications of this comic perspective for Doyle's social vision can be seen by examining the trend his work has taken over the last ten years. As his novels progress, the themes remain consistent and social conditions remain bleak, yet Doyle's emphasis changes: although he never appears overwhelmed, the world, it seems, is getting more serious for Doyle. In the first two novels, the darkness is illuminated by the characters' love for each other and the potential for human interconnectedness, their optimism, their humor, their joie de vivre. In *The Commitments*, Jimmy Jr. is trying to save Dublin by showing the connection between working-class Dubliners and African Americans. Although the band is briefly successful, ultimately it fails, but Jimmy Jr., undaunted, is ready to try again with a different format. Sharon's baby is a bastard who will be raised in a raucous, overcrowded environment and may well wind up on the dole, but Sharon is laughing uncontrollably at the end of the novel, and she loves her baby fiercely. Although Sharon is not aware of the literary grandeur of this birth, the life force—symbolized by the healthy infant—has survived rape, violence, drunkenness, and hostility. Humanity will survive in spite of itself. Doyle's third and fourth novels, however, strike a different balance. In *The Van*, although Jimmy Sr. retains his wonderful sense of humor, his unemployment reduces him to a feeble, childlike old man; he struggles to keep his dignity, not very successfully. Although he has a temporary respite from his misery when he begins to work with Bimbo, by the end of the novel he is friendless and crying like a baby in the arms of his sleepy wife. In the story of an actual child, Paddy Clarke has been robbed of his childhood and has worries that are overwhelming to a ten-year-old; the novel ends not with the tableau of a mother laughing with and loving her newborn but with the cruel nursery rhyme with which the children taunt Paddy after his parents' separation; not even innocence is an adequate barrier to the world's wretchedness. Although Doyle himself is still convinced that Paddy will be "all right," the desolation of the background in *The Commitments* has been pushed to the forefront in *Paddy Clarke Ha Ha Ha*. Conversely, the wonderful humor and optimism that was omnipresent in the former novel is overshadowed in the latter.

Doyle's fifth novel, *The Woman Who Walked into Doors*, offers another variation of the hope/despair equation. Paula's history—the background of the novel, which, through the book's retrospective narrative technique, becomes the foreground—is horrible. At the outset we know that Paula has been sadistically abused for eighteen years. We quickly discover that she is also poor and alcoholic and has just been informed that her abusive husband, whom she still loves, was killed by the police. One of her sons has run away and is probably a drug addict. None of Doyle's other novels contains elements of such "evil" (Doyle 1996, 216); none of Doyle's other characters has so much to overcome. The earlier novels are concerned with quality of life, not life itself; for eighteen years, Paula has not been fighting for respect from her neighbors but fighting simply to stay alive. However, although the novel piles up the miseries, it nevertheless leaves the reader with a strong sense of hope: by the end, Paula is adhering to her self-imposed rules concerning her drinking; she has a job; her husband cannot hurt her now. Doyle himself says that *The Woman Who Walked into Doors* is very hopeful: "There is room for hope. . . . [Y]ou can't help feeling that it's very sad and that she's missed out on a lot, but at the same time that she's going to make a stab at it."

Doyle has telescoped his vision of life: living life, surviving day to day, is hard enough. His later characters are trying to stay alive. They lack the energy and desire either to promote worldwide communication or to celebrate, however unwittingly, the life force. Doyle himself says that, although he is not aware of any "downward trend" to his novels, he has become more aware of life's evils:

> I have obviously aged—it's been ten years since *The Commitments*. . . . I was a teacher for fourteen years. . . . The first couple of years I was hopelessly naive and I wore these frilly blinders and I saw nothing beyond the wonderfulness of all these kids. But as I calmed down and grew older, then you begin to see malnourishment, now and again, to see red eyes of someone who has been up all night, and you begin to wonder why. . . . So I think that is what happens as you begin to grow older . . . a growing awareness— I am very aware of my own luck, my own good luck, and I know that there are a lot of people out there who got my chunk of bad luck. While I'm flourishing, they're not. And I don't know why it can't be evened out somewhat. So as my career began to flourish, I found myself going for darker and darker subjects. I don't think it's a slope; I think it's rather cyclical.

Doyle, while not consciously growing more pessimistic, is growing more realistic about the world he inhabits.

The desperation underlying the carpe diem attitude of Dubliners is emerging in his novels. This pessimism comes from living in a country where, if one does get educated, one may need to emigrate to find a job; or if one quits school and is lucky, one can find a low-paying job instead of living on the dole; where one's future is dim at best, and a bright future means leaving one's homeland. Many Dubliners, and most of Doyle's characters, do not have a "future" by American standards. Is it any wonder they so vigorously live life in the present?

The difference in attitude toward the future makes Doyle's characters so uniquely Irish. Although I am aware of the risk of stereotyping an entire country, it seems that in America, there is always "tomorrow": American history has been marked by huge expanses of land, which promise fresh starts; people are upwardly mobile and always moving; Americans deny the existence of any impenetrable social classes and are always seeking to better themselves and to have their children lead more affluent lives than previous generations have led. Because of this perpetual motion, focused on a future that never arrives, Americans tend to neglect the present—and perhaps as a result, to live less.

By contrast, a stasis not found in America seems to pervade Ireland. People lack the sense of a limitless future that goes with unlimited geography, as Seamus Heaney shows us in "Bogland":

> We have no prairies
> To slice a big sun at evening—
> Everywhere the eye concedes to
> Encroaching horizon.
> (Heaney 1990, 22)

As a result, the Irish may appreciate the here and now more. They interact more with their community; they laugh more; they talk more. They submerge themselves in their daily lives to avoid looking ahead. Doyle's characters, especially the earlier ones, personify this thinking.

Doyle is a wonderful writer who has the Dickensian gift of appealing to the uneducated and the educated alike. His novels, even at their most hilarious, contain serious messages. Doyle is as forgiving of his readers' limitations as he is of his characters' and does not demand that his readers spend as much time with his work as he has spent. Any reader will find humor, an engaging story, and the unforced exploration of important human issues. One can easily sympathize with his likable and realistic characters. Doyle's art seems effortless—the dialogue flows easily—and yet the reader can sense his earnestness and personal struggles. His work is extremely contemporary in its characters and situations, cutting-edge with its language, yet old-fashioned in its values and conclusions. At an early age, Doyle has become one of the world's best novelists.

CHAPTER TWO

Biography

The Booker Prize is arguably "the most significant and most intensely coveted award available to a writer of fiction" (Mulkerns 1994, 21). Roddy Doyle, however, confident in his work and in himself, seems unimpressed by awards and honors. The night he received the Booker Prize for *Paddy Clarke Ha Ha Ha*, Doyle was told by one of the ceremony's officials that he was expected to give a series of interviews on the following day. He replied, "No, I'm going home tomorrow." The official responded, "But you're a Booker Prize winner. The Prize brings its responsibilities." "Do you want it back?" retorted Doyle. Prize in hand, he left the next day for home (Fay 1996, 20). Doyle, although obviously glad to have won the award—which guarantees immense commercial success—is strangely unaffected: "I don't want to be dismissive, but on one level, it didn't mean a hell of a lot. . . . [T]he bulk of the contracts had been signed before the Booker. . . . [W]here the Booker has made a difference is that the first time I went to the States there were very few newspapers interested in talking to me. Afterwards, I was talking to all of them" (Lacey 1996, 56).

This anecdote captures the essence of Doyle himself, including one of the reasons for his great success—his sense of perspective. Whether in his fiction or in his life—personal, political, and public—Doyle is able to distinguish what is important from what is not. Although being a Booker Prize winner is indeed a remarkable achievement, Doyle characteristically sees even that feat in the context of the larger picture of his life and family. His success as a writer is due, in part, to the fact that he lives and writes with this perspective.

25

This down-to-earth perspective perhaps has its roots in Doyle's child-hood, which he remembers as a safe, protected time: "Children then had total and unlimited freedom. They left the house when they woke up, and they came back when it was dinner time. I had that, that same freedom that Paddy Clarke has, but I don't think you'd get that now" (Mulkerns 1994, 24). Roddy Doyle was born in 1958, the third of four children, all raised in the same house (in which his parents still reside) in Kilbarrack, northeast of Dublin. When Doyle was a child, the town was not much more than a country village, but today it is a seedy suburb—"rough, increasingly drug-ridden, but not especially dangerous" (Donoghue 1994, 3). Doyle de-scribes his homeland:

> Kilbarrack is about five stops on the north side of the DART [Dublin Area Rapid Transit]. . . . It's about five miles from City Centre. When I was a kid it was bang at the edge of the city. . . . The city limits were right down the middle of the street. There was a farm across the road from us. There was the odd road that had been there for a long time. The people who lived there would have been railway workers for the local train. But gradually as the city grew, the estates [housing projects] grew—early '40s and '50s—and the people moved in like my parents, working-class, lower middle-class, who were in a position to buy their own houses. In many cases, they were all the same age. It was a great time to grow up—surrounded by all these kids—a lot of freedom as well. As I grew up, the city cooperations bought out the farms, and the private developers bought out the other farms, and it gradually grew more inner-city. People who moved into it would have been more solidly working class—from the inner-city. Dublin had the worst slums of any city in Europe. These awful tenements . . . were all demolished in the '50s, '60s, '70s, and these people moved out into the suburbs, into Kilbarrack and into other areas of the Ring of Dublin.

Kilbarrack today is little more than an average lower-middle-class neigh-borhood. There are several streets, rows of lower-income housing, and the odd convenience market on the corner. It is a much cleaner and more or-derly place than is depicted in the movies of Doyle's works. Kilbarrack "is a blank canvas of ordinariness, like any working-class housing estate in any city in western Europe" (O'Toole 1993, 21).

Doyle was raised in a lower-middle-class Catholic home, which Doyle calls "comfortable": "What we were was always warm and well-fed. My parents owned their own house but the land around it was owned by the city corporation so it was the type of area I was writing about" (Adams 1996, 16). This setting—on which Barrytown is based—is one of the few autobiographical aspects of his work.

The elder Doyles' marriage was full of laughter and is still strong after forty-eight years: "I don't recall my parents ever arguing in front of us," says Doyle. As one of Doyle's sisters puts it, their parents' marriage is "a tough act to follow" (Mulkerns 1994, 24). The Clarkes' fighting in Doyle's fourth novel is most assuredly not based on anything Doyle experienced as a child.

Doyle's father, Rory—who, it seems, would have felt at home in Barrytown—"enlivened lower-middle-life by dapper dressing and exaggerated bonhomie" (Harding 1996, 10). Doyle remembers being embarrassed as a teenager at his father's expansiveness: "He says hello to total strangers. Waves at people he's never seen before" (ibid., 10). Doyle describes his father as the son of a "tram driver, [whose] background was definitely working-class." Rory Doyle began his career as a printer: "He would have been blue collar, since he had ink under his fingernails." Eventually, he was promoted to the civil service position of coordinator of the training of apprenticed printers in Dublin: "He took off his blue collar and put on a white one. I think he was earning roughly the same money—actually, I think he took a dive in pay for a while."

Doyle's mother, Ita, was a secretary to a local solicitor. Although not as boisterous as her husband, she mimics neighbors with deadly accuracy; that skill may have been the source of Doyle's own gift for transcribing Barrytownese. Her background "was more middle class—her father was a civil servant, a state employee. And she stayed in school until she was eighteen, which was quite unusual for a girl, whereas my father left when he was fifteen." In retrospect, Doyle sees the benefits to him of his parents' differing backgrounds:

In my own case, I've grown up with a foot in each class. It's a very useful position, especially socially. People who have grown up solidly working class seem to be hopelessly lost in a different version of reality. Whereas being from the gray area, you seem to be a little more street-wise. You tend to have more sympathy with things. You don't give out about tax as much, because you know that tax goes to people who need it, and so what if a few waste it? Not all of it is wasted. Whereas those from all middle class tend to see it as their money. It's a useful position to be in, especially as a novelist.

Today, despite the financial success of his novels, Doyle consciously tries to retain his dual-class perspective.

Because both parents were voracious readers, books were always plentiful at the Doyle home, a factor in the development of Doyle's own love of literature. Doyle says that he read a great deal as a child simply because there was nothing else to do: "There was only one television station in Ireland, and it started at 5:30. Even record players were quite rare in private houses then [in 1968]. So there was nothing much else you could do but read. I love books, but I think that's because I grew up in the '60s when there was nothing else to do. If there'd been alternatives, I think I might have done something else to fill my time" (Mulkerns 1994, 24).

Doyle attended St. Fintan's Christian Brothers School in Sutton and hated it: "I don't want to be too unfair, but if the teachers had anything going for them, there were very few who ever showed it" (Harding 1996, 10). The negatively portrayed teachers in *The Woman Who Walked into Doors* are based on some of his own teachers. He benefited from a law passed in 1968 that made secondary education free:

> I started my secondary education in 1971, and it was free. My parents had to buy books and pay for transport, but it was free. Up until 1968, it wasn't free. The state might have put some money into it, but it wasn't free at all; I think there was a fee of some sort. So that meant a closed door to a lot of people—whereas people of my generation, there was a new door opened up. I think my parents would have sent me to secondary anyway— they could have afforded it—but what I am saying is that it became the norm to go to high school; everybody went. I was part of that generation that benefited from free secondary education. Education facilitated the move for me from working class to middle class.

Although Doyle's two sisters and one brother decided not to go to college, Doyle himself attended University College, Dublin, "traditionally the Catholic, working-class university, not as socially smart or as ancient as Trinity College" (Davies 1993, 21), where he majored in English and geography. Because, as he jokes, he was not good enough to be either a professional footballer or a rock musician, after graduation he decided to teach. In 1980, he started teaching English and geography at Greendale Community School, a secondary school in a depressed area, at a salary of £1200 a month. Dubbed "Punky" Doyle by his students because of his spiky haircut, earring, and casual dress, he was a "strict but fair" teacher and found teaching, at least for the first years, "exciting and enjoyable" (ibid., 22). Although Doyle was a good teacher, he criticizes the state of the profession in Ireland:

> I taught in a school where we were all roughly the same age. We were all relatively young. We were all very energetic. There were a lot of extracurricular activities. There was a great buzz in the place. But it's easy to imagine going to a school where they've all been there for twenty-five years, where they're all just playing out the time till they retire. I would be worried, as a parent now with kids going to school, that we're going back to that situation again. When I left the school I taught in, I was never replaced. Somebody aged twenty-one straight out of university should've got my job. It's a job that you burn out on very, very quickly. By year twelve, I wanted out. I had enough. I didn't want to do it anymore. (Fay 1996, 19)

Thus, in 1993—after becoming solidly established as a writer with the success of *Paddy Clarke*—Doyle retired from teaching; as he said at the time, "it was becoming soul-destroying because I found I could only sit down one or two times a week to write. Also, I've found that now I've got two kids of me own, I'm not remotely as fascinated with other people's any more." Although when he began writing he relied somewhat on his students for his material (especially for the Barrytown dialect), he did not see leaving teaching as an obstacle to future novels: "I'm not an outgoing person and I wonder where I'm going to get my stuff from . . . but not to the extent that it puts me off. I've got no master-plan, but I suspect that my kids as they get older will give me a lot of interests. . . . And while I won't be going into work as a teacher anymore, I have got 14 years of that locked inside me head" (Heller 1993, 4). As Doyle's recent work has shown, he has success-fully discovered other sources for his art.

Doyle started writing as a teenager, mainly producing nonfiction essays. He wrote satirical pieces for a college magazine in Dublin, and then "grad-uated" into writing fiction, leaving his interest in nonfiction behind. After having taught for several years, Doyle started writing during his vacations: "As a teacher, I found myself with a lot of free time and not needing to fill it with getting another job to make more money. It's an easier path than learn-ing how to play the guitar. I already know how to write—I learned years and years ago. All you need is a pencil and paper. You don't need money. I suppose there was a little ambition in the back of me head—I'd read an awful lot at the time, and somewhere along the line I figured I'd try to see if I could do it."

His first attempt, *Your Granny Is a Hunger Striker*—a political satire written between 1982 and 1986—was never accepted by any publisher. As Doyle himself admits, the book was "this absurd, very snide, undergraduate-type humor story about a group of people who were either by design or acci-dentally around the H Block campaign in Dublin. . . . [O]verall it was dreadful, just dreadful. It'll never be published, not if I can help it. I have all the copies." Doyle has perspective on this "failure": "Well, I was upset, but that novel hadn't been done as an escape or for money. It was enjoyment" (Davies 1993, 23). In a later interview, he looked at it from a slightly differ-ent angle: "It was a good exercise, anyway—just getting from the first page to the last is good practice. It's a rehearsal for doing it again."

Undaunted by this lack of success, in 1986 Doyle began another novel, *The Commitments*, which took him only six months to write. He decided to base this novel on the familiar, and so used his pupils for inspiration; but still, publishers showed no interest. The haughtiness of the publishing companies angered Doyle: "I sent a copy off to every publisher I could find, and invariably it came back unopened. So they didn't reject the book—they rejected the notion of someone sending them a book." Confident of the novel's merit, he started his own publishing company, King Farouk, with his college friend John Sutton: "I had to get a bank loan of £5,000. I wasn't married, only had a rented flat, no car, so I wasn't spending a lot. My father had to stand guarantee as I was not a property owner" (Davies 1993, 23). The two friends published *The Commitments* in 1987; although it sold only a thousand copies, the book received mostly favorable local reviews. Doyle sent the favorable reviews to various established publishing houses, and eventually Dan Franklin, an editor for Heinemann in London and also an avid soul music fan, picked up the book, landing Doyle a £1200 advance.

In June 1986, writer and director Paul Mercier—a college friend of Doyle— persuaded him to write a play to be performed in the SFX Centre (formerly the St. Francis Xavier Hall). Doyle was excited and frightened about writing for the theater:

> I was given the chance to be involved [in Mercier's production com-
> pany, the Passion Machine], and it was hard to stay calm. I was going to
> write a play; Paul Mercier was going to direct it. I was scared as well. I didn't
> think I could write anything remotely as solid as *Studs* [Mercier's play]. I was
> right; I couldn't. But I loved writing *Brownbread* and, later, *War*. I loved the
> whole thing—the rehearsals, everything. (Doyle 1992, 2)

Brownbread, which opened 16 September 1987 to mostly favorable reviews, is a farce (à la Monty Python) about directionless Dublin youths who kidnap a bishop for a lark. Their escapade makes world news as the United States Marines and even Ronald Reagan attempt to save the bishop. The three lead characters, Donkey, Ao, and John, completely lack motivation and can be seen as representatives *ad absurdum* of modern-day Dublin youth. Their "fecklessness is set against a world of authority—from the church to parents, to the guards, to Ronald Reagan—which is stupid, incompetent and completely crazy. Ao, Donkey, and John may be off the wall, but the people who are supposed to be in charge aren't exactly models of purpose and decision either" (O'Toole 1987, 18). Dubliners liked the play so well that it was moved to the larger Olympia Theatre where it sold out the remainder of its run.

Doyle then wrote *War*, a gritty comedy juxtaposing the loutish behavior at home of the lead character, George, toward his unfulfilled wife, Briget, with his fierce competitiveness in the local pub's weekly quiz game. *War*, which debuted 7 September 1989 at the SFX Centre, was inspired by

Doyle's own experiences with pub quiz games at the Foxhound Inn in Kilbarrack and the Cedar Lounge in Raheny: "For about a year I read the papers and watched The News only with next Monday in mind. There was a volcano in Columbia; I didn't give a shite about the dead, I just wanted to remember the name of the mountain. I had a list of African presidents, emperors and prime ministers" (Doyle 1992, 2). This play was also successful, although several reviewers claimed that the Passion Machine was "selling out" because Mercier downplayed the contrast between George's brutality at home and his hilarity at the pub. In the written work, Briget has the last line, "Please God, he didn't lose again. Please" (Doyle 1992, 215); in the stage version, however, Mercier cut Briget's line completely, thus ending the play on an upbeat note with George winning the pub quiz rather than on a note of isolation and fear. Although both plays were successful, Doyle developed a dislike for the theater: "There's too much posing and posturing involved. I can't see myself writing any more plays" (Fay 1993, 5).

Immediately after writing *Brownbread* and during the writing of *War,* Doyle began writing another novel, *The Snapper.* This novel took him three years to complete and was well received when it was published in 1990. In 1991, *The Van* was published and short-listed for the Booker Prize, despite negative reviews—in Doyle's words, "They hammered *The Van* and yet it went over very well here." In 1993, *Paddy Clarke Ha Ha Ha* won the Booker Prize, and Doyle was vaulted into the national spotlight: "I had won the Booker Prize with a rather charming little book, I'd been given a sort of knighthood in Ireland and was something of a little hero" (Lacey 1996, 55). He then started on *The Family,* a four-part series about domestic violence for the BBC. When it was released in May 1994, this series—the ratings of which exceeded even the Pope's visit to Ireland—caused a huge furor because of the violence and poverty it depicted. Doyle's popularity among the Irish plummeted: "Then comes *Family,* which is grim and sordid and violent, and it really shocked people because domestic violence is one of the great secrets of Irish society, and we'd much rather not have to admit it occurs. Going down to the shops to get the milk the day after the first episode was a bit of a struggle. I was waiting for a car to skid to a halt behind me and be hit by a hammer or something" (55). Undeterred by Ireland's fickleness, he based his next novel, *The Woman Who Walked into Doors* (1996), on a character in *The Family;* in something of a turnaround by the public, the novel was received favorably. In the late 1990s, Doyle was working on (among other projects) a huge novel about "a man who claims to be ninety-four. Not only has he been alive for most of the century but he claims to have been involved in an awful lot of what's gone on. He's a monumental liar and he may even be lying about his age. It's very different from anything else I've done but I wouldn't see it as a dark exploration of the century, although there might be little bits of that in it. I'd see it as being more about a liar and a storyteller flexing his creative muscles and seeing how far he can go" (Fay 1996, 20). *A Star Called Henry,* the first "installment" of this project, was published in 1999.

Doyle himself sounds a bit like his most recent character: "I can tell stories" (Giffin 1995, F12). He refuses to interpret his work for the reader because he feels a reader's opinion is as valid as his own: "I just write books. It's up to other people to interpret them" (Fay 1993, 7). Just as Doyle will not interpret his work and his characters, neither does he listen to others' interpretations: "When I'm writing, I write for myself and I don't care who reads it. . . . The critics aren't too influential in my case anymore."

As he wrote his novels, Doyle was also learning another trade, filmmaking. He was increasingly involved in the film adaptation of his first three novels, as well as in scripting the TV series *The Family.* Doyle has always loved films—which he views as "a halfway house between novels and the stage" (Christon 1994, 9)—but working with director Alan Parker on *The Commitments* was his first experience with movies as anything but a viewer. Parker—the director of *Evita, Bugsy Malone, Mississippi Burning,* and *Fame,* to name a few—happened to buy a copy of the novel *The Commitments* and decided that the story would make a good movie. He placed an ad in *Hot Press* for local musicians and received over forty-five hundred applicants. He cast twelve first-time actors who were chosen for their musical talents as well as for similarities to the characters they would play: "What they had in common was a love of music and complete ignorance of what the film business was all about" (McGuinness 1996, 25). Doyle, along with Dick Clement and Ian La Frenais, wrote the screenplay; the music for the film was recorded live, although the vocals and the instruments were set down separately. Released in July 1991 at the Cannes Film Festival, the movie was a huge success and became the first Irish film to make more than £2 million at the box office. It was nominated for an Academy Award for best editing, and although it did not win an Oscar, it did win four awards at the 1992 British Academy of Film and Television Arts (BAFTA) for best picture, best editing, best director, and best adapted screenplay. Doyle accepted the adapted screenplay award with his, by now, characteristic aplomb: "It's obvious who I should thank, but I won't bother, so thank you very much" (44).

Although Doyle terms the project a success, he was disappointed that he had so little control over many aspects of the movie: "I wasn't involved in any of the decisions or around for any of the decisions, so when I saw it I was relieved—they could have done anything. I thought Parker would do a good job—I didn't know if it would be my good job—but I was very happy." And although Doyle likes the movie overall—"I think they've done a terrific job"—he questions some of the scenes: "One thing in *The Commitments* film which made me uncomfortable was the religious scenes and holy statues and such. The confession scene, very funny lines, but it annoyed me—I didn't write that scene—you know, where he goes in and starts talking about the temptation of women and the soul music and the priest contradicts him. . . . It's funny, but it annoyed me. That kid would not have gone to confession. Kids do not go to confession anymore. . . . None of those kids in the film would have gone near a confession box." He did not even attend the film's premiere at Cannes.

Although several people associated with the movie have discussed making a sequel, Doyle will have nothing to do with the project: "I'm not at all involved with it, other than wishing it ill-will. I hope it's never made. I just think that, whereas *The Commitments* was very much a labour of love, *Commitments 2* is definitely an act of cynicism" (Dodd 1993).

Doyle made sure he had more control over the film version of *The Snapper*: "And having just luckily escaped with *The Commitments*, I decided that that was never gonna happen again. With *The Snapper*, I refused to allow it to be made into a film unless I had choice of producer and the right to pull out and bring the book with me if I felt it wasn't going well. I also insisted that I would do the screenplay and that I'd sort out any problems with the screenplay myself. The BBC agreed to all that, so from day one it was a treat" (Fay

1993, 6). He changed the names of the characters (for instance, the family's surname is Curley instead of Rabbitte) and slightly altered the arrangement of the family (he added a son and lost a twin) because he "didn't want it to be seen as a sequel. It's not a problem with the book, but it is a problem with the film, because if it's a sequel, you have to have the exact same actors, the exact same streets, you'd have to bring the Commitments [band members], at least one or two of them, somewhere along the line since it's the same community. I didn't want that—I thought it'd be a dreadful idea. I just wanted it to be an entirely separate film."

Lynda Myles, whom Doyle had met during the filming of *The Commitments* and who was Doyle's choice for producer for *The Snapper*, suggested her friend Stephen Frears as director. The Irish director—whose other films include *My Beautiful Laundrette*, *Dangerous Liaisons*, *The Grifters*, and *Mary Reilly*—says that when he was sent the script for *The Snapper*, "I jumped on it right away" (Christon 1994, 9). *The Snapper* was originally made for TV, which (as Doyle recalls) "caused Stephen Frears to make some cinematic decisions. There are a lot of close-ups and a lot of faces—it was made for the telly and not the big screen." After its standing ovation at the Cannes Film Festival in May 1993, however, the movie was transferred to film format, even though Doyle disagreed with the change: "I didn't like it on the big screen—I thought it was grainy." However, the very graininess and close-up shots (of often unglamorous faces) about which Doyle complains add a certain charm and intimacy to the movie, which Frears must have desired when he opted to banish the "box-office mentality" of *The Commitments* film (Bowman 1997, 61). Overall, Doyle was pleased with the movie, but again he was not overly excited with its success: "My emotional involvement went as far as seeing it on the TV. . . . That was great, but I didn't bother going to Cannes" (O'Connor 1993, 2C). The movie achieved a following in the United States but never was a blockbuster hit.

With *The Van*, Doyle took a different approach to film adaptation, as he wrote the script and (with Lynda Myles) formed the production company, Deadly Films. Interviewed in 1996, the year the film was released, he expressed his pleasure at the process: "I was in control from day one and I've seen four or five rough cuts and it looks great." Doyle was involved in every major decision, including the selection of the cast and of the director

(Stephen Frears again), as well as being present for every day of shooting. Doyle is enthusiastic about this film: it "looks glorious, really, really fantastic. The-camera-never-lies is all me arse because Dollymount looks absolutely staggeringly magnificent. There'll be busloads of Yanks going out to Dollymount when they see it. They're in for a shock" (Fay 1996, 20). The film lacks the "outrageous humor" of *The Snapper* movie, but instead has "a quieter, more introspective tone, where the travails of friendship are more important than slapstick" (Bowman 1997, 61)—perhaps an appropriate attitude from the more mature Doyle. The camera is often at eye-level, giving the movie a "slice-of-life" feel which coincides perfectly with the blue-collar material.

Although the movie opened to enthusiastic reviews at Cannes in 1996, its limited release in the United States received mediocre reviews, with critics citing the film's episodic nature, thin material, and absence of strong characterization as the primary areas of weakness. Perhaps one reason *The Van* did not achieve the following of either of Doyle's previous films is because the dialect and thick accents, which are especially difficult for the non-Irish to follow in this movie, prevented much of the humor from translating to American audiences. Or, perhaps because the economy was booming when the film was released in 1996, audiences couldn't or wouldn't relate to the financial hardships of the characters. Or perhaps, simply, as one Tucson critic wrote, "I don't get it. . . . I think these guys are supposed to be lovable losers, but I couldn't really grasp the lovable part. Maybe if I were Irish, but I'm not, and I found Bimbo and Larry to be loud, drunken, angry characters who mostly panicked and yelled, Irish versions of Fred Flintstone and Barney Rubble" (Richter 1997).

Through his work on the films, Doyle discovered that he enjoys screenwriting—"I love writing a script. I love the lay-out of a script. I get a great kick out of being able to do a page in about 10 minutes" (Heller 1993, 4)—and the whole film-making process in general: "I haven't felt as invigorated since the first few months of teaching. I was just so full of it. . . . The hours are so long and it's so engrossing. . . . If nothing else, it gets you out of your room and you talk nonstop all day, which is a nice change for a writer" (Fay 1996, 19). However, his experiences did not lead him to want to be a director:

I would love to direct but in the same way that I'd love to score a hat-trick for Ireland in the World Cup. I reached that conclusion quite early on, watching Stephen Frears work. That visual sense isn't there in me. And also, it's an incredibly pressured job. When you're making an independent film, you've got creative independence but you're a slave to the budget. . . . It's just a constant heartache. . . . While the producer has a certain amount of the pressure, the writer and everybody else does too, it's the director's ultimate responsibility. Leaving aside the fact that I wouldn't have the skill to do it, I couldn't handle the pressure. I don't know how they cope with it. I wouldn't even want to see if I could cope with that sort of pressure. I love being around the making of a film but I'll stick to writing and producing.(20)

In the late 1990s, Doyle began writing a screenplay based on Liam O'Flaherty's classic novel *Famine* (1937), which proved slow going because of the novel's length and his discomfort with adapting someone else's work: "Leaving aside the fact that it's set a hundred and fifty years ago in the west of Ireland and it's a different world completely, I've never adapted anyone else's work before. Even though the man is dead and he's not gonna come around to my house with a machete, I still can't get over the problem that I'm working with somebody else's property" (Fay 1996, 21). Doyle also wants to communicate the enormous tragedy of the Irish Potato Famine, which he feels has never been done:

> One of the reasons I'm keen to do the film is that I think there's been a lack of emotional response to the Famine. To see a film about an ordinary group of human beings going through it on a big screen would fill a gap that's there. . . . One of the problems is trying to give a sense that there's a bigger world out there and that these people are starving because of political decisions. It's difficult to achieve that without a character becoming some sort of mouthpiece for his class or his nation. (20)

Just as Doyle does not want any of his characters to become a nation's mouthpiece, neither does he want to be one: "I'm a spokesman for nobody except myself—and even then I'd get a third party to speak on my behalf" (Lacey 1996, 56). Although his father is an ardent supporter of and leading activist in Fianna Fáil (one of the major political parties in Ireland), whose "version of republicanism" Doyle detests (Harding 1996, 10), and both grandfathers were IRA members when the IRA was thought of as "essentially, the people who gave us freedom" (Heller 1993, 4), Doyle "refuses to view himself as a political animal, and feels little inclination to preach a message to the liberal class" (4). As a student, he was a member of the Socialist Labour Party, but he admitted to more recently voting democratic left, although he felt a little odd voting for the party in power because his "vote was always something of a protest. But it struck me that it was grow-up time. . . . I feel reasonably happy with this government" (Fay 1996, 20).

Doyle has scrupulously avoided using his celebrity status to endorse anything: "I don't endorse products. As a writer, I don't think you can criticise society and then say, 'And by the way, buy Levis.' It just doesn't work that way. . . . I began getting all these invitations to attend political functions. . . . Again, I keep saying no, no, no. . . . I can talk about issues within the context of my books or the television series. Other than that . . . someone [else] would speak a good deal more impressively than I could ever do" (Fay 1996, 19). However, as a private citizen Doyle fervently supported the Vote Yes campaign in the divorce referendum in 1996. He felt that the referendum involved more than simply the right to dissolve marriages; for Doyle, the central issue was the Catholic Church's attempt to dictate the terms of being Irish:

> It basically was the Catholic Church against everyone else. It was this insistence that if you're Irish, you're white and you're Catholic as well, and if you're not both of those things then you're not fully Irish. Ultimately, that is what it was all about. . . . I felt that it was a real fight, a fight for the future of my children and the future of the country. I was very, very emotionally involved. . . . My children are growing up and they're not going to be Catholic. I felt that I had to insist that they are perfectly entitled to grow up non-Catholic in this country. But the word coming from the No campaign was that they couldn't do that. You had to be Catholic and Irish. . . . I felt strongly that if the No campaign got that one, there'd be more to follow. . . . If that happened, we just couldn't live in this country. If divorce was defeated again, leaving Ireland seemed inevitable. It's something we'd be loath to do. (19)

The referendum narrowly passed, and Doyle did not feel compelled to emigrate.

As implied by his strong rhetoric concerning the divorce referendum, Doyle likes Ireland and being Irish. At the same time, he feels no duty to "do Ireland proud" and will not whitewash situations to save his country embarrassment, the *Family* series being an excellent example of this. Doyle views his Irishness in a characteristically blunt way: "We've got an almighty national inferiority complex. If something bad happens in Ireland, very often the initial reaction of Irish people will be, 'What'll the neighbours think?' And then, some little triumph—something like the Eurovision Song Contest, which is usually treated with utter contempt—we win it and suddenly, it's a wonderful thing, a dawning of a new age in Irish contemporary music" (Fay 1996, 20).

As Doyle observed when discussing the referendum, for him, being Irish does not necessarily mean being Catholic. Doyle, although raised as a Catholic, has been "a very happy atheist" (Fay 1993, 8) since his early twenties; he and his wife chose not to raise their children Catholic and to send them to a multidenominational school on the north side of Dublin. Doyle does not quite understand Catholicism in Ireland:

There's no religion in me own life, for certain. I've no room for it at all. It's difficult in a country like Ireland because you do have to put your face out and tell it to go away—"Fuck off." You have to be quite blunt to allow yourself your own agnostic space. . . . It kind of depresses me when I see all those people in the church. Particularly the kids. What are they going for? They're immortal—they're not, but they should think they are. What are they going there for? When you begin to slow down and there's a rattle in your breathing, then you go off to church to make your peace, not when you're seventeen and you should be avoiding at all costs all that crap.

In 1987, Doyle married Belinda Moller, a business student whom he met when she was helping him publicize *The Commitments*. Currently, they have three young children, Rory, Jack, and Kate, and live three miles from the home in which he was raised. His days at home are low-key: after taking his children to school, he returns home, reads the paper, works on one of his projects, and stops working at about five o'clock. As he commented in a 1996 interview, "I gave up teaching because I wanted to write, but I decided I would keep the routine because it fits everybody else's routine. . . . It's not the stuff of great literature—I know you're supposed to be a tortured soul and work deep into the night. But that's a lot of crap. I have other little tortured souls to look after." For music, he likes Elvis, early R.E.M., and (not surprisingly) soul. He says his life is "blissful": "I live in a happiness and contentment I once wouldn't have thought possible. But all I have to do is look at people to see that my contentment isn't shared: *Family* and Paula grew out of that. I wouldn't want to just build a wall around myself and say, 'Well, I've got this so fuck the rest of you.' I find I think in the opposite way, like: "What would it be like to be without any luck?' " (Adams 1996, 16).

Through his increasing fame, Doyle has focused on keeping his and his family's life sane and relatively unchanged: "I liked what I had before [the Booker Prize] and I want to keep what I have after it. . . . I'll talk about my work but I'm not going to be photographed leaning against my mantelpiece or in the park with me kids" (Fay 1993, 8). He lives in the same house, has the same friends, and visits the same pubs. He is extremely reticent in his relations with the press; as his editor, Dan Franklin, said, "If you ask most people to do some publicity thing—if you tell them it is going to get them into the top five, well most people—I mean, even people you like and respect—they'll do it. Roddy really won't. Not even for the top five" (Heller 1993, 4). Interestingly, at the start Doyle was relatively cooperative with the press—until one impertinent photographer tried to rearrange the furniture in his home; only after he received a death threat shortly upon the release of the film *The Snapper* did Doyle completely separate his public and personal lives: "There's not an awful lot you can do about fame, but there's a hell of a lot you can do about celebrity. Celebrity is a question of choice, and the way to avoid becoming a celebrity is just to say 'no' " (Mulkerns 1994, 24). For his own part, he says that he "wouldn't be like Sinead O'Connor now, beating off journalists if they tried to take a photograph of my children. When I do go out with them, I don't have a sack over their heads. 'Are they male or female?' 'I'm not telling yal.' But I'm not going to start wheeling them out in the hope of getting mentioned in next Sunday's paper" (Fay 1993, 8).

To be sure, although Doyle strives to keep his art separate from his life and denies any autobiographical content in his work, he is nevertheless visible in his most successful characters—individuals who keep their troubles in perspective and enjoy everyday pleasures. However, the art/life parallel ends there. Doyle, a quiet, "regular," yet talented man, has had fame thrust upon him; his response has been to thrust it back. His work ethic, realistic perspective, and talent would seem to guarantee him a long, prolific career. Although no *Vanity Fair* layouts of Doyle *en famille* may be forthcoming, I personally would rather have another of his novels.

CHAPTER THREE

The Commitments

The Commitments, published first in 1987 at Doyle's own expense and picked up shortly afterwards by William Heinemann Ltd. in England, is a striking first novel. Not overly ambitious, it nevertheless provides material for the introspective reader to consider at the same time as it offers engaging and lively situations and characters for the more casual reader. The novel introduces us to Doyle's working-class Dublin, a city without a future but a community full of joy.

As with the subsequent books in the Barrytown trilogy, the story is set in present-day Ireland and centers on the Rabbitte family. Jimmy Sr. and the long-suffering Veronica have six children: the intelligent, ambitious, wise-cracking oldest son, Jimmy Jr., about 20 years old; independent 19-year-old daughter, Sharon; their troubled son Leslie, about 17; their hard-working, good-looking, athletic, and studious son Darren, about 15; and finally the twins, Tracy and Linda, about 13, sassy and rebellious. As the trilogy progresses, the family members age accordingly and the family dynamics evolve realistically.

The Commitments focuses on Jimmy Jr., who has an unspecified but obviously uninteresting job in a shop. Throughout the trilogy, Jimmy Jr. jumps—rabbitlike—from project to project; in this particular endeavor, he agrees to help two of his friends, Outspan and Derek, who want to start a band but so far have little more than a name. Believing that a band can be more than just a way to meet girls but rather a political force—with the ultimate goal of unifying all of Dublin—Jimmy idealistically chooses soul music as the language with which their band will speak to the working classes. According to Jimmy, soul music was introduced in the 1960s as a vehicle through which the oppressed black race in America could assert itself—and because the Irish are the "niggers" of Europe, soul music could empower the Northside Dubliners as well. The reader is never convinced that Jimmy's band can accomplish such lofty goals, but may enjoy watching its members try.

The band, formed after numerous auditions and rejections, is comprised of ten members, most of them inexperienced. The novel focuses on Jimmy, the manager; Joey the Lips Fagan, an older saxophone player who is both a con man and a prophet; Deco, the lead singer, with a terrific voice but an annoyingly belligerent and self-centered personality; and Imelda, the prettiest of the three female backup singers, with whom all the male band members are in love. After many riotous rehearsals and several less than auspicious performances, the band begins to take off, as Dubliners can relate to its sound if not to its message. Its members eventually gain enough fame to attract a small, local record label; before they can sign, however, the inner turmoil caused by sexual rivalries and enlarged egos dissolves the band. The novel ends with Jimmy vowing to give up his political goals and planning to start an apolitical country music band.

This enjoyable first novel does have its limitations. The plot is almost farcical: the premise for the band's creation—uniting all Dublin youth—calls for an extreme suspension of disbelief. The one-dimensional characters, although likable, do not develop. Some of the humorous situations read like scenes from situation comedies and, although funny, are somewhat forced. Despite these criticisms, however, the novel as a whole is effective. Viewed in the spectrum of Doyle's work, we can see traits that Doyle uses and further develops in his later novels: the fast-paced, profanity-laced, realistically transcribed dialogue; the sympathetic and likable characters, isolated from their pasts and not looking toward their dim futures; the laugh-out-loud humor. These elements are some of Doyle's trademarks. Moreover, the novel, although most interesting when viewed as either the first book in the trilogy or as a measuring stick for Doyle's maturity as an artist, does contain noteworthy features of its own. Doyle's facility both with music and with humor are especially remarkable. His use of music is so innovative as to remind the reader of the music in Joyce's *Ulysses*;

his comedic writing is masterful, and the atmosphere of the novel is one of uproarious hilarity, yet *The Commitments* is not merely a comic novel. What is most significant is the way in which Doyle is able to employ both music and humor as vehicles for his social vision.

The novel is about a band, and so of course it includes many references to song titles and lyrics, but Doyle does much more than merely mention songs. Lengthy excerpts from the songs constitute almost 10 percent of the novel, serving to make the novel accessible to many types of readers. For example, almost any reader—from a working-class Dubliner to a middle-class American graduate student to an upper-class British housewife—might have heard the often recorded "Knock on Wood," which is one of "the classics, the ones everyone knew" (Doyle 1989, 116). Doyle's humorous transcriptions sometimes include instrumental breaks:

—I DON'T WANNA LOSE—THIS GOOD THANG—
—THU—UNG UNG UNG
—THA' I'VE GOT—
IF I DO—
DUHH DAA DOOHH
—I WOULD SURELY—
SURELY LOSE THE LOT—
—COS YOUR LOVE——THI—THI—
IS BET HA—THU—UNG UNG UNG
THAN ANNY LOVE I KNOW —OW—
—IT'S LIKE THUNDER—
—LIGH'—NIN'
—DEH EH EHHH—
—THE WAY YEH LOVE ME IS FRIGH'NIN—
I'D BET HA KNOCK—
—THU THU THU THU—
—ON WOO—O—OOD—BA—BEEE—

(69)

The full transcription is intended to ensure that the reader, even if unfamiliar with the song's title, will recognize the lyrics and the melody, or at least will be able to get a sense of the flavor of the music. Doyle does not want any of his musical allusions to go unrecognized.

Because of the music's accessibility, the atmosphere created is absorbingly intense. The result of the instrumental and lyrical transcription (which is as accurate as is his transcription of the speech patterns of the working-class Dubliner) is the overwhelming rush of music that engulfs the reader when he or she opens the covers of the book. It is a true sensory experience—one can virtually hear the music and feel the reverberations of the instruments. Just as the most memorable aspect of the movie is the soundtrack, one of the most memorable aspects of the book is what one might call the "transcribed-track."

Music in the novel figures as more than atmosphere; indeed, it has several functions. Its most important role is to establish the link between 1980s Dublin and 1960s black America. The band plays soul music for the specific political purpose of trying to establish the same sense of brotherhood among Dublin youth as soul music did among African Americans. Doyle, who learned of the music's historical and political importance in part through Gerri Hirshey's book *Nowhere to Run: The Story of Soul Music*, hoped to use the music to alert the non-Irish reading public to the plight of the Dublin youth. Appropriately, the lyrics are uniquely "Dublinized," which has the effect of anchoring the novel in 1987 working-class Dublin and allowing the reader a glimpse into its collective consciousness.

In the 1960s, soul music expressed black America's changing perceptions of itself: "[S]oul serves . . . to provide a positive self-image for the large majority of black persons who find themselves still tightly locked behind the walls of the urban ghetto. Soul helps to free the black urban ghetto dweller from guilt about his apparent failure to find escape from economic and social oppression" (Riedel 1975, 52). Even more important, the music offered a temporary refuge from injustice, as "soul music gave many . . . somewhere to run—to get out of ourselves, to feel free, if only for two and a half minutes a side" (Hirshey 1984, xvi). Soul attempted to give African Americans something to claim as their own and expressed "the blacks' consciousness of non-Americanness while living and working in America, at the same time that it enable[d] blacks to begin living on the same terms as other Americans" (Riedel 1975, 51).

Modern Dubliners have experienced similar economic oppression. Although Ireland's economic booms since the late 1990s has improved conditions, at the time Doyle wrote *The Commitments*, one-third of the Irish lived below the poverty line, and more than a quarter of a million Irish were unemployed, with rates of unemployment up to 60 percent in some areas of Dublin. Faced with the prospect of being on welfare their entire lives, fifty thousand Irish men and women were leaving the country each year. Even today, many young people are on welfare; others have tedious jobs in factories and shops. Therefore, the social oppression and lost feeling of 1960s American blacks are likewise part of the consciousness of Dublin youth. Paul Hewson—also known as Bono, the lead singer of the internationally popular rock group U2—recognized the parallels in a 1988 essay: "[British critics] seemed to find any kind of passion hard to take, they prefer a mask of cool . . . unless you're black. Which is interesting, because though this passion is to me an Irish characteristic, in American blacks it's called soul. I was called a 'White Nigger' once by a black musician, and I took it as he meant it, as a compliment. The Irish, the blacks, feel like outsiders. There's a feeling of being homeless, migrant, but I suppose that's what all art is—a search for identity"(1988, 190). The Irish artist and the Irish émigré both feel like exiles, belonging to no one tradition: "[I]t was like we were lost in space, floating over many traditions but not belonging to any one of them" (189). Unable to establish themselves in their home country, thousands must move away and attempt to find a niche in a country with a foreign culture, foreign mores, and a foreign dialect.

How to respond to such economic and cultural dislocation? For blacks in America, the ability to express themselves, to play with words, is especially crucial, according to southern historian Michael Vlach: "For people denied social and economic power, verbal power provides important compensation" (Rose 1990, 30). Verbal power is the ability to manipulate words, allusions, and expressions in new ways. Black history is filled with powerful, emotive language; for instance, slave songs had double meanings, the surface meaning compliant and submissive for the benefit of the white owners, the real, deeper meaning angry and subversive. Powerful emotions accompany subversion: as abducted Africans began to see themselves as slaves and not merely as captives, their songs evolved away from the music of a free African people toward music that could express their misery, their longing, and their hope: "Since the beginning of their American experience, blacks have cried out their sense of desperation and alienation in music—spiritual, gospel, blues, jazz, and now soul. The message seems to be always the same" (Riedel 1975, 53). In the 1960s, soul music took this history of African American misery and rechanneled it: Instead of a powerless music, soul became powerful. By redefining English words and sounds, revitalizing them, and giving them new meanings, often to the astonishment and bewilderment of the mainstream audience, "blacks have turned the table—white listeners are the outsiders, the excluded" (51). Soul music is able "to change what counts as history and reality . . . what names mean, what reference means" (Rose 1990, 141).

The Irish have also had a turbulent history of enslavement and oppression. Conquered by the Vikings in the eighth century, the Normans in the twelfth century, the English from the sixteenth until the early twentieth centuries, much of their original culture has been disregarded or destroyed: "In the end, the repeated invasions which had given Irish history its peculiar dynamic also led to . . . the tragic recognition of culture's failure" (Deane 1994, 23). Forced in the seventeenth century to make English their official language, the Irish people's struggles to retain their heritage have resulted in strong oral traditions and storytelling: "The destruction of the Gaelic order had, as one of its consequences, the enhancement of the oral tradition" (23). When written Irish—the language of the oldest European vernacular literature—was driven almost out of existence, poets and storytellers had to rely on an oral tradition to preserve myths and legends dating back to pre-Christian times. Thus, the Irish—like the Africans in America—learned to employ all of language's aspects.

Updating this tradition, Doyle's character Jimmy wants the Commitments to give Dubliners the same sense of power that soul gave to American blacks. He wants to instill a sense of pride in people who have no education and little future:

> Where are yis from? (He answered the question himself.)—Dublin. (He asked another one.)—Wha' part o' Dublin? Barrytown. Wha' class are yis? Workin' class. Are yis proud of it? Yeah, yis are. . . . —Your music

should be abou' where you're from an' the sort o' people yeh come from.—
—Say it once, say it loud, I'm black an' I'm proud. . . . —The Irish are the
niggers of Europe, lads. . . . An' Dubliners are the niggers of Ireland. The
culchies have fuckin' everythin'. An' the northside Dubliners are the niggers o' Dublin.—Say it loud, I'm black an' I'm proud. (Doyle 1989, 8–9)

Jimmy is attempting to borrow a tradition that he hopes will be successful
once again in uniting a people. Jimmy's mission accounts for the odd name
of the band: he wants the Commitments to commit themselves to the transformation of their city.

Doyle specifies not only the style but also the specific source of the
music that the band plays. James Brown, Jimmy's musical hero and the
founder of soul music, is the original artist of thirteen of the songs on the
band's limited playlist. Brown is an "icon of Black America" (Rose 1990, 22).
Fred Wesley, one of Brown's band members, says, "All music that we hear
today is influenced by James Brown. I stand on that—everybody who calls
himself a creator of music has been influenced by James" (Rose 1990, 37).
Doyle himself calls Brown "'the godfather of soul' and what not, 'the main
man of soul.' 'The godhead,'" and says that in concert, "He was great. . . .
[T]he show was terrific."

Brown took soul music to new expressive heights. Through music, he
"got out of himself" and enabled others to do the same; a master showman,
he transported his audiences out of their lives for a short time, while simultaneously uniting them in this experience. Brown also knew that music tied
blacks to their important heritage: "Black music shows the past . . . soul
music, living history" (Rose 1990, 15). Moreover, he knew that the historical was political. He tried to make his audience aware of "how deep the
codes and meaning of music run in black America, how they evoke an his-
toric continuum, how they can move to unite" (56). In "I'm Black and I'm
Proud," Brown sings:

> But all the work I did was for the other man . . .
> Now we demand a chance to do things for ourselves
> We're tired of . . . workin' for someone else.

I'm black and I'm proud. . . .
We'd rather die on our feet than live on our knees.
(Rose 1990, 68)

It is fitting that Brown should be Jimmy's hero. Jimmy is trying to change his fellow Dubliners, and Brown, according to band member Fred Wesley, "had the audacity to believe he could make things happen. . . . He forced it on people . . . but he made us all believers" (Rose 1990, 86). Jimmy wants his band to be as successful at transporting audiences as was Brown. He hopes that he has more in common with "America's soul Brother No. One" than only a first name.

Jimmy attempts to immerse his band in soul music and its culture. For instance, he "gave [the band members] their stage names" (Doyle 1989, 42), such as "James The Soul Surgeon Clifford" and "Billy The Animal Mooney." In doing this, he is adopting a long tradition in black musical culture: "Such names were essential identities in an America which had long been Negro but which would emerge . . . newly born as black. These were titles, beings, selves which existed beyond the reach of another [white] America. . . . These names and their world, however public they happen to become, remain very much a matter of private black control" (Rose 1990, 29). In his own experience of soul music, Doyle felt the power of this tradition of naming: "I loved these names, these nicknames that they have to live up to."

As another element of his cultural immersion, Jimmy appreciates the nonverbal sounds of the soul singers, which are, as Brown put it, "a code . . . another language" (Rose 1990, 127). He has Deco study "James for the growls, Otis for the moans, Smokey for the whines" (Doyle 1989, 31). Similarly, Jimmy taps into the African traditions surrounding food and the spirit. He puts Deco "on a strict soul *diet*" (31; my italics). Nourishment and the language surrounding it are integral to soul music: "Soul tradition 'feeds on truth'. . . . Food was a frequent metaphor in an escalating creative drive. . . . But it reaches back . . . towards more African definitions of what nutrition is all about: the feeding of the spiritual and cerebral as well as the corporeal self" (Rose 1990, 86).

In the manner of black preachers, Jimmy often gives inspirational speeches to his band, trying to strengthen its connection to black history: "He'd give them a talk. They all enjoyed Jimmy's lectures. So did Jimmy. They weren't really lectures, more workshops" (Doyle 1989, 35). Indeed, soul's origins are in the church; according to Aretha Franklin, "Soul came up from gospel and the blues" (Hirshey 1984, xiii). James Brown himself had a very strong gospel singing background: "In Brown's art, gospel is central" (Rose 1990, 24). The soul singer and the gospel preacher even share the same origins: "The same techniques [of freestyle collective improvisations] are used by the preacher and the singer—the singer perhaps being considered the lyrical extension of the rhythmically rhetorical style of the preacher," according to Pearl Williams-Jones, a music faculty member at City College in Washington, D.C. (Rose 1990, 118). James Brown felt that religion and soul were interchangeable: "As with the church itself, there was no end: this was meant to be music that would move the brother and sister for days. It was part of your black life, it was black life. As with real religion, you are meant to carry it out of the temple and with you into the daily arena of temptation, jubilation and despair" (Rose 1990, 60). Jimmy attempts to force his fellow Dubliners to see the similarity between themselves and blacks, to adapt the latter's modern tradition, and perhaps to gain a little self-respect. Doyle makes use of these similarities to broaden his readers' awareness at the same time as he cultivates a more respectful understanding of his countrymen.

A final feature of the band's sound that harkens back to African traditions is the substitution of Dublin words and places into the body of the songs, which adds "a bit o' local flavour" (Doyle 1989, 54). This localizing of the lyrics is common in soul music: "[The Afrocentric beat] is rhythm whose expectations of change, of improvisation, surprise and participation are deeply embedded . . . rhythmic participation also symbolizes black spiritual unity" (Rose 1990, 123). In the novel, the recognition of familiar places and common experiences inspires surges of local pride and always evokes cheers and hurrahs from the crowd. Interestingly, Deco, the band's lead singer and the most disloyal character, begins this exercise in unity. For example, in the song "What Becomes of the Broken-Hearted," he sings:

I'LL SEARCH FOR YOU

DOWN ON THE DOCKS

I'LL WAIT UNDER CLERY'S CLOCK.

(Doyle 1989, 54)

Clery's Clock, located on O'Connell Street in Dublin, would have been used by most of the crowd as a convenient meeting-spot. In "The Chain Gang," Deco extemporizes:

I'M THIRSTY

MY WORK IS SO HARD

GIVE ME GUINNESS.

(56)

Many non-Irish know that Guinness is the official national drink of Ireland, as common as Coca-Cola is in America; a fortified version of it is even served in hospitals and is also the sustenance recommended to be taken after donating blood.

As he explained in a later interview, one of the reasons Doyle changed the lyrics of certain songs "was the humorous effect—just seeing the Dublin accent written into a song and then changing the lyrics slightly." Nevertheless, examining the new lyrics can give the reader insights into the collective consciousness of the people about whom Doyle is writing. For instance, "Night Train," the band's signature song, features the most localized lyrics, recounting the northward route of the Dublin rapid transit system:

—STARTIN' OFF IN CONNOLLY—

—MOVIN' ON OU' TO KILLESTER——

—HARMONSTOWN RAHENY—

—AN DON'T FORGET KILBARRACK—THE HOME O' THE BLUES—

—HOWTH JUNCTION BAYSIDE—

THEN ON OU' TO SUTTON WHERE THE RICH FOLKS LIVE—

OH YEAH—

—NIGH' TRAIN——

—EASY TO BONK YOUR FARE—

—NIGH' TRAIN—

AN ALSATIAN IN EVERY CARRIAGE—

NIGH' TRAIN——

LOADS O' SECURITY GUARDS—

NIGH' TRAIN—

LAYIN' INTO YOUR MOT AT THE BACK—

NIGH' TRAIN'

GETTIN' SLAGGED BY YOUR MATES—

NIGH' TRAIN—

GETTIN' CHIPS FROM THE CHINESE CHIPPER—

OH NIGH' TRAIN—

CARRIES ME HOME—

. . .

COMIN' HOME FROM THE BOOZER—

NIGH' TRAIN—

. . . GETTIN' SICK ON THE BLOKE BESIDE YEH—

NIGH' TRAIN—

CARRIES ME HOME—

NIGH' TRAIN—

TO ME GAFF—

(Doyle 1989, 106, 148)

In response, the crowd "laughed. This was great. They pushed up to the stage. . . . They cheered. . . . Dublin Soul had been delivered" (105). The song's references describe general experiences to which most of the band's audiences could relate: the ever-present threat of the police; the drunken toots followed by nausea; hurried, semi-private sexual encounters; the late night binges on greasy food. Knowing about these general experiences makes the characters more accessible to a non-Irish, non-working-class readership.

Deco's lyrics, like Jimmy's renaming, preaching, and extemporizing, push the African American connection as far as possible in an attempt to make the band an authentic purveyor of soul music. Doyle has created such characters and such a band in order to broaden both his countrymen's and his public's awareness of cross-cultural similarities in an attempt to engender sympathy and empathy.

In addition to this central function of music in *The Commitments*—that of drawing the parallel between the African American and Irish experiences—Doyle also uses music to comment on or to foreshadow the dramatic action of the novel. Interestingly, this musical commentary is similar to the whistling habit of Ira Moran, a character in Anne Tyler's *Breathing Lessons*, one of Doyle's favorite novels (written just after *The Commitments*.) Ira has a tendency toward reticence, a trait that his wife has learned to accept because his whistling is so expressive: "But what he failed to realize was, his whistling could tell the whole story. For instance . . . after a terrible fight in the early days of their marriage they had more or less smoothed things over . . . and then he'd gone off to work whistling a song [with the lyrics] . . . 'I wonder if I care as much . . . as I did before'. . . . But often the association was something trivial, something circumstantial—'This Old House' when he tackled a minor repair job, or 'The Wichita Lineman' whenever he helped bring in the laundry" (Tyler 1988, 13). Like the songs that Ira whistles, some of Doyle's musical commentaries are frivolous and amusing, but others have serious connotations.

Doyle's use of music for humorous commentary is simple and obvious to those who are looking for it. For instance, one section of the novel begins with the sentence "The Commitments rehearsed three times a week" (Doyle 1989, 55), rough duty for a bunch of low-ambition teenagers; we have to chuckle when several lines later they begin to practice the song "Chain Gang." Another time, directly before Outspan's guitar string breaks, the lyrics are "—CAN'T GO OHON—" (81). Similar examples abound.

Sometimes the songs insert serious commentaries, as in the following:

> —GET ON UP—STAY ON THE SCENE—
> GET ON UP—LIKE A SEX MACHINE AH—
> GET ON UP—YOU GOT TO HAVE THE FEELING—
> SURE AS YOU'RE BORN—GET IT TOGETHER
>
> (18)

These lyrics encourage the young men who have the dream of forming a band concerned with "real sex and real politics." This music urges the fledgling band to have a voice and to make a positive impact on the empty lives of Dublin youth. In another instance, at one performance Deco does not introduce the band members in the rehearsed manner, a transgression that—added to all of Deco's other infuriating habits—angers the band. The song chosen for the encore, however, features suggestively conciliatory lyrics:

> AT THE DARK EH-END—
> OF THE STREET—
> THAT'S WHER-RE WE BOTH SHALL MEET
> HIDIN' IN SHA-DOWS WHERE WE DON'T BELOHO-O-ONG . . .
> YOU AN' ME—
>
> (118)

As embodied in the song, the band decides to forgive Deco's transgressions and to keep its higher goal in sight: "The Commitments were forgiving Deco. . . . It was beautiful" (118). Despite Deco's maddening egocentricity, the other members subconsciously realize that they must stay together: apart, they have no voice or power and are totally alone "at the dark end of the street"; banded together, however, at least they belong to something, even if this something has infuriating elements.

As a final example of musical commentary on the action of the story, the novel closes with the Byrds' "I'll Feel a Whole Lot Better":

> I HAVE TO LET YOU GO BAY—ABE—
> AND RIGHT AWAY—AY—Y—
> AFTER ALL YOU DID . . .
> AND I'LL PROBABLY—FEEL A WHOLE LOT BETTER—
> WHEN YOU'RE GOH—ON—
>
> (161)

The band has broken up, and Jimmy—disgusted by all the warring and tension that produced the split—is relieved to be rid of the worry and stress of being the band's manager. However, even though he is giving up the idea of a political band—which, as the song tells us, will be much easier on him— Jimmy has by no means lost his capacity to dream; as Doyle would later comment in an interview, Jimmy has "energy [and] resources . . . unemployment is just something to get out of the way—he's other things to do— he'll survive." Indeed, Jimmy is playing this recording of a good-bye song to introduce the genre of music that his next band will play.

Finally, in addition to commenting on the present action, the music also cleverly foreshadows situations in the future. For example, the first time that we meet saxophone player Joey the Lips Fagan, he sings a snippet of the classic Beatles song "All You Need Is Love." Later, Joey has sex with every female member of the band, and at the end of the novel he leaves Ireland because he is afraid that he has become a "da." Notice also that Deco's favorite song, "I Heard It" (Doyle 1989, 31), is a song about betrayal— which is what he ultimately does to the band when he attempts to go solo. When we read the lyrics to the song "What Becomes of the Broken Hearted?" we realize that the novel answers the question for the band members themselves—they go off and start a new band, which will most likely also fail because "HAPPINESS IS JUST AN ILLUSION— / FILLED WITH SADNESS AN' CON—FEU—SHUN" (51). One of the band's most popular songs, "Knock on Wood," features the following lyrics:

> I DON'T WANNA LOSE—
> THIS GOOD THANG—
> THA' I'VE GOT—
> IF I DO—
> I WOULD SURELY—
> LOSE THE LOT
>
> (69)

This love song comes to seem rather grim when one realizes that the Commitments indeed do "lose the lot" and are left living on the dole with few prospects. In a somewhat more pointed case of musical foreshadowing, the song "It's a Man's Man's Man's World" states that

IT'S A MAN'S—

MAN'S WORLD—

BUT IT WOULD BE NOTHIN'—

WITHOU' A WOMAN OR A GURREL

(136)

A few pages later, amid dissension and quarrels, Jimmy realizes that although the female band members—the Commitmentettes—were just backup singers, "Imelda might have been holding the Commitments together. Derek fancied her, and Outspan fancied her, Deco fancied her. He was sure James fancied her. Now Dean fancied her too. He fancied her himself. Imelda had soul" (145). Obviously, it might be a man's band, but it would be nothing without Imelda. On a lighter note, it is Natalie who sings the solo for "Walking in the Rain": "Natalie, in the middle, stepped forward. —I WANT HIM—" (58–59); three pages later, "Dean found Natalie kissing [Joey]" (61).

Thus, song lyrics—through both historical reference and structural reflection—connect, suggest, comment, foreshadow, and create an unforgettable mood in *The Commitments*. Doyle carefully chooses his band's playlist, for by inserting certain lyrics and certain songs, he adds a subtle new dimension to the novel's social commentary.

Alongside music, humor serves as Doyle's other major literary tactic in *The Commitments*. Although Doyle's manipulation of his audiences via humor in his later works is anticipated here, the humor in this novel is straightforward and not overly sophisticated. The book's premise—ten very inexperienced young adults forming their own band under the absurd tutelage of the practical yet bizarrely idealistic Jimmy Jr. and the middle-aged, Bible-spouting Joey the Lips—reads something like a situation comedy. Characters are funny; situations are funny; dialogue is funny. Doyle's deadpan literary style is apt for these comedic situations.

Doyle's Chekhovian manner of allowing the characters to reveal themselves is amusing in itself. For instance, Deco is a lead singer with no experience but excessive self-confidence. When Joey first plays the tape of a song that the band will perform, "they listened, frightened, to Jimmy Ruffin. They could never do that. Only Deco thought he could do better" (49).

Doyle's blunt, straightforward language perfectly captures Deco's lack of awareness of his own egotism.

Like Deco, Jimmy Jr. is also inexperienced, but he is under special pressure to never let others sense this inexperience, and his attempts to hide his uncertainty often lead to comedy. When he interrupts some of the band members smoking marijuana during a break, he is upset:

> Jimmy was doing some thinking. What had annoyed him at first was the fact that they hadn't got the go-ahead from him before they'd lit up. He needed a better reason than that.—For one thing, he said.—Righ'—Yis're barely able to play your instruments when yis have your heads on yis. . . . Second, said Jimmy. —We're a soul group. . . . Not a pop group or a punk group, or a fuckin' hippy group.—We're a soul group.
>
> —Wha' d'yeh mean, WE'RE? said Deco.
>
> —Fuck up, you. Jimmy was grateful for the interruption. It gave him more time to think of something. (73)

Again, Doyle's style is the perfect vehicle for this humor. Doyle lays bare for us the inner thoughts of these young people, inner thoughts that we all have but usually don't admit to having. Seeing ourselves in these characters makes us laugh at them and at our own fallibilities.

The dialogue itself is also funny. One simple, typical example is found at the start of the novel, when Outspan and Derek seek Jimmy's advice regarding the new band they have formed. Jimmy greets them sarcastically: "Puttin' the finishin' touches to your album?" Outspan replies with self-deprecating honesty: "Puttin' the finishin' touches to our name" (3).

Doyle also uses slapstick situational comedy, which works in this novel simply because the audience—its disbelief suspended by the inspirational speeches—is already prepared for the highly incongruous. The band's first gig is a perfect example of this physical humor. The soul band, dressed in dark suits and tight black miniskirts, is playing in a church hall. A banner behind them proclaims that they are performing as part of an antiheroin campaign; the word "heroin" is misspelled, but "the [drawing of a] syringe is very good though, isn't it" (96). The audience at this auspicious premiere is also presented comically: "There were about twelve of them . . . all kids, brothers and sisters of the Commitments, and their friends. . . . There were six other older ones, in their late teens or early twenties, mates, he supposed, of Deco or Billy or Dean. There were three girls, pals of Imelda, Natalie, and Bernie. The rest were kids, except for one, Outspan's mother. The caretaker got her a chair and she sat at the front, at the side" (94). Mickah, the semipsychotic bouncer, shoves the few audience members "up to the front. . . . It'll look better. . . . We don't want the group demoralized" (95). When the first number goes well, the audience does not need Mickah's prompting when it comes time to clap. During the next number, however, Deco, who has been swinging the microphone over his head, inadvertently hits Bernie with it: "[The mike] swooped into the back of Bernie's head. She was sent flying forward and she had to jump off the stage. The Commitments stopped" (100). During the next number, the piano "bashed into the backdrop, the operetta society's South Pacific scenery (last year's Sound of Music scenery with a very yellow palm tree painted onto one of the hills). The song was over. The audience didn't know this until Mickah told them to clap" (103). The highlight of the evening occurs when, during the encore, "something flies up and out of the darkness. It landed behind them, a little pair of light blue underpants." Quite the compliment, until we see how they came to be thrown up there:

> —I'll get them back for yeh after, righ', said Mickah.—When it's over.
> —Yeh said yeh'd give me a pound, the boy reminded him.
> —I'll let yeh in for nothin' the next time, said Mickah. This injustice stunned the boy for a while. He'd just made a sap of himself, flinging his kaks at your women on the stage and now he wasn't even going to be paid for it. (109)

The evening ends prematurely during the song "Knock on Wood" when Deco "knocked over the horn section's mike and half the horn section gave him an almighty kick up the hole. Deco wasn't going to be able to sing again for a good few minutes so Jimmy drew the curtain" (110). The situation is one of the most outrageous of the book, but there are others like it.

Religion also supplies a source of humor. For example, Joey the Lips is constantly spouting religious maxims, including using biblical language to praise the benefits of soul music:

> The Lord told me to come home. Ed Winchell, a Baptist reverend on Lenox Avenue in Harlem, told me. But The Lord told him to tell me. . . . The Lord told the Reverend Ed that the Irish Brothers had no soul, that they need some soul. And pretty fucking quick . . . the Brothers wouldn't be shooting the asses off each other if they had soul. . . . Jimmy was delighted. . . . The Commitments were going to be. They had Joey the Lips Fagan. And that man had enough soul for all of them. He had God too. (26)

It is no accident that the most religious-sounding character has sex with the band's three female members. In one of the novel's last scenes, he is also exposed as a liar.

Joey is a parody of John the Baptist, paving the way for the real Messiah, Jimmy. Doyle, the disinterested Creator, paring his fingernails, has offered up his creation, Jimmy, to save Dublin. Jimmy preaches to his band members—his disciples—and through them tries to reach the masses. Among the disciples are Deco, the Judas figure; James, a physician (like the biblical Luke); and Imelda, the sacred, untouchable female figure, the worship of whom holds the band together. The agnostic Doyle, however, writing tongue-in-cheek, clearly does not mean for the novel to be read as a Christian allegory; the band's attempt at saving humanity fails because the band members are ordinary, extremely fallible, heavy-drinking, sex-crazed Dublin youths. Associating these characters with New Testament figures is a joke that Doyle plays on the reader.

Such humor, far from being merely a way to draw the audience in (though it is that), is crucial in conveying the social vision and message of *The Commitments*. Despite the distressing economic and social situations of the band members and the band's eventual failure, the novel is anything but dreary: each character's outlook is either so positive or so humorously presented that pity is evoked for no one. The characters do not consider their situations dire, so the reader does not either; rather, we enjoy their wit and optimism. As with other of Doyle's early novels, bleakness is confined to the background while life-affirming humor and optimism dominate.

The novel emphasizes solutions. There are many problems, but each is solved in some way satisfactory to the reader and to the characters. The first crisis occurs at the outset, when Outspan and Derek seek Jimmy Jr.'s advice. Jimmy convinces them that soul music is the way to go; they agree; crisis solved. Each subsequent step in forming the band involves further struggle: finding additional members, teaching them to play soul music, planning and executing rehearsals. In this process, Jimmy receives invaluable aid from Joey the Lips, a middle-aged sax player who has played with numerous soul bands. All challenges overcome, everything comes together in time for their first gig (discussed above), which has good results in that they get a little bit of media exposure.

The next big crisis occurs when Billy, the drummer, quits the band because he hates Deco, the lead singer: "I fuckin' hate him—I can't even sleep at nigh' " (128). Less than a page later, however, Mickah—the former bouncer—decides that he wants to play the drums; another problem solved. Then Jimmy discovers that Dean, the fledgling saxophone player, has been studying and playing jazz, the death knell for any soul musician; Jimmy and Joey talk to him, and he agrees to stop doing so. Catastrophe averted.

The last crisis, obviously, occurs when the band implodes. Not even Jimmy's fine talking and slick maneuvering can patch up the final rift. But again, in less than five pages, there is talk of another, better band, without Deco (whose egoism and abrasive personality were the catalyst for the Commitments' split). The emphasis is on the new band, the solution, which will be better than the old, strife-ridden group.

This solution-problem formula obliquely suggests a social vision. This world is hard to live in, and life is not easy, but it can be survived and even enjoyed. The difference between leading a miserable or a joyful life is not located in one's circumstances or environment; rather, the difference is in each person. The young adults who form the Commitments are from poor homes, live with violence and drunkenness, will most likely never have fulfilling or intellectually challenging jobs—yet they are happy. How? In such circumstances, having a sense of humor is invaluable. Doyle's characters laugh at themselves and at each other. They do not dwell on the misery around them; they accept it and move on.

Their delight in belonging to the band shows us Doyle's second necessary ingredient for a joyous life, one that would become more apparent in his later novels: family. The band becomes a surrogate family for its members, with all the usual family dynamics. There are two parent-figures: Joey, the experienced voice of authority, and the more conciliatory problem-solver Jimmy. The other band members play the usual sibling roles: Imelda, so pretty that she is the "glue" that holds the group together; Mickah, the crazy one; Outspan, the shy one; James, the smart one. Even the insufferable Deco must be endured for the sake of the family. Like a real family, the group gives its members a sense of belonging. For once in their lives, they are doing something worthwhile and belonging to something sustaining, and they realize it. After the band's demise, Imelda asks Jimmy, "If you're startin' another group let us be in it, will yeh? It was brilliant crack. . . . It was fuckin' brilliant" (160).

The Commitments successfully launched the career of Roddy Doyle. The popularity of the novel and of the movie adapted from it brought name-recognition to Doyle; particular elements of the book—the Rabbitte family story, Barrytown and its savory dialect, the charm and accessibility of Doyle's writing—created an audience for future installments. In addition, *The Commitments* first demonstrated Doyle's comic genius while unpatronizingly giving literary voice to a community of outsiders. He appealingly presents both the joy and the pain of working-class Dublin.

CHAPTER FOUR

The Snapper

Doyle decided to focus his next novel, *The Snapper,* on the issue of pregnancy because "I knew nothing about it and I wanted to see if I could create a world which had nothing to do with me but which would be convincing." Although he started immediately after he finished *The Commitments* in 1986, the unfamiliar subject matter—which led him to, among other places, Doris Lessing's *A Proper Marriage* for invaluable inspiration—meant that the book took three years to complete ("such a short book—it took me longest of any to write"). Like *The Commitments, The Snapper* is funny, fast-paced, and dependent on dialogue written in Doyle's signature Barrytownese. At the same time, the differences between the two works are equally significant: Doyle's second novel narrows its focus to two characters rather than a whole group, and stresses how those characters develop and grow over time; there is less reliance on situational gags to provide humor; and the story and characters are the basis of the book's popularity, not the soundtrack of the film version. Although still as raucous as *The Commitments, The Snapper* evokes a more complex set of emotions, showing Doyle to have matured as an artist in just a few years.

Although the film version was marketed as "the feel-good movie of the year," *The Snapper* is not a light-hearted comedic novel; some readers even view it as a tragedy. The story again centers on the Rabbitte family, with Sharon and Jimmy Sr. as the principals; Jimmy Jr., the hero of *The Commitments,* is rarely seen. The book opens with Sharon, aged twenty, telling her parents that she is pregnant and intends to keep the baby—the "snapper" of the title, short for "whippersnapper." The reader's interest is piqued when

Sharon refuses to reveal the father's identity. Her parents, wisely realizing that her pregnancy is a fait accompli, accept the news with relative equanimity. The book progresses with the pregnancy; as Sharon tells the news to her friends and the rest of her unruly family, however, the father's name remains a mystery. The shocking circumstances of her impregnation are finally revealed in a flashback in which a drunk, semiconscious Sharon has sex against a parked car with George Burgess—a neighbor, the father of one of Sharon's close friends, her brother's soccer coach, and a spineless, unattractive, frustrated married man who is her father's age. Doyle never states that this sexual act is a rape, but Sharon's inebriation has made her not fully aware of what is happening; at the very least, Mr. Burgess has taken advantage of her horribly.

Instead of experiencing the overwhelming negative emotions that often accompany such a violation, however, Sharon is primarily concerned lest the father's identity become known to all of Barrytown—and she become a laughingstock. She is disgusted by the thought of a liaison with Mr. Burgess and wants only to forget the sordid event. Such forgetting proves impossible, however: when Sharon learns that he is bragging that she is a "great little ride," she is forced to confront him with the truth. The unforeseen result of this interview is that Mr. Burgess begins to believe himself in love with Sharon, and he soon leaves his wife, telling her that he is in love with "a girl . . . [who] is expecting . . . [who] has no one else to look after her" (Doyle 1990, 117). Barrytown is not filled with "eejits," and its inhabitants soon deduce a relationship between Sharon and Mr. Burgess. Sharon, still sickened by the thought of Mr. Burgess, denies the rumor and invents a mythical Spanish sailor as the father of her child; nevertheless, she becomes the joke of the whole town, just as she had feared.

Surprisingly, not the pregnancy itself but the circumstances surrounding it drive a wedge between the Rabbitte family members. Jimmy Sr., believing the rumors that he has heard concerning Mr. Burgess, is upset that Sharon's poor taste in men has made her family the laughingstock of the neighborhood; he becomes very angry at Sharon and gives her the silent treatment. For her part, Sharon refuses to accept blame for her condition, and the tension between the two begins to tear the family apart. Sharon forces Jimmy Sr.'s hand by threatening to move out of the home, at which point Jimmy Sr.

realizes how much he would miss her, and they reconcile in a touchingly humorous scene. Jimmy Sr. then becomes very involved in the pregnancy, which provides more comic interludes. At the end of the novel, Sharon delivers a healthy baby girl—and thumbs her nose at all of Barrytown by naming the baby Georgina. The last scene shows Sharon in her hospital bed, where she is laughing uncontrollably at her joke on Barrytown.

Central to the novel—and indicative of the strides Doyle had made as a writer since *The Commitments*—is the characterization. Doyle concentrates on just two characters, Sharon and Jimmy Sr., and develops them more fully than any characters in the first novel. Although these characters are not yet as complex as those in his later novels, the reader is able to recognize the personal growth that each undergoes and the consequent changes in their relationship.

At the beginning of the novel, Sharon is almost a textbook comic heroine. According to one critic, the comic hero "is marvelously resilient: [he] endures indignities, disappointments, misfortunes, and frustrations, yet his setbacks are almost invariably followed by a marked revival. The capacity for survival and revival [is] kin to all the comic figures who are constantly undone but never finished" (Bell 1991, 44). Sharon is the victim of a gross injustice (if not a criminal rape), but because she "radiates a fundamental comic equanimity" (46), she does not seem to need or want the reader's pity; as a comic heroine, she seems impervious to alienation and adultery, rape and poverty.

From the beginning, we sense that Sharon is not a pathetic character. She is self-assured, plain-speaking, unemotional. Doyle conveys this to us in his plain, unadorned narration: "Sharon was pregnant and she'd just told her father that she thought she was. She'd told her mother earlier, before the dinner" (Doyle 1990, 1). With a narrative tone like that, it is hard to see this pregnancy as apocalyptic. We perceive her self-possession—"she was happy with the way things were going so far" (2). Sharon is not calculating, but she is extremely competent and is not going to be forced into some false sense of guilt or shame over something that could happen to anyone. Sharon shares Molly Bloom's credo on guilt: "[I]f thats all the harm ever we did in this vale of tears God knows its not much" (Joyce 1986, 18:1517–18). In this first, crucial scene, Sharon effectively controls her parents and their reactions. She has the savvy to tell her mother first and to enlist her support in shaping her father's reaction. She refuses to divulge the father's identity, and she cannot be forced to alter her course of action merely because her parents want their curiosity satisfied. She refuses to humiliate herself because others may think her actions wrong. By asserting her rights as an adult, she forces her parents—and the reader—to acknowledge those rights. Just as we often need a prompt to tell us when something is funny or when we should laugh, Sharon's behavior is our prompt to put away our tragic sensibilities and to prepare ourselves to witness a self-sufficient character.

Another reason we do not pity Sharon is because she refuses to pity herself. Though she is not immune to worries, she rarely allows herself to get depressed. Her low point in the book lasts only two paragraphs: "Sharon lay on her bed. She couldn't go downstairs, she couldn't go to the Hikers, or anywhere. . . . She'd no friends now, and no places to go to. She couldn't even look at her family. God, she wanted to die; really she did. She just lay there. She couldn't do anything else" (Doyle 1990, 119). However, her despair lasts only for a moment: "She was angry now. She thumped the bed. . . . She'd deny it, that was what she'd do" (120). Nothing in her situation changes except her mindset. This determination occurs again when she fears that Yvonne Burgess, Mr. Burgess's daughter, might cause a scene at the pub: "She hoped to God Yvonne wouldn't be there tonight. Maybe she'd be better off staying at home—Ah fuck this, she said. And she got up and went out" (106). She recognizes the futility of negative thinking, and she avoids it.

Another quality of the comic hero is "an odd sort of passivity that combines a flexible yet stubborn resistance to being pushed with a general reluctance to pull" (Galligan 1984, 84). The hero reacts, but rarely acts, to survive: "None of them solves his problems by taking purposeful action; each waits for something to happen that will bring about a solution" (100). Comic heroes are patient, waiting for the "luck it takes to survive in this world" (115). In short, they are floaters, but of a particularly shrewd or effective type: "Comedy's heroes are not men of action who can impose their will upon circumstances. . . . They are men and women who have the wit to keep circumstances from imposing on them" (33).

Sharon has these qualities. She blames no one and wants no revenge for her condition. She merely accepts it and expects others to accept it as well. She is pregnant and has refused the option of abortion; instead, she makes the best of her situation. Her actions are reactions—she visits Mr. Burgess only after he has spread rumors about her; she waits until the last moment to tell her friends about her condition; she quits her job only after her manager has made it unbearable; she invents the Spanish sailor only after her continued denials of Burgess's paternity are not believed. Notice that even when she gets angry and vows to fight, she is still passive: "She'd deny it, that was what she'd do. And she'd keep denying it" (Doyle 1990, 120). Sharon's ability to adapt defuses any difficult situation. Mr. Burgess, Jimmy Rabbitte, and the rest of the Barrytowners—not Sharon—have created the problem. Sharon merely accepts and reacts to what life offers her.

Sharon's status as comic heroine is confirmed by Doyle's focus on her body. In the words of one critic, "In comic ignorance of the profundities which should be ruining or at least complicating his life, the comic protagonist concerns himself with such corporeal trivialities as flatulence, constipation and its happy relief, elimination, and sex" (Bowen 1989, 32–33). Doyle tells more than many readers may care to know about the changes occurring in Sharon's sex life, nipples, menstrual history, and urinary and defacatory habits:

> Her nipples were going to get darker. She didn't mind that too much. The veins in her breast would become more prominent. Sharon didn't like the sound of that. . . . The joints between her pelvic bones would be widening. She hoped they wouldn't pinch a sciatic nerve, because she had to stand a lot of time in work and a pinched sciatic nerve would be a killer. She read about her hormones and what they were doing to her. She could picture them; little roundy balls with arms and legs. She hoped her bowel movements stayed fairly regular. Her uterus would soon be pressing into her bladder. What worried her most was the bit about vaginal secretions. They'd make her itchy, it said. That would be really terrible in work, fuckin' murder. Or when she was out. She'd have preferred a pinched sciatic nerve. (Doyle 1990, 13)

Sharon—and later, Jimmy Sr.—consistently monitor her body's progress and changes, cataloguing what is going on in her body, what she eats, how the baby is progressing. The reader experiences, first-hand, her morning sickness; we know she urinates much more frequently; we are with her in the delivery room and witness her pain.

Interestingly, most of the emphasis is on Sharon's physical changes rather than on psychological ones. She notices that her uterus is pressing into her bladder but seems oblivious to the responsibilities that come with bringing a new life into the world; she is more interested in her growing tummy than in her child's possible future. She never despairs over having to share her body with an unwanted life for which she never asked and whose father she despises; she experiences no angst over lost dreams and altered life plans. She experiences no depression over bringing a child into a world with such poverty, violence, ignorance, and spiritual aridity. Moreover, she suggests no self-questioning about whether she is doing the right thing. Sharon is extremely matter-of-fact about this pregnancy, her only concerns (and mild ones at that) revolving around how all these life-changes might affect her work performance and her enjoyment of the pub.

Such a dearth of depth and despair is characteristic of the comic tradition: "The tragic spirit is inimical to the comic hero, because comic characters have a morality which is complete, in the sense that their principles are generally clear and coherent enough so that they do not face soul-wrenching moral decisions. . . . [T]he action in comedies derives from the changes of fortune that the comic heroes encounter" (Bowen 1989, 3). Sharon is trying to "muddle through," as the British say: she wants to mind her own business, make as few waves as possible, hurt as few people as possible, and seize as many of the small opportunities to get ahead as come her way. She doesn't soul-search. She encounters a situation and handles it. She does not deal in "ifs," nor does she concern herself with smaller matters of morality, like whether stealing a box of cod steaks is wrong. She manages what she is able to change and what affects the living of her life. Abstractions don't interest her.

In the context of these personal and biological changes, the major interpersonal confrontation comes in Sharon's struggle with her father. Again, her life has historical precedent: "In traditional comedy the hero overcomes the senex figure, the father or his surrogate, and thus the dynamic renewal of the community is assured" (Waters 1984, 67). In true comic hero passivity, she does not confront Jimmy Sr. until she is forced to by his intolerable treatment of her: "A few weeks ago she wouldn't have blamed him for being like this. But—she flattened her hands on her belly—it was a bit late to be getting snotty now. She'd have to do something. . . . [S]he wasn't going to let him go on treating her like shite" (Doyle 1990, 151).

For several weeks, Jimmy mopes around, pretending that he is truly suffering humiliation because of Sharon's condition. She is aware of what her father is doing—and of how dangerous it could be for her baby and for the family's harmony. She decides to call his bluff: she apologizes profusely and then tells him she cannot live at home anymore because it would be too hard for the family. Jimmy, a loving father, does not want his daughter to leave home. Recognizing how badly he has been acting, he apologizes. He says that he will love the baby no matter who it resembles and that there will be no more attempts at imposing guilt trips. Through her response, Sharon forces her father to accept her and her baby.

Over the course of the novel, however, Sharon proves to be more than a stagnant comic heroine reacting to situations. Rather, *The Snapper* is a bizarre *bildungsroman* during which Sharon undergoes a rite of passage and matures because of her experience. She goes from being an almost stock comic heroine to being a fully realized and individualized character.

Although we do not see Sharon in any great depth before her pregnancy, nevertheless we can infer what she was like. Even though Jimmy Sr. calls her "the only civilized human being in the whole fuckin' house" (160), Sharon seemed to be a typical teenager, perhaps a bit more responsible than most. She probably left school early, and she is currently working in a grocery store. She regularly gets drunk and has had sex, these two acts occurring, more often than not, in the same night; evaluating her character in a later interview, Doyle comments that "I suspect that it is not the first time she has had sex against the car when she has been drunk." She has probably done nothing that every other Barrytowner her age has not done.

During her life through the beginning of the novel, Sharon has developed only superficial relationships and she has no confidante:

She felt a bit lonely now. She'd have loved someone to talk to, to talk to nonstop for about an hour, to tell everything to. But—and she was realizing this now really—there was no one like that. She'd loads of friends but she only really knew them in a gang. . . . Jackie had been her best friend for years but now that was only because she saw her more often than the others, not because she knew her better. . . . She'd often read in magazines and she'd seen it on television where it said that women friends were closer than men, but Sharon didn't think they were. Not the girls she knew. (42–43)

Sharon's particular gang of friends would get together to drink, laugh, and ridicule ex-lovers. However, when "one of the gang was going with someone . . . she'd disappear for a while, usually a couple of months, and come back when one of them broke it off" (42). Sharon's female relationships are shallow and immature because she and her friends are shallow and immature.

Sharon still lives with her family, but judging from her conversations with her brothers and her father, their relationships stay on the surface. Although the familial love and loyalty are obvious, the various Rabbittes do not seem to know each other as people, only as family members. We most often see Sharon and her siblings yelling at one another. At the beginning of the novel, Jimmy Sr. fares no better at conversing with Sharon. When they attempt to have a drink together at the pub, Jimmy thinks, "He loved Sharon but, if the last five minutes were anything to go by, she was shocking drinking company. . . . There was only an hour to closing time but Jimmy Sr. wasn't sure he'd be able to stick it" (10). In this particular instance, Jimmy is indeed unable to "stick it," as he gives Sharon a "fiver" (a five-pound note) and sends her over to a group of her own friends—his usual way of interacting with his family.

From these unpromising beginnings, Sharon is forced to mature during the course of the novel. However, Doyle does not write a typical novel showing how childbirth makes a woman a more responsible adult. First, the pregnancy itself has little to do with Sharon's maturation; the circumstances around it are what spark her growth. Second, Sharon is an unwitting participant in her own maturation; although the reader can discern Sharon's maturation, Sharon herself does not. As mentioned previously, she is more concerned with her physical changes than with her psychological ones, and she is as dimly aware of her growth as she was of her impregnation.

The rites of passage surrounding Sharon's pregnancy have nothing to do with accepting the burden of bringing a new life into the world; rather, Sharon's alienation from her family and community is what makes her stronger. The provinciality of Barrytown, or of any small area, often results in the muting of independent personalities. All want to fit in; consequently, even offbeat personalities generally conform. Doyle initially portrays Sharon as on her way to such a fate: she and her friends had become almost indistinguishable, their voices in the pub seemingly interchangeable; even as a literary character, Sharon was a textbook comic heroine, a set of rules and definitions. Because of the unfortunate Mr. Burgess affair, however, Sharon soon has no one's behavior to copy and no one with whom to blend in. She becomes the community's Other, friendless and alienated; when denied by her father, she is left completely alone, without even the support of her family. Although it is painful, Sharon manages to endure this exile— and eventually to become stronger than the community. She starts acting rather than reacting, and thus begins to be an independent force. She breaks free from definitions and expectations and becomes distinctive. Ultimately, the community does not accept her, repentant, back into its folds; rather, *she* accepts the community back into her life, her actions reestablishing the bonds that it had broken.

We see Sharon's maturation when she stops reacting like every other Barrytowner. Initially, when a bunch of young boys heckle her—"How's Mister Burgess?"—she ignores them, her typical response to shouts from men; but "still, she was shaking and kind of upset when she got home and upstairs" (125). However, she soon refuses to ignore these insulting remarks: "Sharon grabbed the boy. She held him by the hood of his sweatshirt. . . . Sharon slapped him across the head. . . . If you ever call me anythin' again I'll fuckin' kill yeh, d'yeh hear me. . . . She'd never done it before. It was easy. She'd do it again" (130). Her change does not stop with little boys: instead of appeasing her father's ill temper, she devises a plan to change his attitude. Her plan works and he begs her to stay: "I've been a righ' bollix, Sharon. I've made you feel bad an' that's why you're leavin'. Just cos I was feelin' hard done by. It's my fault. Don't go, Sharon. Please. . . . I can't look at yeh, sayin' this. It's very fuckin' embarrassin'. . . . I love you, Sharon. An' it'll be your baby, so I'll love it as well" (162). Sharon has regained control of her position in the family.

The last scene of the novel encapsulates her newfound maturity. By naming her daughter Georgina, she refuses to be ignored by Barrytown and she refuses to apologize for her child. She is demanding that she and her daughter be treated respectfully and that there be no snide whispers about the child's paternity. The name also ensures that her daughter will be special: by advertising and glorifying the baby's difference instead of hiding and covering it, Sharon is forcing others to accept it. This act solidifies Sharon's new sense of personal independence, as well as giving her daughter her own uniqueness. From this point on—or so the novel leads us to believe—Sharon will interact with the community on her own terms, not on theirs.

Alongside the story of Sharon's struggles and growth, Jimmy Sr. plays an important role in the novel. Indeed, at times it seemed to Doyle as if Jimmy were becoming *too* important of a character: "The father was taking over *The Snapper* and would have given birth to the baby if at all humanly possible." Like Sharon, Jimmy too changes, becoming aware of his shortcomings and then altering his lifestyle. In the beginning, Jimmy is a typical Barrytowner, having never engaged in much introspective thought. He is a simple man with simple thought processes, so simple as to be childlike, almost a caricature. For instance, when Veronica agrees to have sex early one evening, his response is similar to a child who has been told he can have a special dessert: "Are yeh serious? . . . Fuckin' great . . . it's not even dark yet. You're not messin' now? . . . I'll brush me teeth" (Doyle 1990, 73). In another scene, he seems like an adolescent boy when he is embarrassed to kiss Veronica good-bye in front of his sons because "[t]hey'd slag him" (39).

Although Jimmy Sr. is the primary breadwinner of the family, he lacks the maturity to be the disciplinarian in his family. He tells Veronica to set the family policy concerning Sharon's pregnancy because "they'd only laugh at me. I'm only their da" (49). When his family has news that they think will anger him, his anger is not something to be feared but instead something to be cajoled or tricked away, like a child's momentary rage; Sharon is able to defuse his potential anger both when telling him of her pregnancy and in the confrontation over his ill treatment of her. Indeed, instead of setting the rules, Jimmy functions in his family as the comedian. With his silly behavior, broad humor, and occasional fiver, he diffuses potentially angry or stressful situations. For instance, he makes fun of the twins' teacher when they announce, "Miss O'Keefe said yeh should be ashamed of yourself" (35); and he cajoles Veronica out of her ill humor over the twins' abandonment of ballroom dancing after she has slaved over their costumes.

Jimmy does not interact with his family in any way deeper than his prescribed roles. He seems unable to show affection overtly, and instead is constantly giving the twins fivers so they can run to the store and buy Twixes and Choc-Ices for the family. We've already witnessed how he is unable to make simple adult conversation with his daughter. When he does interact with his family within the parameters of his roles, however, the result is rewarding. The scene in which he gives Darren the long coveted bicycle for his birthday shows Jimmy at his best, both as breadwinner and as comedian: he is able to provide Darren with the present he most wants and to make a joke out of the situation at the same time.

As long as things are running smoothly, Jimmy is content. However, when something goes wrong or when his efforts are not appreciated, he sulks like an adolescent. For example, when he valiantly tries to protect Sharon's honor from imagined insults at the local pub—getting a bloody nose in the process—what hurts him most is Sharon's anger at him for causing an unwanted scene.

> All Jimmy Sr. had wanted was value for his nosebleed. But something had gone wrong. A bit of gratitude was all he'd expected. He'd felt noble there for a while before Sharon started talking about leaving, even though he'd been lying. But she'd attacked him instead. . . . He was ashamed of Sharon. . . . There was something else as well: she was making an eejit of him. . . . But, fuck, his life was being ruined because of her. . . . He was the laughing stock of Barrytown. . . . Jimmy Sr. got moodier. . . . [H]e knew he could snap out of it but he didn't want to. He was doing it on purpose. He was protesting; that was how he described it to himself. He'd been wronged; he was suffering and he wanted them all to know it. Especially Sharon. He wanted to make her feel bad. (147–49)

However, in a true epiphany brought on by Sharon's trickery, Jimmy becomes aware of his childish behavior:

> He was a changed man, a new man. That trouble a while back with Sharon had given him an awful fright and, more important, it had made him feel like a right useless oul' bollix. He'd done a lot of thinking since then. . . . There was more to life than drinking pints with your mates. There was Veronica, his wife, and his children. . . . [H]e was responsible for them. But, my Jaysis, he'd made one poxy job of it so far. . . . [H]is kids were grand, but . . . that was just good luck and Veronica because he'd had nothing to do with it. But from now on it was going to be different. Darren and Linda and Tracy, and even Leslie, were still young enough and then there'd be Sharon's little snapper as well. A strong active man in the house, a father figure, would be vital for Sharon's snapper. (193)

Jimmy does change for the rest of the novel, and he tries to become an *active* force in his children's lives. He coaches Darren's bike racing team; he reads up on pregnancy and becomes so knowledgeable that he begins to annoy Sharon with his questions and comments. We see him genuinely engaging in conversation with Sharon, mostly about the baby. He even volunteers to be present at the delivery.

Not only do these two characters grow, but also their relationship matures accordingly. Before Sharon's pregnancy, each character saw the other as only one-dimensional. As with most families, each of the Rabbittes must conform to a certain familial role: Jimmy is the breadwinner and comedian who, if necessary, must be appeased by means of trickery; Sharon, the oldest daughter, is a caretaker who lives her own life and causes little trouble to her parents—even in the beginning of her pregnancy, she still has things under control. These two characters cannot interact with each other except when playing their respective roles; such rigidity makes a fiasco of their tête-à-tête in the pub after Sharon discloses her pregnancy. However, after Jimmy's period of sulking and his subsequent epiphany, they begin to view each other differently. Sharon, never cognizant of her need of her father's support until it is gone, no longer takes Jimmy for granted; for his part, Jimmy sees Sharon as a woman, not as a child any more. We witness a conversation where they actually talk to each other like adults, ending with Jimmy asking to be Sharon's partner in the delivery room. Their relationship has strengthened to the point where he can make such an intimate request; at the beginning of the novel, his asking this (or even wanting to) would have been unimaginable. Sharon understandably says no, thank you; we can sense Jimmy's relief, but nevertheless he made the offer.

The novel's most compelling aspect is the way Doyle makes the outcome of a sordid experience—Mr. Burgess's brutal violation of Sharon—into something so positive. Doyle wanted the impregnation scene to be foul: "I wanted the circumstances from her memory to be really seedy and awful with the yawning big hole of embarrassment. . . . The awfulness is as much the fact that the man is so inelegant." Moreover, another reason for the "awfulness" is the question of rape that is raised during the scene. In the novel, Sharon "wondered a few times if what had happened could be called rape. She didn't know" (Doyle 1990, 45). Most reviewers do not even bring up the issue—only two of the twenty or so that I have read mention the circumstances of the pregnancy, and these two do call it a rape. Doyle himself says,

> When I was writing the book, I didn't want to encroach too much. I wanted it to be left up to the reader. Legally, in Ireland, it is not a rape, although I believe that in some states in the States it is a rape. I wouldn't personally consider it a rape. I do believe that he behaved very wrongly in taking advantage of a drunk woman. But, again, does that make it illegal? Where do you step from immorality to illegality? . . . I wanted the circumstances to be left open to interpretation.

Alongside the issue of rape, the scene also carries incestuous overtones: Mr. Burgess—who, as her friend's father, has watched Sharon grow up—says as his parting words, "I've always liked the look of you, Sharon" (Doyle 1990, 45). Whatever the reader's individual interpretation of these issues, the impregnation was a horrible violation—but Doyle is able to take such a circumstance and make it into a celebration.

How does Doyle do this? As we have seen, he succeeds in large part by creating vivid characters who use the experience to grow; moreover, he is able to manipulate his audience's reactions by means of humor. More than merely the occasion for some quick laughs, humor in Doyle's work serves as a literary tactic, directing our responses to certain situations in the novel: "We laugh more when we are in a humorous frame of mind. Indeed, once we begin laughing at a series of ludicrous incongruities we may be made to laugh at anything. . . . [W]e will look forward to the pleasure and we will prepare our minds to receive it" (Schaeffer 1981, 18).

Doyle relies on this principle in the first scene of *The Snapper*. Notice how carefully Doyle shapes our response to Sharon's news: she "was happy with the way thing were going so far" and she and her mother "looked at each other, and grinned quickly" (Doyle 1990, 2–3). The reader takes his cue from Sharon that this passage should not be read glumly—and then is free to laugh at Jimmy's childlike confusion. We can smile with Sharon and her mother at Jimmy. Then, when our mind is teetering on the tragedy/comedy fence, Doyle presents several comic interludes that are nearly impossible not to enjoy. Jimmy Jr., who wants to be Ireland's answer to Wolfman Jack, begins practicing his radio persona in a booming voice. Then, only several sentences after Jimmy Sr. "could feel himself getting a bit angry now" at Sharon's refusal to answer the paternity question, one of the twins enters the kitchen and complains that Darren is hitting her. The ensuing dialogue is hilarious:

—I'll go in in a minute an' I'll hit Darren an' you can watch me hittin' him.
—Can I?
—Yeah, yeh can. Now get ou' or I'll practise on you first. Linda squealed
and ran away from him. She stopped at the safe side of the kitchen door.
—Can Tracy watch as well?
—She can o' course.(4)

Jimmy, in his clown role, simultaneously diffuses the sibling fight and un-wittingly his own anger with humor. Sharon and her parents discuss her situation a little longer, but the potential anger has already been rerouted, and the family harmony remains as it ever was.

These first scenes are very important because Doyle, if he wants his comic spirit to prevail, must get his readers into an accepting, light-hearted mood. We must be expecting more humor and be waiting to laugh, because when he finally divulges the real circumstances of Sharon's pregnancy, we will be so horrified that, had our minds not been primed, the future of his comedy would be dim. In the scene before Sharon's violation is revealed, Veronica is laughing so hard that tears stream down her face. The discovery scene itself is somber and matter-of-fact. Sharon is confused and hurt. She goes over what occurred that night in minute detail, and we feel her disgust. The reader is shaken up—Doyle has thrown us a curve ball—surely we had gotten past the worst with the unwanted pregnancy. Doyle does not allow the reader much time to think about the circumstances of the impregnation, however, as the next scene explodes with hilarity almost before the reader is aware of it. He lures the reader into the next scene immediately—"the reader is drawn into the book by the fluent, seductive rapidity of its successive scenes" (Kiberd 1994, 23)—by beginning the scene with violence and tears; initially, the reader may think that the tears still relate to Sharon's violation, but soon realizes that they are totally unrelated. Instead, the characters are laughing hilariously, and the reader joins in. Doyle has succeeded in making his audience aware of the circumstances of her pregnancy without miring them in either anger or despair.

Throughout much of the rest of the story, Doyle makes it difficult to keep the rape in mind—or, at least, to let the rape take over our minds. We are given a number of uplifting, humorous side plots—Darren's birthday and bike team, the twins' demand for ever-changing costumes, Jimmy's voyage of discovery into the female body—which draw our attention away from the violation. Moreover, the criminal, Mr. Burgess, is so pathetic and laughable that our minds are diverted from the atrocity of his crime: "Sharon's incipient snapper is the result of what could well be called rape in the car park at the soccer club Christmas do, but she was so pissed at the time, and the offender, George, is so pathetic, that she lets that one pass" (Barnacle 1990, 33). Conversely, Sharon is so sensible that it is difficult to pity her.

It is important to realize that Doyle is not holding up rape or incest as laughing matters. As Ernest Becker insists, ignoring or denying unsavory situations, although comforting, is ultimately cowardly because it "smooths over the rough edges of nagging truth" (Lewis 1989, 68–69). Doyle's humor, however, does not deny truth; rather, it serves as a way to deal with it. Humor is such a powerful tool because it is "a force in controlling our responses to unexpected and dangerous happenings" (13). Doyle is not exercising this power to minimize such a despicable crime. He is exercising his power to present to the reader an alternative way of coping with the horrors everyone will encounter in life: humor can "console us by making us feel that what we are dealing with is not worth taking seriously as an object of fear" (69).

Doyle's characters, in their daily lives, illustrate the healing power of humor. They use humor to diffuse anger and to restore harmony. Numerous scenes include anger, shouting, and potential violence, but the characters' senses of humor prevail. For instance, when the family has assembled to hear Sharon's "bit o' news," a fight breaks out between Leslie and Jimmy Sr. Veronica even slaps Leslie several times, and the fight ends when Leslie storms out of the house almost in tears. Jimmy Sr. attempts to vent his anger on Jimmy Jr., who makes a funny, sassy reply that evokes laughter from other family members. The scene could have turned violent, but then Veronica starts laughing—"Sorry, she said.—I can't help it" (Doyle 1990, 46). Everyone either laughs or grins, and Sharon now has the proper atmosphere in which to break the news of her pregnancy.

At the pub, humor works the same as it does in the Rabbitte kitchen. A jovial mood is almost broken when Yvonne starts to gripe jealously about Sharon's job, but Jackie comes to Sharon's rescue by attacking Yvonne:

> —It's nice for some, said Yvonne.—Havin' a job to think abou' givin' it up.
> —. . . . Fuck off an' leave her alone. Are you havin' your periods or somethin'?
> —Yeah, I am actually. Wha' about it?
> —You're stainin' the carpet.
> The row was over. They nearly got sick laughing. (56)

Humor keeps tempers under control, smooths over hurt egos, and allows a graceful exit from a fight.

Similarly, in the reconciliation scene between Sharon and Jimmy Sr., humor eases the tension and makes apologizing easier for Jimmy. After he has told Sharon that he is sorry for his past behavior and for trying to make her feel guilty, she asks him what he would do if the baby, by any weird co-incidence, should resemble Mr. Burgess. Jimmy replies, "—If it looks like Burgess's arse I'll love it, Sharon. . . . —They were both laughing. They'd both won." When asked what if the baby were a girl and looked like Burgess, Jimmy says, "Ah well, fuck it; we'll just have to smother it an' leave it on his step" (163). With this shared joke, the tension between them is broken, family equilibrium restored.

Doyle also uses humor to show group unity. There is a great deal of laughing and joke telling going on at the pub, and this hilarity means more than just superficial fun. As often occurs in real life, laughter bonds the friends together and shows their support of each other: "When we laugh together, we close ranks . . . in the face of something that threatens the solidarity of the group" (Waters 1984, 12). Sharon tells her friends about her pregnancy at the pub and "then they all started laughing. They looked at one another and kept laughing. . . . They were all blushing and laughing" (Doyle 1990, 53). Even though Sharon knows that Barrytown will talk about her, she thinks her friends will stand by her: "Fuck them. Fuck all of them. She didn't care. The girls had been great" (68). This united laughter shows their support of Sharon and their joy at her news. During the scene when Sharon first tells Jackie about the Spanish soldier, laughter again provides solidarity. The beginning of the scene is tension-filled; the two are discussing the "Burgess situation," and Jackie is unconvinced that Mr. Burgess is not the father. "Jackie tried to laugh. They looked at each other and then they really laughed. Sharon thought the happiness would burst out of her" (122). With this laughter, Jackie's doubts are pushed aside and she says that she believes Sharon. She has said, with this laughter, that she will stand by Sharon; she and Sharon use laughter as others use a handshake.

The reconciliation scene discussed above leads us into a final way that humor is used in this novel, namely, as a tool for characterization. We learn about a character when we see how he or she uses and responds to humor. We can also judge a character's growth or regression from his or her use of humor: "Because it contributes to both maturity and to maturation, humor frequently arises in convincing literary treatments of growth or enlightenment. . . . [A] character's use of humor should be related to his or her capacity for cognitive, emotional and moral development. . . . [A] growing person's relation to his or her family and society will in many cases be apparent in his or her sense of humor" (Lewis 1989, 75). This is true in the case of Doyle's characters.

Sharon's sense of humor remains fairly consistent throughout the novel, although at times she (understandably) has to struggle to keep it. Consider the confrontation scene with Mr. Burgess: although raped by this man, Sharon can nevertheless see how ludicrous he and the whole situation are. After he tries to give her money, "she wanted to laugh but she thought that that wouldn't be right. But she couldn't manage anger." And later, after having been given back her underwear, "Sharon was stunned, and then amused" (Doyle 1990, 90–91). Even though just a bit earlier she was almost in tears, Sharon can still appreciate the incongruity of her predicament. This outlook keeps her in control of the situation and also keeps her from appearing ridiculous and pathetic.

Her sense of humor enables her to triumph at the end. In the final scene, we see her humor as a sign both of her maturity and of her future success as a mother:

> Georgina; that was what she was going to call her. They'd all call her Gina, but Sharon would call her George. And they'd have to call her George as well. She'd make them . . .
> —Are yeh alrigh' love? It was the woman in the bed beside Sharon.
> —Yeah, said Sharon—Thanks; I'm grand. She lifted her hand—it weighed a ton—and wiped her eyes.
> —Ah, said the woman.—Were yeh cryin'?
> —No, said Sharon.—I was laughin'. (215–16)

As discussed above, Sharon has just played a huge joke on Barrytown, and she loves it. We see her embrace and revel in the whole ludicrous situation.

Jimmy Sr. is another character with whom we may use humor as a measuring stick. In the beginning of the book, he is, as the family clown, one of the funniest characters. Always joking or the object of a joke, he is full of laughter. Having seen what a wonderful sense of humor Jimmy possesses makes it all the harder for readers to stomach the self-righteous, martyred

Jimmy who tries to chasten Sharon. He totally loses his sense of humor: "That was all; no joking, no smile, not even a guilty look" (151). Jimmy is trying to punish Sharon by withholding his good humor. He gets his comic just deserts when Sharon humbles him in the scene already discussed. Notice what the first sign of reconciliation is—a shared laugh: "They were both laughing. They'd both won. Both sets of eyes were watery" (163). In the next scene, chaos—the Rabbitte version of harmony—reigns again.

Significantly, Mr. Burgess is the one character with no sense of humor or appreciation of the incongruous—and therefore, he is ludicrous. Mr. Burgess's lack of humor leaves him vulnerable and weak. For instance, his idiocy makes it easy for Sharon to control their confrontation; he crumbles before her disdain. His inflated sense of gravity contributes to his ridiculous decision to leave his wife for Sharon, with whom he has convinced himself he is in love, and who, he also has convinced himself, needs his protection. He bears the weight of all of Doyle's infrequent satire; even his letter to Sharon is written on pink stationery bordered with bunny rabbits. Burgess is so pathetic that he seriously rehearses bathetic lines to use on Sharon—and admits it:

> —Sharon, I've been livin' a lie for the last fifteen years. Twenty years. The happily married man. Huh. It's taken you to make me cop on. You Sharon.
> —Did you rehearse this, Mister Burgess?
> —No—Yeah, I did. I've thought o' nothin' else, to be honest with yeh. I've been eatin' an' drinkin' an' sleepin'—sleepin' it, Sharon.
> —Bye bye, Mister Burgess. (128)

Sharon wants no part of him, and avoids him. When he finally forces her to talk to him, she berates him, laughs at him, and even denies his paternity. He cannot see how ridiculous he is—and in this he is the exact opposite of Sharon, who knows how funny her situation looks to outsiders and finally embraces its comedic value. Burgess never understands, and Barrytowners and readers alike laugh at him at every opportunity.

Humor also plays a part in the novel's treatment of religion—only this time it is Doyle himself, not one of his characters, who is having some fun. As in *The Commitments*, religion is not a factor in the Rabbittes' lives; still, if the Rabbittes had not been professing Catholics, the story would have unfolded quite differently. Notice how Sharon will not even consider having an abortion: "—There's no way I'd have an abortion, said Sharon. . . . .— Abortion's murder" (6). Sharon, a woman with no knowledge of biology, would have objected to abortion only for religious reasons, hinting at a possible religious undercurrent in her unconventional life.

However, it is interesting to note that the most inconvenient tenets of Catholicism, most of which concern impulsive actions such as sex, are dispensed with. For example, premarital sex and adultery—other sins in the Church—are not even mentioned. In fact, abortion itself is not unheard of in the country: "In an average year, three to four thousand Irish women go to England to have an abortion" (Donoghue 1994, 3). This leads one to wonder how inconvenient having a child actually was to Sharon; and indeed, there are suggestions that from the start Sharon actively wants the child. Early during her pregnancy, when she thinks her period has started, she thinks "she'd been robbed" (Doyle 1990, 26); Sharon also likes the attention that her condition brings her, before Burgess's paternity is known. In this light, Sharon's hasty statement—"Abortion's murder"—seems more like a case of religion being used to validate what she wants to do rather than an indication of a true Catholic belief.

Moreover, *The Snapper*—like *The Commitments*—also has elements of a tongue-in-cheek religious allegory: it would be in keeping with Doyle's iconoclastic sensibilities for him to rewrite the story of the virgin birth of Christ, with Sharon as the Virgin Mary and Jimmy Sr. as Joseph. The circumstances and paternity of each pregnancy were disputed and became an issue within each woman's community. Both women are accompanied by older men who, though not the babies' biological fathers, will be the male role models. Few believed either woman's version of her impregnation; of course, Sharon's initial story is a lie, but Mary's, according to the New Testament, was not.

The combination of memorable, sympathetic characters, witty, fast-paced dialogue, a story line that is neither predictable nor drawn out, and a hopeful, optimistic vision makes *The Snapper* a joy to read and to reread. This richly comic novel contains a great deal of wisdom: it shows us that—through humor and love—we can make our own lives bearable, under almost any circumstances. If "attitude is the paintbrush of the soul," Sharon shows us how to create a masterpiece with crayons.

CHAPTER FIVE

The Van

The Van, published in 1991 and short-listed for the Booker Prize, is the last installment of the Barrytown trilogy. This novel is concerned with Jimmy Sr.'s experience of unemployment, and although it utilizes Doyle's trademark brand of humor, it is (in Doyle's own words) "a darker book by necessity and there's no room for a little sequel at the end." The novel is not, as the publisher and some reviewers assert, "a tender tale of male friendship" (Fitzgerald 1991, 16); rather, it is in a sense the bleakest of Doyle's novels, containing no hope for an ultimate triumph brought about by his characters' Irish resiliency. *The Van's* more somberly realistic portrayal of the world makes it a pivotal novel in Doyle's career: he has traded his unabated optimism for characters who are more complex and substantial—and consequently more vulnerable and frangible—than ever before.

The Van takes place in 1990, about one-and-a-half years after *The Snapper*—judging by the vocal skills of Gina (short for Georgina), Sharon's baby, whose birth ended the latter novel. *The Van* centers on Jimmy Sr.; Jimmy Jr. and Sharon, the protagonists of Doyle's previous novels, have only minor roles here. Jimmy Sr. has been laid off, losing his job as a plasterer because of his age. Moreover, his family is moving on, leaving him behind, as it seems to him: Jimmy Jr. has moved in with his girlfriend and gets engaged during the novel. Veronica has gone back to school and is intent on succeeding by herself, without help or interference from any family member. Darren has grown up into an honors student and an accomplished athlete with an attractive girlfriend—and has become disrespectful to his unemployed father, who desperately wants his son's affection. Leslie had gotten into some trouble with the police and was sent to England; he has never since contacted his parents, and they have no idea where or how he is. The twins, Tracy and Linda, are experimenting with make-up, cigarettes, boys, and truancy. Sharon is still good-natured and responsible, but mothering is much harder than she had anticipated and she is struggling. Everyone is leading his own life and seems not to need Jimmy's help; the first third of the book concerns his efforts to retain any of his fast disappearing self-respect.

Jimmy, alone or babysitting Gina, merely tries to find ways to spend his time. He goes to the library, plays pitch and putt, attempts to read. He still is able to appreciate the humor in many situations, but often he is plagued by awful feelings of uselessness and loneliness. Exacerbating his loneliness and depression, the money he receives on the dole is not enough to enable him to socialize at the pub, and he rarely sees his old buddies anymore. His redundancy and the consequent loss of self-esteem cause him to doubt his virility and to experience an unnamed but pervasive fear. He is frightened, yet he cannot pinpoint why.

Things take a more positive turn for Jimmy when his best friend, Bimbo, loses his job as a baker. The two spend a great deal of time together and are often able to cheer each other up. Bimbo, with his redundancy money, decides to buy an old chipper van—a large vehicle equipped with deep-fat fryers and a grill, where hamburgers, French fries, and other such food can be prepared and served to waiting customers. He and Jimmy Sr. become partners in the enterprise, although Jimmy has no money with which to split the cost of the van. After fixing up the van—which, "with no wheels, no brakes, no engine, no water, no electricity, filthy, too, almost beyond purification . . . might stand for the valiant illusions of Barrytown" (Fitzgerald 1991, 16)—they enter the chipper van business.

The initial months of their partnership are hilarious, as the reader sees them cleaning, scraping grease, learning how to peel and fry potatoes, deciding on a menu, cooking burgers, and fast becoming successful business men. However, with success comes dissension, and Jimmy slowly gets squeezed out of the partnership. It is never made clear who is behind Jimmy's demotion from partner to paid help: Bimbo's wife Maggie, whom Jimmy sees as a grasping Machiavelli, or the long-suffering Bimbo himself, who—after playing sidekick their entire friendship—enjoys finally being able to make Jimmy listen to what he says. Although Jimmy blames Maggie, Jimmy and Bimbo's friendship suffers the consequences. Eventually, Bimbo starts to pay Jimmy wages, instead of splitting the profits fifty-fifty as they had initially agreed; Jimmy, deeply hurt, retaliates by taking government-prescribed coffee breaks, asking for overtime pay, and talking about joining a union. The two finally come to blows near the end of the novel. After the fight they go to the pub and get drunk together; Bimbo, severely intoxi-cated, begins to apologize to Jimmy and vows to repair their friendship. He then drives the van into the ocean and leaves it there. Jimmy tells him he can get it the next day when the tide goes back out. The last scene shows Jimmy climbing into bed with his wife Veronica, asking her for a hug.

As Doyle observes, *The Van* is such a dark book because Jimmy repre-sents a large portion of the Irish population: "It's just a lot of people in Ire-land—unemployment is a reality for the rest of their lives. . . . [b]asically, the rest of their lives is filling their days. There're hundreds of thousands of people in Ireland like this." Moreover, unemployment affects the older gen-eration more severely than it does the youth; Jimmy Sr.

> doesn't have his son's energy or resources or education. With the younger Jimmy, unemployment is just something to get out of the way—he's other things to do—he'll survive. He may be knocked about when he gets older, but he's flooding with self-confidence. . . . But it just happens that [Jimmy Sr.] is unemployed at the same time in his life that he's slowing down, and he looks back and imagines, "Where were they when I was young?" and he feels like he's missed out, and he feels redundant in every element in his life.

Jimmy Sr., a strong, jubilant character in Doyle's first two novels, is weak and pitiful here. In the eyes of his daughter, "he looked miserable, and small and kind of beaten looking" (Doyle 1991, 30).

At the novel's beginning, Jimmy Sr. has been unemployed for months—long enough for its novelty to wear off—and he suffers all the hardship of being unemployed. Obviously, having no job means having no paycheck. The welfare money is enough to cover basic expenses but leaves no money for entertainment. Jimmy is left to his own devices, which are few, to pass his days. Unfortunately, Jimmy lacks inner resources and is bored much of the time; he has not been educated enough to be able to appreciate literature, art, music, or self-reflection. Yes, he does read *David Copperfield*—which Doyle includes to show how "brilliant" and accessible Dickens is as an author—but a mind not used to reading will not be able to find refuge in it for long periods of time. Thus, not having extra money means not being able to buy the video machine that could provide entertainment; it means not being able to take day trips when one is bored.

Not having extra money also means not being able to go to the local pub to hang out with friends. Too proud to drink at the pub without being able to buy a round, Jimmy remains at home, lonely: "It wasn't the pints Jimmy Sr. loved; that wasn't it. He liked his pint—he fuckin' loved his pint. . . . [B]ut it wasn't his gargle he was dying for: it was this . . . the lads here, the crack, the laughing. That was what he loved" (Doyle 1991, 34). Spending time at the pub with "the lads" is a source of rejuvenation for him. The pub—not the church or the arts—allows Jimmy to escape from life's burdens and to find a place where he can enjoy himself and be carefree for a short while. Losing a source of income alienates Jimmy from his friends and from the solace that they provide.

Losing his source of income also alienates Jimmy from his family. Giving his children money is one of the ways that the undemonstrative Jimmy shows affection; in *The Snapper*, he often gives the twins a fiver to buy the family Choc-ices, Twixes, or other edible treats, and gives Sharon money when he wants to show her his approval after she breaks the news of her pregnancy. He likes being able to provide Veronica with enough money to run the household the way that she wants to. Without money, Jimmy is at a loss as to how to show his love.

Money is also the source of Jimmy's authority in the family. His status as breadwinner allows Jimmy to assert some sense of dominance in the household, derived from knowing that his wages are feeding and clothing his children and wife and that without him, perhaps, they wouldn't survive. Once he is no longer earning wages, however, his sense of personal authority vanishes. Jimmy's redundancy makes him an easy target for the sarcastic Darren: during an argument at dinner, Darren answers Jimmy's admoni-

tion—"Don't you forget who paid for tha' dinner in front of you, son"—
with the insult, "I know who paid for it. . . . The state" (102). Another blow
to any pretensions that Jimmy might have had about providing for his family comes from Jimmy Jr. (whose life has greatly improved since the days of
The Commitments), when he gives his father a fiver with which to go to the
pub. Jimmy Sr.'s response reflects his inner contradictions: "It was funny;
he'd been really grateful when young Jimmy had given him the fiver, delighted, and at the same time, or just after, he'd wanted to go after him and
thump the living shite out of him and throw the poxy fiver back in his face,
the nerve of him" (31). Although Jimmy Jr. is not trying to insult or to hurt
his father, his generosity nevertheless makes his father that much more
aware of his own inadequacies.

Because Jimmy has been stripped of his sense of authority, he feels im-
potent even in situations unrelated to money. Despite the closeness
achieved by the end of *The Snapper*, Jimmy is no longer a force in Sharon's
life—merely, it seems, a free babysitter. In one brief scene, Jimmy hears
Sharon crying in her bedroom. The Jimmy of *The Snapper* would have demanded to know the reason for the tears, and most likely would have suggested postpartum depression or some other phenomenon that he had read
about in his pregnancy book as the cause. But this Jimmy doesn't: "Jimmy
Sr. held the door handle. He was going to go in. But he couldn't. He wanted
to, but he couldn't. He wouldn't have known what to do any more. He went
back down to the kitchen very carefully, and stepped down over the stair
with the creak in it" (51). Jimmy has become an emotional coward.

His relationship with Darren is the most problematic. Darren is beginning to date, studies subjects his father cannot comprehend, and regularly
is brutally sarcastic to his parents. No longer an adoring adolescent boy, he
is growing distant from his father. Jimmy often tries to curry Darren's favor
with jokes and humor, but the scenes in which Jimmy does this are some of
the most humiliating for him—both because they show how desperate
Jimmy is and because the attempts are rarely successful. For the twins as
well, their parents have become, if not enemies, merely dupes to fool and
subvert.

Finally, Jimmy feels alienated from and intimidated by Veronica. She
has returned to school and wants to finish her education by herself: "She

wanted to do it on her own, even going up to the school on her own and walking home; everything" (16). She will not discuss her educational worries, anxieties, or joys with Jimmy. The depressed Jimmy senses her increased power and tries to latch on to it by becoming involved with her studies:

> —Did yeh ever read David Copperfield, Veronica? . . . D'yeh want to read it after me, Veronica?
>
> Veronica . . . knew what he wanted her to say. —Okay, she said. . . .
>
> He was delighted. He didn't know why, exactly. . . . He wondered if maybe he should take notes as well. . . . No; that would just have been thick; stupid. (54)

Veronica senses Jimmy's need and is able to help him in this instance, although we never actually see her reading the novel.

Besides alienating him from his friends and his family, Jimmy's redundancy emasculates him. In addition to doubting his position as the head of his household, he also begins to doubt his virility, his position as a man. He tries to reassure himself sexually. He often fantasizes about young women, even peering, hidden behind his bedroom curtain, at factory girls as they pass his house. He finds himself thinking about both of his sons' girlfriends: "A ride; she was. It was weird thinking it; his son was going out with a ride. . . . He could've given himself a bugle now, out here in the hall, just remembering what she was like and her smile" (52). He even starts comparing Veronica with his friend Bertie's rather sexy wife Vera. At a Christmas party at Bimbo's house, Jimmy, in the bathroom, starts playing with Maggie's razor and begins to fantasize about Vera: "It was Maggie's, that was it; for her legs or—only her legs probably. . . . Vera probably used one of these when she was shaving her legs—" (63). An even more humiliating scene occurs when he lures Bimbo, under the guise of a night on the town in hopes of restoring their friendship, to an expensive disco where he hopes to pick up a woman: "What he wanted was to see if he could manage a young one or one of these glamorous, rich-looking, not-so-young ones. He'd back off once he knew it was on the cards; actually getting his hole wasn't what he was after at all—he just wanted to know if he could get his hole" (256).

Jimmy reaches a low in this scene: in an attempt to pick up a woman (who later turns out to be married), he spends a great deal of money on overpriced bottles of wine, lies about his profession, tries to force the woman to kiss him, and ends up fighting with Bimbo over the woman. In an attempt to bolster his flagging sense of self, Jimmy embarrasses himself and worsens the situation with Bimbo.

Jimmy's fantasies and his excursion into the uptown nightlife only serve to reduce him further in his own estimation. He is embarrassed that he fantasizes about the young factory girls, and he feels dirty when he thinks about Darren's and Jimmy's girlfriends. The day after the disco fiasco finds him extremely hung over and guilt-ridden; he pledges to take Veronica out for a nice dinner, with wine. These attempts to regain his manhood only diminish it in his own mind: "He'd felt like a right cunt then, gawking out the window; like a fuckin' pervert" (111). Notice the emasculating word he calls himself after his attempt to feel more virile.

These scenes are as humiliating to Jimmy as the scenes in which he tries to curry Darren's favor. We see Jimmy at his most vulnerable; we learn things about him that he does not even want his closest friends to know, things of which he is ashamed. Doyle, however, neither judges Jimmy nor excuses him. The reader does not judge Jimmy either, perhaps because Jimmy is so ashamed of himself, as in the scene in Bimbo's bathroom: "—Ah fuck this! He threw the Girl Care [the razor] back onto the shelf over the sink. God, he was a right fuckin' eejit. . . . He felt weak, hopeless, like he'd been caught. Was something happening to him?" (64). If he were oblivious to his abasement, he would be despicable, or at least ridiculous. As it is, we tend to worry about him and to pity him.

Finally, Jimmy's job loss causes him to lose part of his identity. For Jimmy Sr., his job means more than a steady source of income; for most of his life, a major part of his identity has come from being a skilled plasterer. Losing his profession is difficult to come to terms with.

When one part of an identity disappears, other such shifts inevitably occur. Jimmy's innate comic vision cannot survive the blows that his identity and self-esteem have suffered. He is still able to recognize the absurdity in situations, but he can no longer laugh at those absurdities. For instance, consider Jimmy's thoughts on renting pictures from the library:

"That was a bit fuckin' stupid when you thought about it; sticking a picture up on your wall for a fortnight and then having to bring it back again; on a bus or on the DART, sitting there like a gobshite with a big picture on your lap, of a woman in her nip or something" (12). Despite recognizing the ab- surdity of the situation and the potential for humor, Jimmy is bitter; there is no raucous laughter; he doesn't store this observation away to share with the lads or even laugh to himself. Jimmy's low spirits have robbed him of his ability to enjoy life. Deeper, they have robbed him of his comic spirit, which in previous novels enabled him to discover humor even in the worst circumstances: "The comic spirit encourages blurred lines of demarcation between the self and the not-self. . . . The more carefully one defines one's identity, the more likely the definition is to turn into a cliché. The more protective one is toward the self, the more likely one is to pity oneself. Negligence about identity is likely to be much more liberating; the self is free to become whatever it will become" (Galligan 1984, 124). The comic sense of self—fluid, ever-changing, and adaptive—is completely lacking in Jimmy in this novel. He has become so fixed in his roles as breadwinner and family head that he cannot exist outside these roles. The other family members can adapt to their changing roles—e.g., Veronica is the student now and not merely the mother—but in the absence of his comic spirit, Jimmy Sr.'s personal identity depends on his traditionally male roles, devas- tated by his unemployment.

Depression and anxiety naturally occur when such huge gaps in one's identity emerge. For Jimmy, low-level depression and generalized anxiety, induced by his no longer being able either to enjoy his present or to avoid his future, are new experiences; as Doyle says, when "he had his steady job and a couple of quid in his pockets for a few pints, he never ha[d] to worry about self-confidence." However, now that Jimmy is unemployed and aging, doubts and worries plague him. The employed, more virile Jimmy had been accustomed to purge his volatile emotions immediately; however, shouting or sharing pints with his mates is not sufficient to chase away de- pression and anxiety. Also, the source of his worries is not going to change. Jimmy must learn to live with these new emotions.

Jimmy's fears and anxieties take on physical properties, not surprising in a man unused to experiencing mental or spiritual malaise. Unable to articulate his mental pain in such terms, he compares it to physical discomforts:

> He'd thought his teeth were going to crack and break; he couldn't get his mouth to open, as if it had been locked and getting tighter. And he'd had to snap his eyes shut, waiting for the crunch and the pain. But then it had stopped, and he'd started breathing again. He felt weak now, a bit weak. . . . There were days when there was this feeling in his guts all the time, like a fart building up only it wasn't that at all. It was as if his trousers were too tight for him, but he'd check and they weren't, they were grand; but there was a little ball of hard air inside him. (Doyle 1991, 30, 53)

Jimmy is experiencing a generalized anxiety, punctuated by periods of severe anxiety. Generalized anxiety and anxiety attacks are the result of an overwhelming, omnipresent fear of imminent danger or disaster, real or imagined. Jimmy can no longer live entirely in his present, as he was accustomed, because his present is so miserable; yet he is terrified of a future of repetitive, unfilled days.

Jimmy compares the dread with which he is living to a similar feeling that he experienced as a boy:

> It was like when he was a kid and he'd done something bad and he was waiting for his da to come home from work to kill him. He used to use his belt. . . . He didn't wear a belt; he only kept it for strapping Jimmy Sr and his brothers. . . . he'd stare at Jimmy Sr and make him stare back and then Jimmy Sr'd feel the pain on the side of his leg and again and again. . . . [I]t was agony, but not as bad as the waiting. Waiting for it was the worst part. . . . He'd go through the whole day scared shitless, waiting for his da to come home. . . . And that was how he sometimes—often—felt now, scared shitless. And he didn't know why. (53–54)

At least the young Jimmy understood why and of whom he was scared; the adult Jimmy has no one to blame for his anxiety, which makes the fear worse.

Thus, unemployment has made Jimmy weak and pitiful, "redundant in every element in his life" (in Doyle's later observation). However, a third of the way through the novel, Jimmy's circumstances change significantly when his best friend Bimbo also loses his job. Life begins to become more pleasant for Jimmy: "The next couple of weeks were great. . . . If he'd been looking for someone to be made redundant it would have been Bimbo. That didn't mean that he'd wanted Bimbo to get the sack; not at all. What he meant was this: he couldn't think of better company than Bimbo, and now that Bimbo wasn't working he could hang around with Bimbo all day. It was fuckin' marvelous" (Doyle 1991, 86). Jimmy is no longer lonely, and although he and Bimbo both have depressed days, they help each other through them.

When Bimbo buys the chipper van and invites Jimmy Sr. to be his partner, Jimmy is reinvigorated. This new enterprise returns Jimmy to his breadwinner role, which renews his self-esteem and enables him to function in his other familiar roles as well. The business is quite successful, and Jimmy feels vindicated by being able to give Veronica the weekly sum that she had been accustomed to receiving before his unemployment. After the first night in business, which was very profitable, he fantasizes about giving Veronica his wages: "At the end of the week—next Friday—he was going to put money on the table in front of Veronica, and say nothing" (172). With the restoration of his role as breadwinner, Jimmy's feelings of self-worth have returned, and he once again becomes the magnanimous husband: "You're not to waste it all on food now, d'yeh hear, he said.—You're to buy somethin' for yourself" (176). Now that he can again provide luxuries for Veronica, he feels that he has taken back the familial power.

Significantly, Jimmy's sense of humor returns along with his self-esteem. He continues to notice life's little incongruities, but now he vocalizes them. For instance, he tells Sharon, who has been tanning at the beach, that she is "like a well-cooked burger" (200). He jokes much more with his family, and his exuberant attitude is resurrected. The scene in which he and Darren practice their ketchup bottle tossing routine (à la Tom Cruise in *Cocktail*) is reminiscent of the Jimmy of *The Snapper*: Veronica "looked up. . . . Jimmy Sr. had his face squashed up to the window. . . . She screamed, and laughed. His nose was crooked and white against the glass. He was miming to the Georgia Satellites. . . . He kissed the glass. . . . But he lowered himself from the ledge and backed into the garden still miming, with his hand clutching his crotch. . . . He turned and dropped his shorts and wriggled. God, he was terrible" (247). Such antics signal the return to normalcy of Jimmy and Veronica's relationship; she no longer worries about his moping about, and the two are again on an equal footing.

Jimmy's relationships with his children also improve. He gives both Sharon and Darren jobs working in the van. He has stopped kowtowing to Darren: when the two get into a minor argument while working and Darren leaves the van, Jimmy "prayed for him to come back but he wouldn't go to the door to look out; he wouldn't even look at it" (203). Their relationship has become more adult: Jimmy apologizes for the argument, which was his fault, and Darren accepts the apology. Mutual respect has developed between the two. Jimmy begins to interact more with the twins as well: with his new funds, he can buy them expensive haircuts and new clothes, instead of Choc-ices. He now can discipline them, and he makes them clean the van when he catches them misbehaving; the depressed Jimmy Sr. wouldn't have bothered to punish them.

For all the benefits it brings to his family life, however, Jimmy's economic success proves to be double-sided, especially in his dealings with Bimbo. Jimmy and Bimbo's relationship remained close as long as they shared the sheltered, although miserable, life on the dole. When they begin the business of the van, though, problems and tensions never encountered before arise. These two men have no mature conflict resolution skills, and their childish behavior aggravates these problems until their relationship is destroyed.

Bimbo reneges on his original offer of partnership because he is jealously possessive of the first power he has ever had. Before his redundancy, Bimbo had been employed as a low-level baker and had never been a leader among his friends. Doyle portrays him as childlike and gullible; the reader even wonders if he is slightly retarded. Thus, Jimmy's feelings are understandably hurt when Bimbo starts acting on his newly acquired power, and in retaliation he plays childish pranks on Bimbo: pretending he is going to join the union, calling Bimbo "boss" and "sir," taking his coffee breaks during the busy parts of the day, giving Bimbo the silent treatment (which he previously used on Sharon in *The Snapper*). The easily fooled Bimbo does not know how to handle these childish actions. When the health inspector shuts the van down, Bimbo believes that Jimmy has betrayed him by requesting the inspection. The two come to blows and their friendship ends.

Searching for an answer, Jimmy blames the friendship's demise on Bimbo's wife. He believes that Maggie is behind the change in Bimbo and begins to dislike her meddling in the van's business. Although he leaves it unclear in the novel, in a later interview Doyle says that Maggie is not at fault and that it is less painful for Jimmy to blame her than to blame himself or Bimbo:

> I feel that Jimmy blames Maggie because it's easier than blaming Bimbo. . . . It's clearer in the film . . . because it's from the film's point of view, not from Jimmy's point of view, and in one scene, after Bimbo has made Jimmy a wage slave, . . . he asks Maggie, "Do you think I'm right?" and she says, "Yeah, you are." But it's very obvious that it's his decision. She's involved in the management and that sort of thing and Jimmy resents it, but what right does he have to resent it? It's understandable because she is bursting in on their territory and he doesn't like it at all, but she has every right to be there. . . . It's much clearer in the film that she's not to blame.

Although Jimmy eventually faces the fact that Bimbo is enjoying his power—"Jimmy Sr. realized that Bimbo was enjoying it, being the boss; like he was giving out to a thick lad, a thick kid he liked" (Doyle 1991, 283)— he still hates Maggie: "The cunt, he hated her. It was easier than hating Bimbo" (282).

Jimmy's inability to adapt to the new Bimbo stems from his being stripped of another role that he is accustomed to play. The dynamics of Jimmy and Bimbo's relationship has changed; Jimmy no longer holds the dominant position that he had held previously:

> That's right . . . I am the boss. It had always been that way. . . . Jimmy Sr had always been the one who'd made the decisions, who'd mapped out their weekends for them. Jimmy Sr would say, See yeh in the Hikers after half-twelve mass, and Bimbo would be there. Jimmy Sr would put down Bimbo's name to play pitch and putt and Bimbo would go off and play. Jimmy Sr had rented the pair of caravans in Courtown a couple of years

back and the two families had gone down in a convoy and stayed there for the fortnight. (254)

Neither Jimmy nor Bimbo can handle the change in their relationship maturely.

Jimmy and Bimbo's disintegrating relationship, although not exactly allegorical, does lend itself to comparisons with British politics in the 1980s: "Doyle depicts the miserable dissolution of his male bonding with Bimbo as a direct result of their success in escaping the misery of unemployment that cemented their lifelong bond in the first place. . . . All of a sudden they're a two-man microcosm of Thatcher's class-warring United Kingdom, kicking and gouging in the mud and the blood and the beer" (Appelo 1992, 15). Doyle, while not "political," is certainly aware of world politics: "I do follow it some—the razzmatazz of it all." Thatcherism glorified capitalism as the system providing the greatest financial rewards and happiness for all, including those at the lowest level of society. Doyle seems to be dramatizing the idea that instead of bringing people together for mutual advantage, capitalism pits people ruthlessly against one another. In *The Van*, the economic relationship of employer/employed mirrors and parodies the class structure and demonstrates the divisiveness and brutality of contemporary capitalism.

The novel's penultimate scene—in which Bimbo drives the van into the sea—is startlingly Sam Shepardesque in its extremity. Bimbo's action is a childish, futile attempt at reconciliation, as he tries to destroy that which he believes has destroyed his friendship with Jimmy. He doesn't realize that it was not the physical van but rather the pent-up intangible feelings of inequality and resentment built up over his lifetime that ruined the relationship. Jimmy—perhaps unconsciously recognizing that the van is only the symptom and not the cause of their mutual animosity—undercuts Bimbo's "heroic" gesture by saying, "You'll be able to get it when the tide goes out again" (Doyle 1991, 311). Doyle further downplays Bimbo's act by ending the scene with Jimmy walking alone up the beach.

The breakup of Jimmy and Bimbo's relationship implies subsequent losses for Jimmy. He will not have a job and will have the same problems he had at the beginning of the novel. Indeed, Jimmy will actually be worse off than he was initially, for he has lost his best friend: "He was lonely. That was it. . . . Lonely" (284). This loss is permanent and cannot be restored simply by getting a job, as were his other losses. The gatherings at the pub with the lads will no longer be spiritually healing for Jimmy, as Bimbo will not be a part of them. As Doyle later commented, "[T]heir friendship is over—maybe they'll try to revert to some sort of civility—it'll never be the same again and that's a big loss. Jimmy won't be involved with the van again."

Jimmy also will not have his family for much longer. As previously stated, his children are growing up and will be moving away soon. Sharon is seriously dating a nice man at the novel's end; Jimmy Jr. is engaged; Darren has graduated from high school and may go on to the university; the twins are maturing rapidly. Veronica is educating herself, and who knows what she will attempt next. Although his family will always support him, everyone will have moved on before Jimmy can even recover from the loss of his best friend.

The Van is a transitional work for Doyle in that it is the first novel in which his characters do not rally and make a joyous comeback. In *The Commitments*, although the band dissolves, Jimmy Jr. does not despair and our last view of him has him busily making plans for a new band; in *The Snapper*, Sharon is lovingly holding her newborn daughter and thumbing her nose at all of Barrytown by naming her baby Georgina. By contrast, in *The Van's* final scene, Jimmy Sr. is weak and infantile, begging for a hug from his sleepy wife: "Give us a hug, Veronica, will yeh" (Doyle 1991, 311). It is dawn, and this new day casts an ironic light on Jimmy's future prospects: he has no big plans—he does not have a job, and most likely will not have one again. Jimmy will be faced with the same problems he was having at the beginning of the novel, worsened by the fact that his friendship with Bimbo has been irrevocably severed.

This book is ultimately Doyle's bleakest. There is no room for hope, and no reason to expect that things will change for Jimmy Sr. Unlike Paddy Clarke, the hero of Doyle's other drearily ending novel, Jimmy is not young, and he lacks youth's adaptability. Nor does he have the resilience and optimistic determination of Paula Spencer, the battered and alcoholic heroine of Doyle's fifth novel. He is neither soothed by religion nor empowered by education. Jimmy does have the support of his wife, but as we have seen, this support is not enough to give his life a sense of purpose. Although Jimmy does not have to worry about food and shelter, he is defenseless in his world.

The novel's darkness even casts Doyle's use of humor in a different light than in his previous novels. Doyle uses much of the same type of humor as before: the riotous family scenes, the drunken revelry, the witty repartee between friends, and occasionally the somewhat forced and predictable situational humor, as when Jimmy serves a customer a fried diaper by mistake. However, the wounding element of humor also figures prominently in *The Van*. The great deal of bitter sarcasm, although clever, is not funny because it causes pain to the characters. For instance, many of Jimmy's ploys to annoy Bimbo are clever and would be funny if used against a boss who were anonymous and nasty—but because the target is Bimbo, who was Jimmy's best friend, the fake letter to the union and the scrupulously adhered-to coffee breaks are not funny at all. Darren's dinnertime remark about the state providing the meal is witty, but because it wounds Jimmy it produces no laughter, only grimaces. Such humor does not serve to lighten the characters' lives but only to make them more ponderous.

This depressing ending, completing a novel that is the story of a man whom life has defeated, marks the transition from Doyle's riotous and raucous novels to his more serious work. *The Van* is important because with it Doyle sheds his authorial baby fat and begins to write fiction with a harder edge. He begins working with the more compelling characters and situations that emerge in his later novels. He uses his distinctive dialogue and language to (in his own words) "bring the books down closer and closer to the characters." In this novel, he comes close to achieving this goal by allowing the characters to experience feelings and thoughts that are not always funny; he dispenses with his tendency to simplify his characters for comedy's sake. By showing both the scarcity of joyous humor and the absence of the comic spirit in Jimmy's life, Doyle demonstrates the tremendous need for both.

CHAPTER SIX

Paddy Clarke Ha Ha Ha

Paddy Clarke Ha Ha Ha, Doyle's fourth novel and the winner of Britain's Booker Prize in 1993, departs stylistically and thematically from the Barrytown trilogy. Aside from the obvious difference in the book's title—"No more *the's*" (Flanagan 1994, 21)—this novel dispenses both with the Rabbitte family and with their omnipresent chatter. Although we are still in Barrytown, this novel is set in 1968, when the Corporation houses (housing projects) that the Rabbittes inhabit were just being built, and centers on the respectable, middle-class Clarke family. In *Paddy Clarke*, a more patently artistic novel than any of his previous works, Doyle fully matures as a novelist.

The novel is narrated entirely by Paddy, a young boy skillfully depicted by Doyle, and is comprised of a series of vignettes, "free floating paragraphs stirred by sequence rather than consequence" (Lane 1994, 92). Instead of the great blocks of dialogue of the trilogy novels, in *Paddy Clarke* the protagonist, describing and commenting on his life, speaks directly to the reader. Paddy's narrative is "minutely descriptive, from the hairs on his father's hands to the look of melting tar" (O'Toole 1993, 21). These vignettes relate to each other in a somewhat stream-of-consciousness fashion. They are not as tightly knit as Benjy's section of *The Sound and the Fury*, in which the reader can trace the exact word that sets Benjy off on another memory; in *Paddy Clarke*, it is sometimes possible to pick out the word or circumstance that sparks a vignette, sometimes not. As Doyle recalls, he wanted the novel's organization to be basically . . . the way a kid's mind would work. . . . I've tried to make links, but indirectly. It may be a question of color or light and something sparks off another memory, and so he goes on to that. I wanted it, particularly the first half, to seem haphazard—winding memories, and by degrees the winding memories become straighter and straighter as the parents' marriage becomes worse and worse. And that's just the way a kid's mind would work. Also I wanted to get away from the linear time I used in the previous books, and it just fit the story better.

In addition to the structure, *Paddy Clarke* is a major stylistic departure for Doyle because of the character of Paddy himself. Because of the intensity of the first-person narrative, Paddy is one of Doyle's most fully realized characters; the 282 pages of almost uninterrupted Paddy provide the reader more insights into him than the trilogy's rapid-fire, profanity-laced, multi-character dialogue affords the Rabbittes. A typical ten-year-old schoolboy, Paddy is part of a gang of neighborhood friends that also includes Kevin, Liam, Aidan, and Ian. With his friends, Paddy terrorizes the neighborhood gardens, idolizes certain soccer stars, and is fascinated by fire, small animals, and curse words. Within the Clarke family, Paddy beats up his younger brother Francis ("Sinbad"), loves his mother, doesn't quite understand his father, and doesn't care to understand either of his two younger sisters. His days are filled with playing, exploring, and testing his boundaries, including vignettes such as a Viking funeral for a rat, setting fire to an insect with a magnifying glass, and racing all over town through an obstacle course consisting of various gardens and their walls. Charming the reader with Paddy's candid, perceptive views of the world, Doyle strives for the tone and perspective of a ten-year-old boy rather than those of a thirty-eight-year-old novelist.

Through such full immersion in Paddy's world, the reader also perceives disharmonies in that world. First, Barrytown is being developed by the government, and all the open fields and playing grounds that have been Paddy's domain are now being destroyed for Corporation housing. Although in Doyle's previous novels this urban village has developed into a positive community atmosphere for the Rabbittes, in Paddy's day the Corporation housing threatens to erode his own safe, middle-class world through the advent of families such as that of Charles Leavy: "Charles Leavy didn't care. . . . He stayed up all night all the time. Listening to his ma and da. Not caring. Saying cunt and fuck. . . . He terrified me. He was there, all by himself. Always by himself. He never smiled; it wasn't a real smile. His laugh was a noise he started and stopped like a machine. He was close to no one. . . . He had no friends" (Doyle 1994, 238–51). Charles Leavy and his ilk are the precursors of "the living dead," a group of fearless, unfeeling teenagers who terrorize Jimmy Sr. and the chipper van in *The Van*. These are the people whose homes are encroaching on Paddy's playgrounds and who first break into the innocence of Paddy's childhood.

The second, more important cause of disquiet in the Clarke household is the escalating tension between Mr. and Mrs. Clarke, Da and Ma to Paddy. He first mentions their fighting almost offhandedly, inserting "They were having another of their fights" (42) before jumping immediately to another topic. However, as the novel progresses, the fights occur more and more often and begin to influence Paddy's behavior in school. As his parents' fighting increases, the reader sadly watches Paddy change from a happy, mischievous, curious little boy to a needy, solitary, worried, friendless outcast. The title of the book is the refrain from a cruel rhyme with which his peers taunt him at the end of the novel, after his parents have separated:

> —Paddy Clarke—
> Paddy Clarke—
> Has no da.
> Ha ha ha!

Although Paddy claims that he "didn't listen to them. They were only kids" (281), he has been robbed of the innocent, jubilant childhood of the novel's opening pages—and the reader feels the poignancy and bitterness of Paddy's loss.

Paddy Clarke has notable literary ancestors—perhaps most prominently the Stephen Dedalus of Joyce's *A Portrait of the Artist as a Young Man*. Indeed, *Paddy Clarke*'s opening sentence, "We were coming down our road," directly echoes the beginning of *Portrait*: "Once upon a time and a very good time it was there was a moocow coming down along the road" (Joyce 1965, 1). Although we do not see him at ten years of age (but instead both younger and older) nor through a first-person narrative, Stephen has much in common with Paddy: both are Irish Catholic Dubliners; both live with dysfunctional families; more significantly, both possess poetic natures and are fascinated by physical sensations and by words.

Stephen Dedalus's most remarkable quality, his poetic and artistic nature, manifests itself first in his sensitivity to sensations and in his love of words. The first page of *Portrait* includes references to all five senses. Moreover, Stephen frequently remarks on the smells, temperatures, and sounds of objects that are not likely to be smelled, felt, or heard: for instance, his mother's jeweled slippers had "a lovely warm smell," and "there was a cold night smell in the chapel. But it was a holy smell. It was the smell of the old peasants who knelt at the back of the chapel at Sunday mass. That was a smell of air and rain and turf and corduroy" (Joyce 1965, 10, 18). Stephen recognizes the red and green backs of Dante's brushes and the way that sheets are cold initially but later become "lovely . . . hot." He is perceptive enough to see the differences in walking styles of "the higher line fellows [who came] down along the matting in the middle of the refectory. . . . And every single fellow had a different way of walking" (13).

Paddy perceives his surroundings similarly: "There was a smell of church off the desks in our school. When I folded my arms and put my head in the hollow, when Henno told us to go asleep, I could smell the same smell as you got off the seats in the church. I loved it. It was spicy and like the ground under a tree. I licked the desk but it just tasted horrible" (Doyle 1994, 61). Paddy remarks on the colors of his hot water bottles, red and green, and how he "loved the smell off the bottle" (33). He also discerns the difference in the ways people walk: "When my da was standing up he stood perfectly still. His feet clung to the ground. They only moved when he was going somewhere. My ma's feet were different. They didn't settle. They couldn't make their minds up" (103). Both boys are hypersensitive to physical sensations.

As each grows older, this perceptiveness translates more fully into a delight in words. Stephen, who longs to be "like the fellows in poetry and rhetoric" (Joyce 1965, 17), notices that "suck was a queer word" and that if he were to read verses written by a schoolmate backward, "then they were not poetry" (16). The meanings of words intrigue him: "What did that mean, to kiss?" (15). He also ponders the "different names for God in all the different languages in the world" (16). Indeed, as *Portrait* progresses, one of its main themes is the ways in which Stephen—the budding artist—becomes more involved with language.

Paddy takes an even greater delight in words. When he reads "It was Ginger's turn to push the pram and he seized it with a new vigour," a new word bursts into his world: "—Vigour, I said. . . . For a day we called ourselves the Vigour Tribe. We got one of Sinbad's markers and did big Vs on our chests, for Vigour" (Doyle 1994, 58). Manifesting the traditional Irish love of language, Paddy is so enamored of this new word that he prints it on his skin: "The word was made flesh" (129). Paddy and his friends invent a number of ceremonial games, the most striking of which involves the group of boys kneeling on damp ground around a small fire. Kevin, as the high priest, walks around the circle brandishing a fire poker with which he hits the kneelers in the back as part of their initiation. The other part of the ceremony involves chanting "magical" words whose meanings are unknown to the boys: "Trellis trellis trellis!" or "Ignoramus ignoramus ignoramus!" or "Substandard substandard substandard!" (Is it accidental that the protagonist of Flann O'Brien's word-enamored *At Swim-Two-Birds*, one of Doyle's favorite novels, is named Trellis?) These boys collect words solely on the basis of their sounds: "I could never guess what word was going to be next. I always tried; I looked at all the faces in the class when a new word or a good one got said. Liam and Kevin and Ian McEvoy were the same, doing what I was doing, storing the words" (128).

The next part of this ceremony is the most critical. Each boy shouts out a "bad word" that will be his name until the next ceremony. Paddy screams out "Fuck" because it

was the best word. The most dangerous word. You couldn't whisper it. . . . Fuck was always too loud, too late to stop it, it burst in the air above you and fell slowly right over your head. There was total silence, nothing but Fuck floating down. . . . It was the word you couldn't say anywhere. It wouldn't come out unless you pushed it. It made you feel caught and grabbed the minute you said it. When it escaped it was like an electric laugh, a soundless gasp followed by the kind of laughing that only forbidden things could make, an inside tickle that became a brilliant pain, bashing at your mouth to be let out. It was agony. We didn't waste it. (132)

Although the *verboten* aspect is a large part of the word's magic, Paddy is also delighted by the word itself—its explosive sound, the liberating feeling this short expulsion of air can give.

Since Paddy shares Stephen's poetic sensibilities, we naturally wonder if Paddy also will become an artist. Perhaps he will grow up and write five successful novels before he is forty years old—five novels in which a love of words and language is evidenced in an extraordinary transcription of local dialect. Understandably, Doyle does not admit to his being the basis for Paddy, but he acknowledges that he researched the novel by taking "trips up to my parents' attic to remind me of books and what not." In 1968, Doyle was—like Paddy—a ten-year-old with a precocious literary imagination. We can draw our own conclusions.

Along with clear echoes of Stephen Dedalus, the character of Paddy reminds us of other literary childhoods. To be sure, Mark Twain's Huck Finn may seem on the surface to have little in common with Paddy: Huck is a thirteen-year-old backwoods American, uneducated, irreligious, orphaned, and rebellious; Paddy, ten, has grown up in a middle-class Dublin suburb, lives with his loving parents and his three siblings, and is a fairly good student at school. However, the two characters in fact share many important personality traits. Both boys are feisty, inquisitive, and wisely perceptive beyond their years; each plays boyish games that, during the course of his experience, he discards when he prematurely enters adulthood.

Huck's and Paddy's typical boyish natures dominate the reader's mental picture of the two characters: both get dirty, bruised, or scraped every day (although Paddy is not as "tough" as Huck and still relishes the healing properties of his mother's magical kisses). Despite (or perhaps because of) their boyish natures, each possesses remarkable perception. For instance, Huck knows enough about human nature to be able to fool almost anyone;

he deters the two men in the canoe from finding the hidden Jim by imply-
ing that his father is aboard the raft with smallpox. Instances of Huck's perceptiveness abound, as he discerns the true identities of the "king" and the
"duke" and realizes that the Phelpses are so good-natured and easy-going
that Tom could free Jim without all his machinations. Paddy Clarke also
possesses uncanny perception; he reads people as well as Huck does. He
knows that when his father "folded his legs . . . and leaned a bit to the side
into his chair" it meant that he was receptive to Paddy's questions (Doyle
1994, 25). He is able to direct his parents' conversation away from an argument and to make his mother laugh. He can tell when his father is being
lazy. He also makes observations about human nature that, although true,
are rarely admitted by adults: "It was great. Liam was finished now. Kevin
and me wouldn't even talk to him any more. I was delighted. I didn't know
why. I like Liam. It seemed important though. If you were going to be best
friends with anyone—Kevin—you had to hate a lot of other people, the
two of you together. It made you better friends" (182). Paddy's perceptions,
although simplistically stated, often reveal a side of people that we prefer to
ignore.

Both boys, as a balance to their uncommon insights, also engage in the
superstitious thought processes of the uneducated. Huck and Jim are terrified of touching a snakeskin—they call it "the worst bad luck in the world"
(Twain 1959, 59). They also believe other superstitions; for instance, one
isn't supposed to "count the things you are going to cook for dinner" (52) or
shake a tablecloth after sundown or look at the moon over one's left shoulder—performing any of these actions bodes certain evil. By contrast,
Paddy's superstitions are more apparently products of his immediate environment. For instance, Paddy, afraid that a neighbor who has discovered
one of his transgressions is on her way to his house to tell his parents, invents his own ritual to ward off Mrs. Kiernan's potential "evil": "If the bell
didn't ring by the time I'd finished all the ice-cream she wouldn't be coming. But I couldn't rush it. I had to eat it the slow way I always did, always
the last one to finish. I was allowed to lick the bowl. The bell didn't ring at
all. I felt like I'd done something; my mission had been accomplished"
(Doyle 1994, 61).

Both boys order their respective universes with superstitious rituals.

When either feels powerless or frightened, he attempts to regain control with magical thinking. Significantly, the most superstitious talk in Twain's novel occurs in the beginning of Huck and Jim's journey, when the orphaned boy and runaway slave are most afraid of being captured and returned to an oppressive and dysfunctional society. Paddy too relies on magical thinking when he is frightened—as when he believes that his ice cream ritual has prevented Mrs. Kiernan from telling his parents about his misbehavior. The "successes" of his ritualized behavior give Paddy a sense of power over his circumstances. He uses all his powers to prevent his parents' fighting:

> I was on guard. I was making sure that they didn't start again; all I had to do was stay awake. . . . I stayed awake. The cock crew. There was no more fighting. . . . Mission accomplished. . . . I had to stay still. If I moved it would start again. I was allowed to breathe, that was all. It was like after Catherine or the other baby stopped crying; forty-five seconds, my ma said—if they didn't cry out inside forty-five seconds they'd go back asleep. I stood. I didn't count; this wasn't a game or babies. I didn't know how long. Long enough to be cold. . . . I was in charge. They didn't know. I could move now; the worst bit was over: I'd done it. But I had to stay awake all night; I had to keep an all-night vigil. (232, 234)

Paddy's phrase—"this wasn't a game"—takes us into Paddy and Huck's most significant similarity: their rapid and premature entrance into the adult world. In the beginning of Twain's novel, Huck role-plays with Tom Sawyer, imagining that they are a gang of murderers and thieves; although he soon tires of the pretense, Huck still greatly admires Tom and his "learning." In time, however, Huck realizes that the river contains no place for such games when he encounters a real gang of murderers and thieves who put his and Jim's lives at risk. Later, when Huck regresses and tries to fool Jim into believing that he dreamt a huge storm, Jim feels betrayed—and Huck realizes that such childish pranks are not funny and can hurt people: "It made me feel so mean I could almost kissed *his* foot to get him to take it back. It was fifteen minutes before I could work myself up to go and humble myself to a nigger; but I done it, and I warn't ever sorry for it afterward, neither. I didn't do him no more mean tricks, and I wouldn't done that one if I'd 'a' knowed it would make him feel that way" (Twain 1959, 90). Huck has entered an adult world with no place for silly games. When he meets Tom again and reverts into game-playing, "we resent the relapse into childishness because it is a relapse but also because the joke just ain't funny" (Elliott 1959, 284). However, at the novel's end, Huck leaves civilization (and Tom) and its (and his) negative influences.

Paddy similarly begins the novel playing games, and for the same reason that Tom does, namely as a way of "playing hooky from stern, respectable, right/wrong morality" (ibid.). Paddy, raised in an Irish Catholic household, pretends to be various saints, priests, soccer players, and explorers in order to escape respectability's strictures. However, by the end of the novel, Paddy is no longer respectable—his parents' separation has thrust him outside of the circle of acceptability—and he has no more use for childish games. He expects his mother to tell him, "You're the man of the house now, Patrick" (Doyle 1994, 281). (Notice his suddenly adult name.) He tells the reader that the cruel rhymes of the other children don't bother him because "they were only kids" (281). Significantly, however, where Huck is able to take control and to abandon his society by deciding to "light out for the territory" (Twain 1959, 283), it is the more passive Paddy's tragedy that he has been *abandoned by* his "respectable" neighbors.

Along with—and perhaps more important than—the similarity between Paddy and Huck as characters is the similarity between the narrative techniques of the two novels. *Huck Finn*—which Doyle undoubtedly taught during his fourteen years as a middle-school English teacher—and *Paddy Clarke* are both first-person narratives that feature boy narrators. *Style indirect libre*, "the capacity to describe a character's environment as he would describe it himself" (Lane 1994, 93), can be difficult: "When novelists try to find a voice for the inarticulate—for the young, the sick, the daft—they often can't sustain it; they become knowing, sentimental, or both" (Mantel 1993, 12). The author cannot indulge in false psychologizing or make the narrator wiser or more knowing than his years, nor can he make the narrator's stories too obviously significant; to err in any of these ways would destroy the character's voice. Although Doyle and Twain sometimes slip and make their protagonists too perceptive or too articulate, these slips are not egregious; on the whole, both novelists convincingly register their narrators' voices. Like Twain, "Doyle has the perfect pitch" (Lane 1994, 92).

If authenticity were the only noteworthy aspect of these novels, however, *Huck Finn* and *Paddy Clarke* would at most be mere artistic exercises, interesting for not very many pages; most young boys do not possess the observational or verbal skills to interest adults for the several hours that it takes to read a novel. Thus, each author must write on two levels, organizing his protagonist's thoughts and observations so as to engage adults at the same time as remaining true to the narrative voice of the child. *Huck Finn* is superficially the story of the adventures of a runaway boy drifting down the Mississippi with a runaway slave; however, Twain also wanted his novel both to criticize the spiritual and ethical blindness of the righteous and respectable slaveholding society and to illustrate the corruption and moral decay of all classes of people. Doyle's work is similarly multilayered: on the surface, he presents a series of the random experiences of a young boy, which become increasingly dominated by his parents' unhappiness; more deeply, these experiences are not random at all, as Doyle uses Paddy's words to say more than a child would know. The novel casts a cold eye on a society in which divorce is commonplace.

Because Huck is older, more independent, and worldly-wise, Twain can blur the two levels of his writing more often than can Doyle. For example, Huck will often philosophize on such subjects as the morality of helping a slave escape; although he comes to the socially acceptable conclusion (that he will go to hell), the reader knows that Twain thinks just the opposite. Paddy, too young to philosophize, does not (and cannot) reflect on moral, religious, or political issues, but Doyle guides the reader in other subtle ways. Doyle comments on adult behavior by having the almost too candid Paddy make embarrassingly accurate observations that lead the reader to think about the topic in question and to examine his or her own behavior. Often, Paddy will ingenuously tell us about events in his neighborhood or in his life that suggest weighty topics in the larger world; for example, the passage (discussed above) that observes how excluding people strengthens friendships is obviously relevant in today's xenophobic world.

Paddy's experiences with and thoughts about death are especially striking. Paddy's fascination with death emerges on the novel's opening page:

"Liam and Aidan had a dead mother. Missis O'Connell was her name. —It'd be brilliant, wouldn't it? I said. . . . We were talking about having a dead ma" (Doyle 1994, 1). Death to a ten-year-old is not so horrible. It is merely a personal trait, much like having blonde or brunette hair. Paddy's mom is pretty; Charles Leavy's mom is dirty and stinks of cigarettes; Liam and Aidan's mom is dead. At first, death in such a light seems partly comic, and the reader may chuckle at how childish Paddy's thoughts are. He has never experienced death firsthand, and so he thinks of it as a type of urban myth, something that happens to other people: "A fellow in Raheny swallowed a bee by accident and it stung him in the throat and he died. He choked. He was running with his mouth open and the bee flew in. When he was dying he opened his mouth to say his last words and the bee flew out. That was how they knew" (123). In another incident, "they said that two men were killed doing this work but we never saw anything. They were killed when some of Donnelly's field fell on them, after it had been raining and the ground was loose and soggy. They drowned in muck" (112). If you went swimming after eating a full meal, "you drowned if you were full of your dinner. Your belly was too full and too heavy. You swallowed water. It got into your lungs. It took ages for you to die" (174). Notice how the fellow who was killed lived in Raheny, not Barrytown, and how "they said" that some nameless adults died in the field. Paddy is merely repeating what he has heard; he has no conception of what actual death is or that it could happen in his own circle.

When Paddy is finally confronted with real death, when a boy from one of the Corporation homes drowns in a pond, he is deeply affected and struggles to comprehend it: "He'd slipped in face first and his coat and jumper and his trousers got so wet and heavy he couldn't get up; that was what they said. The water soaked his clothes. I could see it. I put my sock in the sink, hanging into the water. The water crept up the sock. Half the water went into the sock" (196). Paddy cannot easily come to terms with this death. He first tries to understand it by experimenting with his sock, trying to reconcile what "they said" with what he experiences for himself. Of course, Paddy's childish ideas about death exist in the adult world as well; Doyle—not believing that physical maturity necessarily brings wisdom and acceptance—is suggesting that death is unintelligible to adults too, and that we use the same sophomoric "tricks" to distance ourselves from it that Paddy uses. We perceive the beginnings of our supposedly adult avoidance behaviors in a ten-year-old boy.

Paddy Clarke's multilayered structure extends to its brand of humor as well. In contrast to the raucous, overt, self-conscious humor of the trilogy, in this novel humor arises more subtly, when the omniscient adult reader watches as Paddy tries to make sense of his experiences. Thus, Doyle makes Paddy *unconsciously* humorous, as in his commentary on Daniel Boone: "Daniel Boone was one of the greatest of American pioneers. But, like many other pioneers, he was not much of a hand at writing. He carved something on a tree after he'd killed a bear. —D. Boone killa bar on this tree 1773.— His writing was far worse than mine, than Sinbad's even. I'd never have spelled Bear wrong. And anyway as well, what was a grown-up doing writing stuff on trees?" (Doyle 1994, 56). We knowing adults enter into complicity with Doyle as we laugh at Paddy's observation, which the child does not intend to be humorous. We also laugh at the way that Paddy collects bizarre data and regurgitates it at odd moments: "The life expectancy of a mouse is eighteen months" (44), or "Snails and slugs were gastropods. They had stomach feet" (53). The reader "laughs in recognition: if none of us can retrieve our innocence, we can all remember our eagerness to get rid of it—that ludicrous, undiscriminating appetite for scraps of knowledge" (Lane 1994, 92). Doyle "is brilliant on the obsessive concentration a child can bring to doing nothing, on the weird mixture of obscure facts and pure ignorance which clutters a child's head" (O'Toole 1993, 21).

By contrast, the reader is not expected to laugh at some of the things that Paddy himself finds humorous, such as dead legs, "pruning" (grabbing someone's testicles), and many of the other cruel things that he and the other boys do. Paddy and his friends pour lighter fluid into Sinbad's mouth and light it; they shoplift; they build dangerous booby traps around their forts; and all in the name of fun. Such violence in Paddy's world is yet another instance of Doyle's two-level writing. Paddy and his friends engage in these savageries because they find them amusing, which Doyle regards as typical behavior:

[L]ittle boys are violent. Read *Lord of the Flies*. When the kids don't have any parental guidance, they are little savages. . . . Peter Brook [the director of one of the movie versions of *Lord of the Flies*] put the kids on the island and just filmed, and his conclusion was that the book was very unrealistic because the kids became savages much more quickly in reality. The book took too long—he said the little fuckers were on the island for only a couple of hours before they were beating each other on the heads. So kids are very violent. I think also there is a certain amount of curiosity in their cruelty. Cruelty to animals is more curiosity. My own kids—they have rabbits and fish and they love them, but they'll push the rabbit, not to be cruel but to see what would happen if they push the rabbit.

Similarly, in *Paddy Clarke* the children kick their neighbor's dog just to see what will happen; they put lighter fluid in Sinbad's mouth for the same reason. Paddy does not realize the harm he may be causing because he cannot comprehend all the possible consequences.

Paddy's violence, however, escalates during the course of the novel: pushing a dog and trying to break a friend's nose constitute markedly different types of negative behavior. Paddy's environment grows harsher, as children such as Charles Leavy enter the neighborhood and as his parents yell at each other and occasionally revert to physical violence. Paddy changes: "Paddy's naughtiness shades into delinquency, although he himself can hardly tell the difference, let alone give a reason; he catches unhappiness off those closest to him, the very people who are supposed to make him happy" (Lane 1994, 92). Significantly, as Paddy's parents grow further estranged, Paddy grows more infatuated with Charles Leavy, the tough boy who seems to need no one. Paddy's increasing violence reflects his disintegrating surroundings: the novel "uses Paddy's half-formed consciousness as a prism through which he can refract the ordinary pain of adult experience, so that . . . loss and grief can be bent at a new angle and show their true colours" (O'Toole 1993, 21).

Mr. and Mrs. Clarke, as Doyle has acknowledged, are ordinary people, but their fighting is increasingly damaging to Paddy. Even though Paddy's mother seems saintly and his father deeply flawed, we must remember that we are seeing them through Paddy's eyes—we never even learn their first names. Consequently, we do not receive an objective picture of either parent. Paddy spends more time with his mother, as she is his primary caregiver and seems to be a very nurturing woman. She listens to him, is patient with him, and tries to understand him. By contrast, his father—whose favorite song contains the revealing lyrics "I married a wife—she's the plague of my life—I wish I was single again" (Doyle 1994, 84)—is less patient than his wife and has a quicker temper and a sarcastic sense of humor. He does not spend much time with Paddy and does not understand the way that his son's mind works, and so he loses his temper with Paddy more often. For example, when Paddy asks about wearing jeans on Sundays, his father answers "No" while his mother says "It depends—Not till after mass anyway." The father again says "No." "My ma looked at him with a face, like the look she had when she caught us doing something; sadder, though. —He doesn't have any jeans, she said. —He's just asking" (61). Mrs. Clarke knows that Paddy often asks questions just to be talking or engaging his parents. At the same time, although Mr. Clarke may not be the best of fathers, he is not a bad one; the reader must work to overcome an instinctive negative reaction against him because of Paddy's perceptions.

Mr. and Mrs. Clarke are simply two people who can no longer live together, and Paddy and his siblings experience the negative effects of this incompatibility. In Doyle's hands, this complex human situation constitutes another instance of two-level writing, this time with a political agenda: beginning in the late 1980s, Doyle was a passionate supporter of the divorce referendum in Ireland. Having worked for the Vote Yes campaign since he stuffed leaflets through letterboxes in 1986, he used his celebrity status on behalf of the success of the 1996 referendum. Doyle was so impassioned about this debate that had the referendum not passed—which it did by a very narrow margin—he and his family would have considered leaving Ireland.

Paddy Clarke depicts the pain that warring parents unintentionally inflict on their children—and the contradictions within which such parents are caught. The obvious question at the end of the novel is, "What happens next?" If there is no reconciliation between Paddy's parents, they face a life of grim solitude; because divorce is not possible in the Ireland of 1968, they could separate but could never remarry. Paddy's mother, a religious woman, would most likely never have a male companion again, and her life would be spent raising her four children alone. Mr. Clarke, who is not religious, will nevertheless be forced to abide by the antidivorce law; perhaps he will be like Mr. O'Connell, whose sister-in-law takes his children away from him because his long-time girlfriend, whom he cannot marry, moves into his spare bedroom. Whatever happens, these two average people will never be able to have another legal relationship.

The Clarkes' alternative, however—staying together for the rest of their lives—seems no more encouraging. These two people cannot live to-gether peaceably, and unless their personalities change drastically—which seems improbable—the fighting will begin again. Having witnessed how a relatively short period of fighting has affected Paddy, we must wonder what a lifetime of fighting will do to the other children. Thus, with divorce against the law and with little hope for the principal characters changing their fundamental attitudes, no good alternatives exist; Doyle forces the reader to confront the optionless futures that laws forbidding divorce ensure. As we shall see, Doyle goes on to address the issue of spousal conflict more fully in his next novel, *The Woman Who Walked into Doors.*

The final element of the two levels of meaning to be found in *Paddy Clarke* comes in the novel's treatment of religion, in which Paddy's childlike view—which concentrates on the mysteries and entertaining stories of tra-ditional Catholicism—is countered by Doyle's own agnosticism. Although, as Doyle says, "*Paddy Clarke* is filled with religion—a childish version of it," Catholicism offers Paddy no help in his time of need; the ten-year-old boy cannot grasp the real significance of the mass, the sacraments, or the saints. To Paddy, religion is merely another set of bizarre rules, imposed by adults, which he must blindly follow. Noticing that his father is still chewing at thirty-six seconds past eleven-thirty on Sunday morning—which breaks into the proscribed fasting period before communion—Paddy says, "I kept it to myself. If he went up for communion I'd see what happened. I knew and God knew" (Doyle 1994, 155). Mr. Clarke has broken the rules, and Paddy expects him to receive his punishment accordingly. Interestingly, Paddy, raised in a Catholic household, is concerned only with the picayune regulations of religion—but it is Huck Finn, raised with no religious training at all, who actually grapples with the heady questions of good and evil, right and wrong.

Doyle draws parallels between the rules of religion and the rules of Paddy's teacher, Mr. Hennessy, who relies heavily on the stick to maintain order. Indeed, seen from Paddy's viewpoint, religion and classroom order have much in common. Both sets of arbitrary rules, if broken, result in horrific punishment; both sets of rules are enforced by omnipotent, frightening, and at times inconsistent figures. To be sure, by the end of the century physical punishment as a teaching method has come to be considered inhumane, but the religious dicta have changed relatively little since Paddy's childhood.

Although religion is incomprehensible to Paddy, it can still be an enjoyable game. One of his favorite pastimes is to act out the story of Father Damien and the lepers, but to do this, "I needed lepers. Sinbad wasn't enough. He kept running away. . . . So I needed lepers. . . . I got the McCarthy twins and Willy Hancock. . . . They thought it was great being with a big boy, me. I made them come into our back garden. I told them what lepers were" (51). Paddy, playing the title role of Father Damien, coerces first his younger brother, then some younger neighbors, into playing the game. This vignette reveals Doyle's cynical view of saints and of the religious community: to be a priest, a saint, a savior (or even a schoolteacher), one needs worshipful followers over whom one has complete control. The lower the followers, the higher the saint and the more complete his power.

Paddy plays other games with religious themes. He and his friends stage a mock funeral for a rat (although it is a Viking ceremony with no formal priest). He cuts penny-sized communion wafers out of a vienna roll and leaves the round shapes on a windowsill for two days: "They got hard like the real ones but they didn't taste nice any more. I wondered was it a sin for me to be making them. I didn't think so" (48). In a scene reminiscent of Mary Lavin's story "My Vocation," Paddy tells his parents that he has a vocation because he "wanted [his mother] to cry. I wanted my da to shake my hand. I told him when he got home from his work" (52). The surprising outcome of his revelation to his father is a fight: "He sounded angry. —Encouraging this rubbish, he said. . . . —You did! He roared it" (53). Paddy's father is outraged and disgusted when Paddy considers (although not seriously) entering the religious life.

It is noteworthy that Doyle makes one of the novel's most sympathetic characters, Mrs. Clarke, very religious, and the least sympathetic, Mr. Clarke, the most irreligious. With his goal of a truthful portrayal of human life, Doyle would never use his novels as mere vehicles for his own personal agenda by blatantly assigning his beliefs to the most likable characters; in the real world, a person as patient and even-tempered as Mrs. Clarke probably would be religious, whereas the caustic, cynical Mr. Clarke would not. However, Doyle's main point still comes through: the fact that religion is the basis for a number of fights in the Clarke household underscores the irony of the disputes and bloodshed that religion has always inspired.

Aside from the games, the Church does nothing for young Paddy. Indeed, in one of the few times that we ever see the Church called upon for consolation in Doyle's novels, it fails. While listening to one of the early fights between his parents, Paddy reports:

> Their fights were like a train that kept getting stuck at the corner tracks and you had to lean over and push it or straighten it. Only now, all I could do was listen and wish. I didn't pray; there were no prayers for this. The Our Father didn't fit, or the Hail Mary. But I rocked the same way I sometimes did when I was saying prayers. Backwards and forwards, the rhythm of the prayer. Grace Before Meals was the fastest, probably because we were all starving just before lunch, just after the bell. (154)

Prayer gives no consolation here; it is separate from the real world that Paddy inhabits and cannot fill empty bellies or make his parents stop fighting. Paddy finds more consolation in his ritualized vigils than in any type of prayer. Doyle says, "It kind of depresses me when I see all those people in the church—particularly the kids"; neither Paddy nor Doyle finds religion adequate to the problems of the modern world.

Paddy Clarke is obviously one of Doyle's most disturbing novels. It begins as a celebration of childhood but ends as a memorial both for childhood and for marriage. Paddy's parents' fights dominate both the novel and Paddy's life; these fights suffocate him spiritually at the same time as the development of the Corporation homes encroaches upon him physically. Although Doyle asserts that there is no pessimistic trend to his works, he does say that he tries to depict all aspects of life; his first two books show its more positive aspects, the next two show the grimmer side. It is this sense of realism that leads him to entitle this novel, and to end it, with the cruel rhyme with which the other school children taunt Paddy. This chant appears in the penultimate section of the novel, but its power is so overwhelming that the last section—in which Paddy and Mr. Clarke meet in a formal, stilted visit and awkwardly shake hands—is overshadowed by the haunting rhyme. Thus, Doyle concludes *Paddy Clarke* with a powerful image of childhood cruelty that somehow contaminates the entire novel. Although Doyle says that there is room for hope—Paddy is still very young and has two loving and responsible, if incompatible, parents—the novel feels far from hopeful.

Paddy Clarke Ha Ha Ha was a breakthrough novel for Doyle. His first patently artful novel, *Paddy Clarke* made both the literary critics and his popular audiences take him seriously as an artist rather than brush him off as an entertainer. In this book, Doyle shows his mastery of the technique of entering another's consciousness; he skillfully makes Paddy the unwitting vehicle for humor, political statements, social commentary, and religious criticism. At the same time, Paddy is a fully realized character: his candor, perception, and final confusion, betrayal, and hurt will remain in readers' minds, while his gift for observation and way with words suggest that he may grow up to be a remarkable person. Although always humorous, Doyle concentrates more on developing character than on providing laughs. *Paddy Clarke* is a masterful, enduring coming-of-age novel that will continue to speak to generations of readers.

CHAPTER SEVEN

The Woman Who Walked into Doors

The Woman Who Walked into Doors (1996), Doyle's fifth novel in nine years, is more ambitious than his earlier ones. In his previous attempt at first-person narrative, *Paddy Clarke*, Doyle could draw both upon his own experiences as a ten-year-old boy and upon those of his son (roughly Paddy's age) as a living model. However, Doyle has never even known a thirty-nine-year-old female victim of repeated spousal abuse; thus, creating Paula Spencer, the narrator of *The Woman Who Walked into Doors*, demanded more of an imaginative stretch in Doyle than had any of his earlier works.

To be sure, the novel was not without precursors. In 1994, when the BBC invited Doyle to write "anything I wanted," he responded with a screenplay "about a family in crisis . . . [in] four episodes." The resulting miniseries, entitled *The Family*, follows a contemporary family over a period of several months; each episode focuses on a different family member, starting off with the violently controlling husband Charlo and ending with his wife Paula. *The Family* was both widely watched and controversial. In particular, Doyle received many letters and queries concerning Paula, asking "How could she have married him in the first place?" The novel grew out of those inquiries: "I felt strongly that she had an awful lot that she could say and I had grown very fond of her and very protective of her because she'd been through so much, and I could imagine her sitting down when she had free time . . . and she would start writing and explore her past. . . . [T]he book lets her explain to an extent why she fell in love with this man and why he fell in love with her and it made him something less of a monster as well." Paula Spencer attempts to explain—both to the reader and to herself—how, by age thirty-nine, she had become an alcoholic and abused widow with four children. By understanding what happened to her, she hopes to start to make changes in her life and in herself.

As in many novels where the narrator attempts to explain his or her life, the structure of *The Woman Who Walked into Doors* is not linear or chronological but rather spiral. A present situation sparks off a memory, which in turn provokes another memory, and so forth, until the narrative returns to the present—which then begins another chain of memories. Paula, as she is speaking to us, is coming to terms with and learning about herself and her life. She is confronting her "memories of the people, places, objects, events and feelings that make up the story of [her] life. Memories that answer the questions, Who am I, and How did I get to be this way?" (Kotre 1995, 168). In this process, along with providing the reader with general background information, Paula articulates her memories of more specific and powerful events, from which we learn a great deal about her: "Memories of ordinary events don't reveal much about a person's character, but memories of extraordinary events do" (168).

Paula Spencer, née O'Leary, remembers her youth in an unidentified Dublin suburb as relatively happy and secure, where family went on day trips and the occasional holiday, she performed well in primary school, and she and her girlfriends chased after little boys. However, her older sister Carmel—whom Paula asks to confirm her memories—remembers this period as horrible, with a tyrannical father, a harried and harassed mother, and constant fighting and yelling. Paula also tells us about her days in secondary school: how she was put in the "stupid" class, and the changes in her that this assignment wrought; about the rigid societal codes that girls followed for fear of being labeled a "slut"; about her physical changes after puberty and the reactions of her peers. Paula, a precocious, attractive, normal teenage girl, is hardened by a miserable school and class system.

Then, at a local dance, she meets the Byronesque, mysterious Charlo, about whom she has heard exciting rumors: he is tough and has been in jail. Paula and Charlo are attracted to each other and begin to date exclusively. Because of his reputation as a vicious fighter, dating Charlo commands such respect from the neighborhood that Paula feels free from societal restrictions—for the first time in her adult life. They get married, and Paula is proud that she was not pregnant at the time: "So there. It was love" (Doyle 1996, 129). Charlo has a job, and they move into a small flat. Paula gets pregnant very quickly, and just as quickly their relationship begins to go awry; only months into their marriage, Charlo hits her for the first time. They both are horrified by this blow, which knocks Paula to the ground, and Charlo is repentant. His remorse is short-lived, however, and he begins to beat her more often and more severely. The title of the novel comes from one of the excuses that she frequently uses when Charlo takes her to the emergency room after his more violent beatings: "I walked into the door" (181). As she explains to the reader, "I didn't exist. I was a ghost. People looked away; I wasn't there. They stared at the bruises for a split second, then away, off my shoulder and away. There was nothing there. . . . The woman who had nothing wrong with her. The woman who was fine. The woman who walked into doors" (187).

Paula endures the beatings because she feels that she has no choice. Her father has become a distant, cold, humorless man who, Paula thinks, feels triumphant at the sight of her wounds; her mother, enduring her own dismal marriage to Mr. O'Leary, has become a nonentity with no opinions or life of her own, and consequently can offer no consolation. Paula stays with Charlo for eighteen years and eventually has four children and one stillborn child. She lives in fear and becomes an alcoholic in an attempt to escape the pain of daily existence, never gathering the inner courage and external support necessary either to leave Charlo or to kick him out of the house. One morning, however, she sees him looking at their oldest daughter Nicola with an expression of seething hatred; this look forces her out of her fear- and alcohol-induced paralysis, and she hits him with a frying pan. Paula forces a bloody and stunned Charlo, the man she has feared for the last eighteen years, out of the house. He never returns.

As common and even typical as this series of events (in some ways) is, Doyle does not express it through a straightforward chronological narrative; to do so would be to misrepresent Paula's actual experience of it. Rather, the book starts after the main action is over and is composed of memories, questions, and flashbacks, as Paula struggles to come to terms with her past so that she can be able to live in the present; in Doyle's words, "The book is . . . her attempt to sort herself out, her recent past, not her present." She is trying to recover her life. At the novel's commencement, Paula, on her own for two years, is trying to control her alcoholism, although at this stage "she's not ready to do anything about it because she needs it." She is trying to be an active force in raising her youngest son; she works four days a week as a maid and is becoming financially independent; and she has just been told that Charlo was shot and killed by the Garda in a foiled bank robbery and kidnapping attempt. In this swirl of circumstances, Paula—trying both to understand where her life went wrong and to redirect the spiraling course that her life has taken—turns to memory as a tool of change: "The historical structures that mold our lives pose questions we must respond to and define the immediate possibilities for change" (Hartsock 1979, 61).

The most remarkable thing about *The Woman Who Walked into Doors* is the character of Paula Spencer herself. Fully formed, complex, even intricate, she is more complex than any of Doyle's previous characters. Although the Rabbittes still do not seem like "caricatures" (Shepherd 1994, 164), Paula's voice is closer to reality (a word that Doyle himself frequently intones when discussing his work). Paula's narrative also is a "more complex interior monologue than that of Paddy Clarke, the chirpy 10-year-old—the voice of a woman with adult responsibilities to deal with, as well as all the crack and agonies that come with growing up as a girl" (Turner 1996, 2).

A man writing convincingly and unpatronizingly in a woman's voice is an accomplishment in itself; a man writing successfully from the perspective of a woman who is uncertain about her status both as a person and as a woman, and who is trying to discover her own identity by examining her history, is extraordinary. The writer must invent and account for the whole life of his character; he must give her memories and experiences appropriate to her gender and to her current psychological condition but which are not inanely obvious—there are no quid pro quo experiences in real life. He must make the narrator self-conscious, but he himself cannot be self-conscious. The writer must be able to unfold the narrative yet make it seem as if the narrator is doing this on her own. Inventing a character who lives in the present and who is reacting logically to current situations is difficult enough; inventing a character who is trying to reinvent herself through reference to the past is an even greater accomplishment. Doyle successfully completes his task—and allows Paula to complete her task as well.

One might say that Paula is an extraordinary set of characters—indeed, one can discern at least four Paulas. When reinventing herself, the narrator Paula must take stock of the other three Paulas in order to understand how she became who she is. The first Paula is the very young Paula, the Paula of the memories of a happy home and of caring, loving parents—the precocious, joyful Paula who, with her girlfriends, chases after boys and gets her first brassiere. The second Paula is the teenager who is placed in the stupid class, who becomes brash and bold to avoid being overlooked, who is aware of society's strictures, and who meets and falls in love with the dashing young Charlo. The third Paula is the alcoholic, abused, insensible woman who is married to Charlo—the victim Paula. We know very little about this Paula because the current Paula remembers nothing of this time: "I missed the 80s. I haven't a clue. It's just a mush" (Doyle 1996, 203). This Paula lived in fear and agony; she lived to forget what was happening to her. Finally, the current Paula, the narrator, is trying to make sense of her old selves. Doyle shows us how these four separate identities are connected and how each has evolved into the next.

The young Paula, filled with a touching joie de vivre, is reminiscent of Paddy Clarke before his parents started fighting—perceptive, imaginative, curious. Significantly, each child remembers his or her own "safe place." Where Paddy has his fort under the dining-room table and loves to stare at dust particles illuminated by sunbeams, Paula's first and safest memory is of her bedroom:

> There were noises from downstairs, the radio and my mammy humming and putting things on the table. I was warm. Carmel was asleep in her bed. . . . My father in the coal shed scraping coal off the floor into the bucket, the screech of the shovel on the concrete. . . . I always loved that noise . . . maybe knowing that there was a lovely big fire coming. The cot was white, chipped so that some of the wood underneath showed. There was a picture of a fawn at the end where my head was. . . . When I think of *happy* and *home* together, I see the curtain blowing and the sun on the wall and being

snug and ready for the day. . . . I see flowers on the curtains—but there were never flowers on the curtains in our room. (Doyle 1996, 6–7)

Although part of the difference between these memories can be attributed to the circumstances of their relation—Paddy is still a young boy only a few years removed from the scene, while Paula is remembering thirty years later—they are also gender-based, almost to the point of stereotype. Paddy, the young boy, is alone in his memory; he has barricaded the dining room chairs into a fort that is rather dirty and always cool; he often falls asleep on the bare linoleum on which the table stands. There are no frills, no amenities, no comforts, but he likes what he can observe from his haven, such as the difference in his parents' walking patterns and the secret life of dust particles. This is the safe place of a mischievous little boy. By contrast, in Paula's memory she is with her family, covered in warm blankets and thinking of future warmth and love. Everything is clean and orderly. She imagines flowers on the curtains and animals on her bed. As an adult with her recent history, she would naturally find this memory, with its safe and sane order, comforting. She misremembers flowers on the curtains because flowers would more naturally appeal to her sense of beauty than the masculine stripes that were the actual pattern.

Notice too that Paula's memory does not include intellectual curiosity. This fact should not be taken as a statement of Doyle's own attitudes about women but rather as a reflection of the social conditions of the times; during Paula's childhood in the 1960s, boys were more encouraged towards intellectual pursuits than were girls. While Paddy's father teaches him about fingerprints, Paula's father tends to ignore her and her sisters' minds. Paula was never encouraged in school, which also had the effect of stifling her intellectual curiosity. Thus, for the adult Paula, a memory of a loving atmosphere would be more compelling to her than one of intellectual stimulation—revealing much about both the young and the adult Paulas.

The young Paula is a winsome, intelligent, exuberant little girl. Instead of describing the "stuff" that comes out of a dead rat (as Paddy does), Paula describes her mother taking her to get her first bra. She describes the problems of her first menstruation. In the time of her life when she felt the most empowered, we see her and her girlfriends going steady with and breaking up with different boys every day:

> I went with dozens of fellas after that for about a year. We swapped them around and they didn't know. I suppose it made them feel good, being chased by little young ones. Sometimes it actually was like a game of chasing; you'd dump one and run after another. It was a gas. Absolutely harmless. . . . We were still a bit young to be called sluts for it. Anyway, the young fellas all thought that they were in charge; they asked us to go with them—but they wouldn't have if we hadn't made them. . . . I went with [a boy] for eleven days, then I broke it off . . . because I wanted to. I just wanted to. I wanted to be able to say it. I wanted the word to go around; she broke it off with him. I wanted the power. (75–77)

Paula also does well in her all-girls primary school. Encouraged by her female teacher, Paula writes imaginative, creative stories and begins to learn: "I loved primary school. . . . I was good in school, especially at stories. She [the teacher] always got me to read mine out to the class. . . . I was good in school; she made us think that we were good" (25). This young Paula is curious, happy, intelligent, sought-after, and self-confident.

Things begin to change—and the second, teenage Paula begins to emerge—when she enters a coed high school: "I changed. I noticed it then; I'm not just looking back. I changed. I stopped trying to hide myself. I pushed myself forward. . . . I wasn't the only one. It happened to all of us. We went in children and we turned into animals" (36–39). The first blow to her self-confidence occurs when the headmaster calls out the list of names for the various levels—and Paula is assigned to the next-to-lowest level. In sharp contrast to her beloved, encouraging female primary school teacher, the headmaster has labeled her: "[W]e were the dopes, the thicks. There was only one class after us, 1.7. They were nearly retarded" (27). Her new teachers, particularly her English teacher, thoroughly quench her intellectual curiosity: "The prick; I was good at English until he came along with his Brylcream head. He never let us forget that we were dense, that we were a waste of his time" (33). As for the rest of her teachers, "The ones that weren't perverts were either thick or bored or women" (34).

Paula cannot stand out among the students with her stories any longer, and she realizes that to avoid being swallowed up, she must use her body. She starts by "grabbing" Derek O'Leary, her piggish seatmate, to retaliate for his grabbing her. She "wanks off" a boy in the back seat of her classroom: "I did it to him; he didn't do it to me. I did it. . . . That was how you made a name for yourself in 1.6" (41). She practices seductive smiles and poses. Paula stops being a thinking human and starts becoming a reacting body.

Paula's beliefs about the treatment of women in marriage are unconsciously modeled after her parents' relationship in this second phase of her life. Her father is metamorphosing from the seemingly loving, coal-shoveling man of her early memories into "a bitter little pill and a bully. He made rules now just to make us obey them, just to catch us out. He used to laugh a lot but now he couldn't or wouldn't and he hated hearing laughter in the house" (120). This father does not say a word while in the limousine with his daughter on the way to her wedding. He makes a banal, cold speech at the wedding supper. Paula makes the mistake of marrying Charlo in order to leave this father.

Her mother is also undergoing a transformation in response to her husband's changes. She is becoming "different. She wasn't the same person she'd been when I was smaller. She used to be bigger, happier, noisier. . . . She was grinning away . . . and she looked miserable. She looked so sad. She hadn't worn a new piece of clothes in years. She didn't drink, she didn't smoke; she didn't do anything except sit in front of the telly and watch the programmes that he put on and say yes and no when he spoke to her: she didn't even knit" (Doyle 1996, 120). The mother's identity is being fully erased. Because Mr. O'Leary's abuse has been primarily emotional, his wife has had nothing concrete against which to rail. Consequently, over time, her personality is being snuffed out of existence. The destruction of her identity is a direct result of her role as wife: "Sex roles would preassign tasks to women which would necessitate continued alienation and isolation. . . . [T]he sexual division of labor in society organizes noncreative and isolating work particularly for women" (Eisenstein 1979, 11). Paula is not conscious of her mother's plight until it is too late.

It is in this period of her life that Paula meets Charlo at a local dance, and the two immediately become smitten and inseparable. Because of her experiences at high school, she has become so accustomed to inappropriate treatment that she says about their first meeting, "Charlo respected me, I have to say that. All the way home . . . he didn't try to get his feel or pull me behind a wall or none of the usual stuff. It was nice for a change" (52). "The usual stuff" has become so commonplace that its absence—which self-confident women, in an appropriate social context, would demand as a basic level of conduct—seems a significant compliment to Paula. Of course, Charlo would discontinue this decent treatment eventually: "He'd do that to me later. . . . I always knew what to expect" (53). She falls in love with Charlo because he "made me someone. Not a Queen or a Princess, just someone. It was a start" (54). Her environment has so worked on her that she barely considers herself a person; she falls in love with Charlo not because he makes her feel worthy or special but because he makes her feel less like a thing. Paula also chooses Charlo because he is familiar: unconsciously, she realizes that "him and [her] father were very alike. She said—twenty-one years later. The wise old woman of the bottle" (Doyle 1996, 121).

Her low self-esteem and her growing awareness of what she can expect in relationships and from the world around her lead her to accept the eventual ill treatment from Charlo without remark. Their sex life consists of quick trysts in which "he came, and we went" (155). When they meet each other's families, Paula tries to make a good impression on Mrs. Spencer, but Charlo tries deliberately to anger Mr. O'Leary. On their wedding night, Charlo gets severely intoxicated and deserts his wife; Paula goes to sleep alone—and never gets to throw her bouquet, a marriage ritual that she had anticipated eagerly.

The older Paula, narrating this period of her life, continually asserts, "He loved me. He respected me." She is fooling herself. This is not to dispute Paula's memories of this time; she and Charlo were, no doubt, very happy in what Doyle later terms "that first totally obsessive phase" of their relationship. During this time, Paula, who had been taught not to expect much, sees Charlo as a benefactor and liberator, treating her better than that to which she had become accustomed. Paula fulfills all of Charlo's needs—she is attractive, sexual, eager to please—why shouldn't he want "to keep her"? Paula attempts to prove that they were in love: she wasn't pregnant at the time of their wedding, therefore there can be no dispute about the fact that they married for love. However, because this couple was operating under the false impression that lust is mature love, when the first romance fades, a greater understanding and respect for each other do not evolve. Instead, abuse follows. Paula has such a debased view both of herself (exacerbated by her relationship with Charlo) and of marriage that she becomes a perfect candidate for abuse.

The third Paula, the victim, occupies most of her life, yet the reader sees her only a few times, and mostly in the last section of the book—as if the narrator Paula couldn't bring herself to confront this period earlier. We do not learn much about her because the narrator Paula does not know much about her, for she is experiencing the partial amnesia that traumatic occurrences inspire. She cannot remember much about her life during this period at all: "What did I do in the 80's: I walked into doors. I got up off the floor. I became an alcoholic. I discovered that I was poor, that I'd no right to the hope I'd started out with" (Doyle 1996, 204). She has become so submissive that she has squeezed her identity out of existence:

> I was looking for everything I got. I provoked him. I was useless. I couldn't even cook a fry properly, or wash a good shirt. . . . I was hopeless, useless, good for fuckin' nothing. I lived through years of my life thinking that they were the most important things about me, the only real things. I couldn't cope, I couldn't earn, I needed him. I needed him to show me the way; I needed him to punish me. I was hopeless and stupid, good for only sex, and I wasn't even very good at that. He said. That was why he went to other women. (177)

Living with Charlo's abuse has made Paula a nothing. She lives in fear and pain. She is grateful for the Flake bar that Charlo leaves her to apologize for his beatings. Doyle presents the reader with the near death of an identity. Paula has become an extreme version of her mother, except that the latter's opiate is television, not alcohol, and her scars are psychological, not physical.

Moreover, Paula can never leave Charlo as long as the situation remains this way. First, her weak identity makes her incapable of leaving him. Second, she always hopes that things will get better and return to the way "they used to be": "In most cases, the woman feels if she just holds on to the old pattern a little longer, why surely the paradisiacal feeling she seeks will appear in the next heartbeat" (Estes 1996, 49). Such hope is her last, slim thread connecting her to who she was before; to give up this hope—as would be required to actually change the situation—would be too much for her to bear.

The primary thing that saves Paula from her family, is, ironically, her family. Paula has nothing left of herself, but she still is biologically and emotionally a mother. Although this label is used often enough to erase many women's sense of personal identity, it helps to resurrect Paula's. She observes Charlo looking at their oldest daughter, Nicola, in the same manner with which he looks at her—"not with desire, as a lesser writer would have suggested, but with hate and a wish to annihilate" (Gordon 1996, 7). Doyle says, "Charlo resents his daughter growing up, and it's about basically keeping her in the same position that he has his wife in. He uses that leer, just before Paula hits him with the frying pan, not as an expression of his attraction, but as a way of pinning her down, of making her feel uncomfortable, of rattling her independence" (O'Toole 1994, 12). Something in the victim Paula suddenly snaps: "I don't know what happened to me—the Bionic Woman—he was gone. It was so easy. Just bang—gone. The evil in the kitchen; his eyes" (Doyle 1996, 213). She picks up a frying pan and hits him—her first independent action since the abuse began. In this moment, she stops being selfless and recaptures her lost identity: "My finest hour. I was there. I was something. I loved" (213). Moreover, the narrator Paula never second-guesses the significance of this action, nor does she (as she does in other instances) wonder how much of her recollection is imagined or how much her battered psyche invented to keep her sane. With this assertion of her own veracity, "Realism becomes, not a literary convention, but a human triumph. The ability to say what novelists say—this happened, then this happened—is, for Paula, the mark of escape from victimhood" (O'Toole 1996, 10). Paula realizes that in this instance, she cannot overestimate her strength.

Ironically and paradoxically, her moments of identity involve her reaction to Charlo: she first feels like a person when she dates and then marries him, and she at last feels like a somebody when she drives him from her home. This final epiphany would be as false as the first had it caused no en-during alteration, but the narrator Paula is still changing. Through her nar-ration, Paula is learning from her history how to better her present: "Slowly, ever so slowly, she appears to be a woman in the process of getting a grip on her past" (Turner 1996, 2). However, her healing is much more difficult than that of any earlier Doyle character because Paula's occurs in relative isolation. Doyle's other characters, especially the Rabbittes, can rely on each other: "The Rabbittes existed mainly in the supportive, sociable medium of dialogue. But Paula has to pull herself together from the inside of her own mind" (2).

One example of Paula's metamorphosis is the continued interest that she takes in her youngest child, Jack. She is a much better mother to Jack than she was to her other children; she has become a hands-on mother, in-volved in Jack's daily life. Her other children's childhoods are a blur because she was either drunk or severely injured during most of them. Now, how-ever, she makes it a point to read Jack a bedtime story every night and re-fuses to take a drink before Jack is asleep. She picks Jack up from school every day, and they have a tea-time together. (She also manages to be at home every day when Leanne gets home from school.)

As another element in her transformation, Paula has also proved to her-self that she doesn't need Charlo or his money to survive. She has a four-day-a-week job that she does uncomplainingly, and she brings home enough money for her family. She runs her household very well—everyone has a routine, and everyone helps out: "We usually clean the house together when there's so much dust that it has no room to settle. It's nearly a tradition now, a game. Leanne loves it" (Doyle 1996, 93). They all seem to enjoy each other. Nicola has a good job and a nice boyfriend; Leanne is doing very well in her school work and may go farther in her education than any-one else in the family.

For her own part, Paula is regaining a little self-confidence and starting to realize that she is not stupid. She says tentatively about Leanne's intelli-gence, "I wonder where she got the brains from. Maybe from me" (104). Paula is indulging her love of fiction by reading, even making critical judg-ments on what she is reading: "Danielle Steele. It was shit, but I loved it. I've seven in my bedroom, in alphabetical order. All saved from the bins.

Catherine Cookson is my favourite. I've two of hers. She's very good" (109). (In this, Paula is another Jillsey Sloper, the cleaning woman turned book editor in John Irving's *The World According to Garp*, one of Doyle's favorite novels). Paula recognizes her progress: "I get up at eight o'clock every morning. I used to sleep it out a lot; sometimes I couldn't get up. But not any more. I made the decision. I make the effort. I get up when the alarm goes. It's a little victory; I'm in charge of myself" (91).

As in his previous works, humor and laughter demonstrate mental health in a Doyle character, and Paula is healing herself with humor. As she narrates her life, she begins to realize how ludicrous certain situations are and becomes able to laugh at herself. Paula, always perceptive, has a keen sense of the incongruous, but her ability to laugh has been retarded because of all the pain and isolation in her life. However, with Charlo out of the picture and important parts of her life back on track, she is starting to look at her life from a distance, to discern its absurd components, and to recognize them as such.

From her newfound perspective, she can easily recognize the humor in the early stages of her life. For instance, she reveals that when she was chasing the little boys, "I'd go into a field with one fella and sometimes we'd do absolutely nothing, not even talk; we'd stay a bit and go back to the rest. They'd nudge one another when we were coming towards them. I'd make myself blush" (76). She can perceive the inanity in society's hypocrisy, where "[e]verything made you one thing or the other" (48): a single girl was called a slut on almost every occasion, but once she began dating the disreputable Charlo, "I could have walked around in my nip with twenty Major in my mouth combing my pubic hair and nobody would have said a word. I was Charlo's girl now and that made me respectable" (49). She even sees the humor in the younger, pre-abuse Charlo. Telling the reader about strolling arm in arm with him on their first night, she remembers his walk: "His side-to-side walk . . . they all walked like that then, the fellas . . . walking like they're afraid they'll topple over because their balls are so heavy. . . . I began to walk like him so we wouldn't keep bashing into each other. . . . We must have looked ridiculous, the pair of us, strolling . . . like two hard penguins" (54). Or later, shortly after they were married: "I think it was during the Hunger Strikes. Charlo was big into the H Blocks. He'd have loved to have been in there with them. I said that to him. . . . He didn't even know I was slagging him. . . . He still ate like a pig, though, and drank like one" (180).

Paula even ridicules herself. The first time that she meets Charlo's mother, she tries to make a good impression but fails miserably: "I said Hello and not Howyeh. All mothers said that their sons' girlfriends were common. . . . All the mothers were the same. I was drunk as a skunk, I'd no jacket on me, there was probably grass on my back, I was smiling crooked but I made sure I said Hello instead of Howyeh" (64).

Paula sees the humor in situations that many would fail to find funny. For instance, she could have surrounded the memories of her youth in a maudlin atmosphere; instead, she is straightforward and wry. Because she finds humor in these potentially bathetic situations, we hope that she will eventually be able to work through the horrors of her beatings. Doyle has given Paula the gift of laughter, and with it she will be able to heal herself.

Overall, then, we have a good understanding of what the narrator Paula is like and how she has evolved. She is perceptive and intelligent. She is determined—she is battling her history and is winning. She knows her limitations—she realizes that alcohol is vital to her at this stage and accepts it, as much as she hates it. She knows she has a desperate need for a solid history, for memories of a "good" childhood—but inventing an alluring past where all was safe and comforting is ultimately harmful, and so she seeks validation from her family members about her memories.

Thus, Paula is fundamentally different—and deeper—than any of Doyle's previous female characters. In *The Snapper*, Doyle's only other novel that attempts to enter the feminine consciousness, Doyle makes Sharon Rabbitte a convincing but still limited character. Ironically, although Sharon is pregnant, the reader views her more as a young person than as a young woman, as a body more than a mind. Sharon is in a crisis and is reacting, not reflecting; she and the other Rabbittes "do not have time to ponder life; they live it instead" (Bradshaw 1994, 128). Sharon lacks the maturity that true reflection requires. Significantly, the thoughts and feelings that she does experience—for instance, curiosity about her condition, shame regarding the circumstances of her pregnancy, fear about the future—are so basically human that they are appropriate to either gender; indeed, Jimmy Sr. feels the same emotions (curiosity, shame, and fear) and expresses himself in terms similar to Sharon's.

By contrast, Paula's novel is a series of female reflections. Whereas for *The Snapper* he read about the physical effects of pregnancy, for *The Woman Who Walked into Doors*, Doyle studied women's psychology: "I did a hell of a lot of reading while I was writing—I read a lot about women and violence, women and alcohol, sexual fantasy. And I used very little of it in the strict sense. It was just to make the ice I was walking on thicker as I walked along." Doyle seems to have used more of his research than he imagined, because he does a convincing job of creating a female psyche: "Unsure as to whether a self-portrait by a woman . . . could be handled by a male . . . I submitted the novel to a gender test which it passed triumphantly" (Gowrie 1996, 6).

Indeed, Paula's life may successfully stand as a metaphor for most women's lives, not just those of the victims of physical abuse: "By calling attention to the specific experiences of individuals, feminism calls attention to the totality of social relations, to the social formation as a whole" (Hartsock 1979, 61). Paula's loss of identity has happened to many women, whether in the patriarchal society of 1970s Ireland or the patriarchal society of America at the turn of the millennium: "Beneath its colloquial 'Dub' style is a universal story of invisible women everywhere, lost in vast council wastelands on the fringes of cities. This is the tale of a little life, of childhood, motherhood and widowhood" (Foster 1996, 36). Paula's physical beatings do more than spotlight domestic violence; they reflect the psychological beatings that many women receive and are taught to receive uncomplainingly in patriarchies. Paula's scars—"the gaps in my mouth . . . the tiny bruises on my arm. The scar on my chin" (Doyle 1996, 197)—in part represent women's psychological scars. Paula's body is the manifestation of many women's psychological damage.

Paula struggles to keep the power that she earned in her youth, before patriarchal rules began to apply. During this time, her naturally vibrant and dominant personality thrives. In her same-sex classroom, Paula excels; her stories are selected to be read in class, and "the applause and the smiles" (25) stand out in her memory. She is popular and has many friends. Perhaps most pointedly, when she and her friends chase boys, they are in charge.

The empowered Paula even feels magnanimous enough to elevate poor Bickies O'Farrell for a brief moment: "I even went with Bickies O'Farrell for a bit because I felt sorry for him" (76)—a benign despot handing out favors. Power in Paula's sheltered world is non-gender-based, and she flourishes.

When she leaves her primary school and enters a coed school, however, she also leaves her sanctuary. The male headmaster first makes her feel unimportant: "I was only in the tech half an hour when I realised that I wasn't good at all. . . . The headmaster stood on the steps and told us to shut up" (25). The very first day, she gets in trouble because she tries to protect herself against her obnoxious male seatmate: "He kept trying to feel me till I punched him in the face and told him to fuck off. I was made to stand up for making noise" (27). Paula, a female, is ostracized and punished for trying to assert herself over a male.

Paula feels uncomfortable in the new school and—for the first time—begins to doubt herself: "There was something about me that drew them to me, that made them touch me. It was my tits that I was too young for; I'd no right to them. It was my hair. It was my legs and my arms and my neck. There were things about me that were wrong and dirty. I thought that then; I felt it. I didn't say it to anybody. . . . I was a dirty slut in some way that I didn't understand and couldn't control; I made men and boys do things" (35). Paula is blaming herself for uncontrollable and exclusively female conditions; she knows that physical maturity is not her fault, yet she still takes the blame—"I made them do things." Such guilt and self-blame are typical of abused children, persisting until they have come to terms with their abuse. One of Doyle's favorite novels, *Bastard Out of Carolina*—about a young girl physically and sexually abused by her stepfather—illustrates the self-hatred of the victim mentality: "It was my fault, everything. . . . I kept trying to figure out how I could have prevented it all from happening . . . not let anyone see . . . the bruises. . . . I should have gone to Mama and made sure she knew that I deserved that beating. . . . What was it I had done: Why had he always hated me? Maybe I was a bad girl, evil, nasty, willful, stupid, ugly—everything he said. Maybe I was" (Allison 1992, 249–52). Moreover, Paula's childhood mistreatment makes her a ready victim for later domestic abuse: "Charlo may have acted out his self-hatred on Paula, but Paula does a fine job of heaping it on herself" (Slater 1996, 4).

The teenage Paula's situation is not unusual in modern patriarchal societies. On the one hand, many contemporary men have internalized feelings of power based on a historical hierarchy. On the other hand, women internalize the feelings of subordination. When males assert their dominance in an already patriarchal world, females, having internalized their own submissive role, have little choice but to accept the mistreatment. Children naturally trust their "protectors," and if women are not allowed to mature intellectually and emotionally, then, forever juvenile, they will continue to see men as their blameless protectors while accepting blame for things beyond their control. This insidious process prevents any sort of self-actualization or the development of a sense of personal identity.

Paula, however, learns quickly—perhaps reflecting the powers of resistance that many women still possess. She refuses to be erased or swallowed up. She learns how to hold her own: "The school made me rough" (Doyle 1996, 35). She starts by grabbing her disgusting deskmate after he tries to feel her, "pre-emptive strikes" that make him afraid of her. She finds girlfriends with whom she shares adolescent fantasies. She "stopped trying to hide [herself]. [She] pushed [herself] forward" (39). She still plays at dating, "going with fellas," but innocent talks and self-inspired blushes are no longer enough. She almost proudly masturbates a boy at the back of the classroom.

Paula tries to keep her power, but given the structures of male-dominated society, she must continually subvert herself to do so. When she masturbates the boy, she is in control, and he is out of control; she literally holds him in her hand. However, this is not a true power because she must become submissive to possess it. As Socrates demonstrates to Polus in Plato's *Gorgias*, tyrants and orators have very little power: "For they do just about nothing they want to, though they certainly do whatever they see most fit to do. . . . If a person does anything for the sake of something, he doesn't want this thing that he's doing, but the thing for the sake of which he's doing it" (466D–467E). Sexual power is not true power if the woman must degrade herself to wield it. Paula gets nothing from the act in the back of the classroom; she is taking notes while she is doing it, and she repeatedly hits her hand on the desk top, which she says was painful. When it is over, she unceremoniously wipes her hand on her sock. Similar to the power that exotic dancers claim to possess, Paula's power is humiliating and debasing. She has started her descent into powerlessness.

As Paula grows up, she becomes aware of the silent yet powerful strictures ruling young women's conduct. As "bitch" is the catch-all name today for a nonconforming woman, "slut" was the term in 1960s Ireland. Paula knows the nuances of being labeled a slut:

> It was alright to sit or lean on the wall during the day but not when it began to get dark. It wasn't respectable. . . . Getting yourself a bad name. Smoking was another. It was alright for a gang of girls to smoke, share the fag, laugh and cough. But it wasn't on for a young one to smoke by herself, say, to walk down the road by herself, smoking. She had the makings of a slut if she did that. Keeping the cigarette in her mouth when she was talking, that made her a definite slut. Smoking Major, the strongest, made her an absolute prostitute. If you didn't smoke at all you were tight and dry and a Virgin Mary. Everything made you one thing or the other. It tired you out sometimes. . . . If you smiled at more than one boy you were a slut; if you didn't smile at all you were a tight bitch. If you smiled at the wrong boy you were back to being a slut and you might get a hiding from his girlfriend, and she'd be a slut for pulling your hair and you'd be one for letting her. Boys could ask you to go with them and you couldn't ask them. You had to get your friends to let the boys know that you'd say yes if you were asked. That could make you a slut as well, if you got the wrong friend to ask for you. . . . Jesus, if you went wrong once you were a slut.—Slut. My little brother. —Slut. My father. —Slut. Everyone. They were all in on it. (Doyle 1996, 49)

Paula knows and plays by the rules of the games. The stakes are a good husband who will take her out of her less-than-ideal family situation and who will give her the respectability of being a wife. Getting married was the most for which someone like Paula, an uneducated female in country with a horrendous unemployment rate, could hope.

To play this game, Paula again must spend even more of her dwindling identity reserve. She cannot decide for herself if she likes smoking Major or even if she likes smoking at all. She cannot pursue her own likes and interests because she is too busy staying within the tacit guidelines for "getting a fella"—and "getting a fella" is the only option open to her because her education in the patriarchal school has been so inadequate that she knows of nothing else. She must conform to prescribed behavior and act in certain ways or else she will be ostracized.

Sadly, the prize for which Paula was vying—the securing of a "good husband"—is the same prize offered to women throughout the modern world: "Class categories are primarily male-defined, and a woman is assigned to a class on the basis of her husband's relation to the means of production; woman is not viewed as an autonomous being" (Eisenstein 1979, 31). Being attractive to the opposite sex is important to both sexes, but it is a raison d'être for many women. Being submissive is one of the ways in which women are attractive to men in a patriarchal society; this serves to perpetuate the patriarchal system. Unfortunately, the securing of the prize is not the end of the game: feminist author Ellen Willis writes, "A man who is labeled upper- or middle-class . . . has more money, power, security, and freedom of choice than his female counterpart. Most women are wives and mothers, dependent wholly or in part on a man's support, and what the Man giveth, he can take away" (Eisenstein 1979, 32). Throughout their whole lives, women must submit to men for fear of losing their place in society; paradoxically, women must lose their voices to acquire voices.

When Paula meets Charlo, she believes she has "captured" a man who is not only "a ride" but also is so tough that she will be free from gossip. He provides security; no one dares to call her a slut. For this freedom, however, she must give up everything. Even in their first evening together, when they do the "penguin walk," she has started compromising herself to accommodate him—she gives up her old walk in exchange for the side-to-side walk that Charlo favors. Sex—even though the narrator Paula later describes it in glorious terms—is no more mutual than the "wanking off" episode in the classroom; Charlo, however, at least gets something from sex, namely orgasms, while Paula gets nothing. Paula, not Charlo, occupies the position of weakness; she has unwittingly traded her sexual power for powerless sex. Symbolic of the general imbalance in their relationship, at their wedding the Spencer family pushes aside the O'Leary family and takes over: "The Spencers were in charge now. My crowd were huddled in corners, sipping their drinks and waiting for going-home time. The Spencers had taken over. . . . They took over the whole place" (Doyle 1996, 142). The same usurpation happens during the marriage—Charlo takes over and Paula is huddled in a corner, physically and mentally.

This "taking over of the whole place," of Paula's whole being, happens gradually. Paula believes that the first time that Charlo hits her is a mistake, a one-time occurrence, and that Charlo's solicitude and tenderness after the episode more than make up for the abuse. The next time, however, it seems easier for Charlo to lose control of himself—and, although she does not say so, easier for Paula to accept this loss of control. Is she mistakenly thinking that she will have a sort of perverse control over him because he will feel guilty?

In marrying Charlo, Paula has traded one form of servitude, that of daughter, for another, more horrible form, that of wife. This inequality is first manifested when she is pregnant, reflecting historical reality. As Karl Marx once observed, "It is through this act [child-breeding] that the first appearance of property arises within the family. . . . [T]his is when wife and child become the slaves of the husband. . . . [T]his latent slavery in the family . . . is the first property . . . The relation between man and woman . . . becomes an object of commerce. The woman is bought and sold. . . ." (Eisenstein 1979, 10, 12). The mentality of 'having' twists species relationships into those of ownership and domination, and marriage into prostitution" (Eisenstein 1979, 10). The pregnant, married Paula experiences a severe form of the enslavement that women suffer universally.

The two most important men in Paula's life, her father and Charlo, have both treated her badly. Both men are responsible for her—Paula goes from one's protection to the other's. In the best-case scenario in a patriarchal world, a woman, incapable of sustaining herself because she is not expected to do so and is consequently untrained, has a responsible, loving, wise father who places her in the hands of a responsible, loving, wise husband. The woman, although dependent, nevertheless lives out her days contentedly. As this is not the best of all possible worlds, however, most people—including men—are as incapable of handling the burden of another's well-being as they are incapable of handling their own. The fallibility of mankind is one of the places where patriarchy breaks down. In fact, Paula's "governors" are irresponsible: her father is at best emotionally distant and manipulative, and Charlo is "still living the lifestyle of a big kid" (Doyle, commenting on the *Family* series in O'Toole 1994, 12).

Having entered Charlo's domain, Paula has no one to whom she can turn: her father has successfully blocked any avenue of communication with himself or with his wife, and friends possess little power against the bonds of marriage. Thus, Paula—young, naïve, and guilty—feels that she must accept Charlo's physical abuse as her deserved lot in life. The amount of abuse is in direct proportion to Paula's self-esteem. When the beatings get horrifically severe, Paula is so depressed that she has no hope for her salvation. Only when Charlo threatens to hurt her daughter does Paula assert herself. Paula literally strikes a blow for womanhood by hitting Charlo. It is simplistic to say, "She stops being a battered wife when she becomes a protective mother" (Gordon 1996, 7). Instead, she refuses to continue the cycle of patriarchal abuse that has victimized both herself and her mother.

Equally as important, Paula realizes that just stopping the abuse is not enough; she must choose to lead an independent and active, as opposed to a dependent and reactive, life. She has marshaled her courage and taken a step that proves irrevocable. Striking back at Charlo makes his return impossible. Her love for her daughter gives her the strength to free herself from her husband and, by extension, her father. She finally begins to take control of her life.

The *Woman Who Walked into Doors*, a book about power and powerlessness, can be read as a metaphor for all the violence—both physical and spiritual—done to women in a patriarchal society, "the experience of the powerless and voiceless" (O'Toole 1996, 10). Sometimes a woman must see violence happening to another, as Paula does with her daughter, to be able to recognize the extent of abuse that she herself is enduring—and to rebel. Doyle surely wants his readers—both female and male—to understand the dreadful dynamics of spousal abuse.

The relationship between truth and memory also figures prominently in the novel. Doyle says, "Memory can't always be trusted" (Bradshaw 1994, 129). Paula believes that truth is vital to her full recovery, and consequently is obsessed with defining and understanding her upbringing.

"I want to know the truth, not make it up" (Doyle 1996, 57), Paula says repeatedly throughout this novel. She desperately needs to define her history for several reasons. First, she wants to know where her life got "off track." Adults use memories "to establish contrast—I am no longer that; I have overcome that. We can use memory to create independence" (Kotre 1995, 168). Paula believes that if she could discover the reality of her childhood, then she could somehow figure out how her life became so hellish. If she was once lovely and lovable, she can be so again.

Second, she needs to validate herself: "As adults, we look to memories for metaphors and symbols revealing recognizable patterns in our lives. We find continuity—I am this, and I have always been this" (Kotre 1995, 168). She yearns to believe that at one time she was happy, secure, self-assured, confident, attractive, and loved. She needs her past to bolster her shaky present: "My past was real. I could stand on it and it wouldn't collapse under me. It was there. I could start again" (Doyle 1996, 59). Paula is trying to use her memories to recreate herself. She instinctively realizes that "fully developed individuals can only be the product of history and struggle" (Hartsock 1979, 61).

Paula wants to know the truth about two connected areas of her life: her childhood relationship with her father and her relationship with Charlo. To understand her relationship with her husband, she must first make sense of her youth with her father, as they react to women in similar ways. If, in fact, her father had once been the loving man she remembers, then Charlo could have been, too. (Notice that Paula, still the victim of a patriarchy, is trying to define herself in terms of her relationships to men. She should examine her mother's life, as Paula's life with Charlo had begun to mirror her parents' lives together. Because her mother's identity has nearly disappeared, however, Paula never considers examining this life with the same intensity she devotes to considering her father's.)

Paula's older sister Carmel says that the father who "used to play with us and act the eejit, always saying and making up stupid things" (Doyle 1996, 121) and "had been a nice man" (59) never existed: "I know what you're up to . . . rewriting history. . . . I'm sure you have your reasons" (56). The father Carmel remembers is instead angry and abusive, irrational and easily enraged. She hints at his having sexually abused her. Paula denies this man's existence: "My father never did anything to her" (85). Paula believes that Carmel "remembers nothing good" (82) about their father because "she'd had a hard time from our father when she was a teenager; they never really recovered from it—they were always at each other, at Christmases and christenings—and now she was giving herself a good reason for hating him, making it up and believing it. Loving herself for hating herself" (85).

Paula attempts to come to terms with her father (who has since died) by engaging in dialectics with her sisters. She realizes that "one way people . . . can establish an independent identity is by comparing family recollections with personal recollections" (Kotre 1995, 168). Carmel and Paula adamantly defend their very different recollections, and they attempt to bring in the third sister, Denise, for corroboration:

> Every Sunday, we used to go out. Bray and Skerries. We always got chips and 99's. . . .
>
> D'you remember Mammy crying because she'd put too much vinegar on his chips, do yis? Ask her.
>
> He was nice then, I said.
>
> When it suited him.
>
> He was nice. At home. Watchin' the telly. We were always laughin'.
>
> What do you think, Denise?
>
> I don't know. . . . Yes, he was nice. . . .
>
> All the time?
>
> No, said Denise. (Doyle 1996, 55)

Carmel seems more convincing at first, merely because she is more vehement. We know more about Paula's doubts since we are privy to her thoughts. However, Paula raises some interesting questions. Is Carmel, wittingly or unwittingly, only remembering the bad things? Perhaps Carmel gets satisfaction out of remembering all the wrongs done to her. A history (not to mention a scapegoat) that is totally black is much more comprehensible than a gray one. Or perhaps it is Paula who is embellishing here: she needs to see her father in a positive light as desperately as Carmel needs to see him negatively. Perhaps Paula is like the landlady on her honeymoon, of whom Charlo says, "I think she makes up half the things she says" (151). This landlady, a widow who lives alone and runs a small bed and breakfast, tells Paula and Charlo all about her dead husband, her children, and grandchildren. Because she never offers to show Paula any pictures of her family, Paula suspects that the old woman may have fictionalized her stories. Her suspicion leads us to ask, "So what?" If the old woman is so lonely that having a loving, but imaginary, family makes her feel less alone, good for her. If vilifying her father helps Carmel cope, then there seems to be no harm in that either.

Understanding her parents is vitally important to Paula because it may be the key to understanding her life with Charlo. Similar to her questioning of her and her sisters' memories of their father, Paula questions whether she and Charlo were ever really in love. There was the infatuation stage, which Paula tells us about—how he ate chips out of her knickers, how he respected her, how passionate he was on the honeymoon. She paints for us (but more for herself) a glowing picture of a young love.

However, she also tells us more about his abusiveness: how he ruptured her eardrum, broke her fingers, ribs, and arms, knocked out her teeth, kicked her, tore her hair and clothing, taunted her about her inadequacies, stupidity, and helplessness, threatened to burn her and to kill her. Paula is uncertain about how things really were—could they have ever been so good if they ended up so miserably? Could they have ever been so bad, if they were ever that good? Sometimes she even doubts the abuse:

> Do I actually remember that? Is that exactly how it happened? Did my hair rip? Did my back scream? Did he call me a cunt. . . . How can I separate one time from the lot and describe it? I want to be honest. How can I be sure. . . . I choose one word and end up telling a different story. I end up making it up instead of just telling it. I don't want to make it up, I don't want to add to it. I don't want to lie. I don't have to; there's no need. I want to tell the truth. Like it happened. Plain and simple. . . . Did any of this actually happen? Yes. Am I sure? Yes. Absolutely sure, Paula? (Doyle 1996, 185)

The reader also wonders what actually happened between Charlo and Paula, at all stages of their relationship. Paula has a penchant for making up optimistic scenarios. When she visits the home of the man whose wife Charlo shot, she does not want to see him. Instead, "I was glad now I hadn't seen him. It was better imagining him. It made more sense" (147). Is Paula unwittingly making up parts of the story that she is telling us? The reader cannot distinguish between what actually happened and what she may be "improving" out of her own need.

Doyle is questioning the accuracy of even one's sharpest memories. Can we ever be certain what really happened? All that remains after an event are memories of one's impression of the event, and no two people's impressions are ever the same. "That is the genius of this novel: the layering of what is concrete and dream, a daily diet of romance and violence, fleeting illusions of liberation and affluence" (Foster 1996, 36).

Although he asks questions about narrative reliability, Doyle seems to be more concerned with Paula finding her own truth, making sense of this truth, and building on it to survive. Doyle, who has been likened to Chekhov in his forgiveness of everything human, wants his characters— and, by extension, his readers—to find their own personal truths, which will enable them to live their lives. The Rabbittes of the trilogy use their comic perception to make the world endurable—simplistically, what they cannot make sense of, they laugh at. Drawing upon her own skills and reserves, Paula learns to use her imagination and memory to order (or reorder, as Carmel sees it) the disarray in her life. This approach seems to be working for Paula, as it is working for the landlady of the bed and breakfast; one's imagination may make reality more endurable.

Ultimately, then, this novel offers a message similar to that of Doyle's earlier novels. At the same time as it points out life's horrors, *The Woman Who Walked into Doors* celebrates humanity's resiliency. As Doyle himself says, "There is room for hope, however. This woman has gone through a brutal marriage for seventeen years and the husband is gone. She actively threw him out. . . . [S]he's going to make a stab at it." Doyle manages to make his abused, damaged heroine a remarkable, believable woman who in a qualified way triumphs. Paula lacks extraordinary abilities to handle her extraordinary difficulties, yet she does live, and she celebrates her successes, however small, when she has them. Moreover, her triumphs are humble enough to serve as models for the ordinary reader.

Finally, the novel contains another, special hope for women. Jack, Paula's son, embodies this hope. Perhaps by raising him the way that she does, Paula can break the cycle of thoughtless and cruel men that have victimized her. With Jack, a new, healthy cycle of mutual respect and tenderness may begin.

The Woman Who Walked into Doors is the most compelling of Doyle's first five novels. Paula Spencer is an ordinary woman made heroic. She is his most fully realized character, and we can agree with Doyle when he says, "I felt strongly that she had an awful lot that she could say and I had grown very fond of her and very protective of her because she'd been through so much." This novel, like *The Snapper* but with more human depth and power, addresses a horrible situation and makes it hopeful.

CHAPTER EIGHT

Conclusion

Roddy Doyle is one of Ireland's most talented and successful contemporary writers. His vibrant characters, wonderful dialect, hilarious comedy, and old-fashioned yet never oppressive morality have led to international acclaim. Doyle has been able to combine critical and popular success, a feat seldom accomplished, and has won his way to fame and fortune.

Although *The Commitments* (1987) and *The Woman Who Walked into Doors* (1996) are very different in style and in substance, both are still recognizably "Roddy Doyle novels." Doyle's first five novels consistently contain several basic components. The characters are all working-class or middle-class Dubliners (in the first four novels, northside Dubliners); their immediate environment and surroundings—including strong familial relationships, good or bad—are central to his characters' lives. Doyle has been able to give an accurate, compelling, uncondescending voice to these social (and literary) outsiders, a voice that vividly expresses their chaotic lifestyles and is filled with joy and with Doyle's trademark humor. The absence of intrusive references to religion or to Irish politics is another aspect common to Doyle's novels; instead of belaboring trite or traditional questions of sin or nationality, Doyle explores significant problems in contemporary Irish society.

Not so obvious are some crucial qualities possessed by each successful character. Courage, resiliency, hopefulness, self-understanding, and humor are the five keys to survival in a Doyle novel. Jimmy Jr. can bounce back from the Commitments' breakup in less than a page because he believes that another, better band is waiting to be created. Sharon's sense of humor and ability to laugh enable her to recognize how ludicrous her situation is and to join in with the laughter—and thus to win in the end. Paddy, really too young to be labeled, nevertheless has the courage and resiliency of youth—he will go on because he must go on and is too young to despair; he, with his estranged parents' love and support, will handle their separation and his classmates' desertion. Even Paula Spencer is sustained by these qualities; she knows herself almost too well (witness her battle with the key to her alcohol stash) and obviously possesses the courage and resiliency to reclaim her life after being brutally abused for most of it. To be sure, *The Van's* Jimmy Sr. is an exception to this rule: he has his daughter's optimism and resiliency for most of his life but loses these qualities when he loses his job and best friend, thus making him Doyle's only character with dubious prospects.

Although this current of strength runs through his main characters, Doyle does not (and seems determined not to) repeat himself as an artist. His novels have significantly evolved since the publication of *The Commitments* in 1987. Each novel of the Barrytown trilogy, though similar in many respects, is separate and distinct; none seems a mere sequel. Although the popularity of the trilogy would have guaranteed the success of at least several more Rabbitte novels, Doyle put aside the inhabitants of 118 Chestnut Avenue after only three. His next work, *Paddy Clarke*, with its first-person perspective and title character, is unlike any of the trilogy novels; although he followed it with another first-person narrative, *The Woman Who Walked into Doors*, Paula is so different a character that neither the form nor the novel seem repetitive.

Doyle abandoned the Barrytown trilogy,—with all its broad humor, wisecracking characters, and profanity-laced dialogue—in order to grow as an artist. Despite these novels' strengths and appeal, ultimately they are not as complex as his next two works. Although Doyle grounds all of his novels in social realism, the world of the trilogy (particularly the first two novels) is a world of comic resolution; Doyle uses comedy to smooth over many uncomfortable, jagged edges. For instance, the Commitments' demise is almost forgotten in the subsequent riotous comedic scenes, and Sharon's rape in *The Snapper* similarly gets glossed over, her final laughter demonstrating both her own well-being and the well-being of her baby. In *The Van*, Doyle's transitional work, the same humor is present but the conclusion is not smoothed over: Jimmy and Bimbo do not repair their close friendship, an ending that stuns the reader who anticipates a happy reconciliation. Doyle's next two novels depict long-term conflict and hardship: despite Paddy Clarke's magical rituals and charm, his parents' separation is far from cheering; in *The Woman Who Walked into Doors*, Paula struggles daily to overcome her problems, and even humor—although healing—cannot eliminate her cravings for alcohol. In these two novels, Doyle's characters must struggle with difficult problems, resulting in more ambitious, more complex works that do not provide easy solutions for realistically painful problems.

The first two novels simplify reality and treat unpleasant situations as temporary—characters triumph almost as a matter of course. The next two works view life more seriously; in them, painful conditions must be overcome in long, arduous processes. In *The Commitments*, for example, Jimmy Jr. is temporarily involved with a band that breaks up; another band will follow shortly. Pregnancy is obviously a temporary condition, as is the disharmony in Sharon's family. The transitional *Van* attempts to have it both ways; as Doyle says, "*The Van* . . . even though it's dark, is also very funny. It's hilarious. So I think the two [aspects] balance each other well." Although Jimmy's redundancy and the loss of Bimbo's friendship are deeply worrisome, the reader hopes and expects that the redundancy is temporary and the van is permanent; only at the end, with the "drowning" of the van, do we suspect that Jimmy's depression will remain. By contrast, in *Paddy Clarke* and in *The Woman Who Walked into Doors* we never doubt that both Paddy and Paula have difficult times ahead of them and will remain emotionally scarred. Still, a thread of optimism does connect the later novels with the earlier ones; although life is getting more arduous for Doyle's characters, he continues to endow them with the personal qualities necessary for survival and success.

Besides depicting a more serious world, Doyle has "upped the ante" in each consecutive novel—each novel takes on a more serious problem with more serious consequences. For instance, when the band fails, no one's life is drastically altered. Being pregnant and unmarried is hardly an ideal situation, but overall Sharon sees her condition as fortunate. The breakup of

Jimmy and Bimbo's partnership and friendship is distressing, but it will not have the consequences on family members that Mr. and Mrs. Clarke's separation will. In Doyle's fifth and most serious novel, Paula's very life and the literal survival of her family are at stake.

Thus, I find a pattern of Doyle's confronting graver and more serious social problems in his novels. He says that his conscience has increasingly compelled him to bring social reality to light: There is "a growing awareness—I am very aware of my own luck, my own good luck, and I know that there are a lot of people out there who got my chunk of bad luck. While I'm flourishing, they're not. And I don't know why it can't be evened out somewhat. So as my career began to flourish, I found myself going for darker and darker subjects. I don't think it's a slope; I think it's rather cyclical." *A Star Called Henry*, which deals with abject poverty, murder, betrayal, and revolution, although told by an extremely resilient narrator, continues the cycle. Thus, although critics might expect his future novels to be progressively harsher and more socially aware, he is apt to be simultaneously writing comic and "very grim" novels. He is under no obligation to follow a pattern determined by critics.

We can also surmise that Doyle's success with both the literati and the public will continue. He has demonstrated his ability to create fiction with artistic depth, but he remains dedicated to making his novels enjoyable to the average reader: "I've no problem with cleverness or intellectual muscle men, but I just think now and again it becomes gratuitous and you go beyond any sort of reality and you are just wasting your time." Doyle believes that "somewhere, in the twentieth century, they built a wall between popular and high art. It's a great pity. . . . I've never liked the division between the high and the low, between the literary and the popular. One of the big issues about my books is whether they're literary or not. . . . It's utter drivel." One assumes that Doyle's future works will continue to tear down that wall. (Again, *Henry* continues the process started with the earlier novels.)

Not content to rest on his past successes, Doyle has attempted increasingly ambitious works. Each work shows growing maturity and skill, while retaining the qualities that brought him success. In all his work, Doyle demonstrates his compassion for and understanding of humanity. His readers and his characters benefit from the "lessons" found in his works, namely that humor, some type of family, and self-understanding will provide the independence and strength to live a satisfying life in today's difficult world.

Appendixes

References

Index

An Interview with Roddy Doyle

March 20, 1996, Dublin, Ireland

CARAMINE WHITE: Has anyone written any books on you yet, or am I the first?

RODDY DOYLE: Books or dissertations?

CW: Either.

RD: There was a guy last year who did his M.A. thesis on my work, the lot, and has been submitted and accepted, the lot. So he was the first in Ireland, but there have been several in Italy and in Finland. I don't remember all the different students I have spoken to. I don't remember if I have spoken to any postgraduate students in the States or not. I don't think so. Or if I did, it seemed as if they were doing some undergraduate work or something—nothing major. The guy who did the M.A. here has gone off to work in Korea, but he was talking about expanding his work into a book. But he'd be the first. A couple of French students. It's hard to keep track of all that's going on.

CW: What is fame like? You were a schoolteacher and now all of a sudden . . .

RD: Well, it wasn't all of a sudden. To be honest, when you're a schoolteacher living in an area, in a suburban area like Dublin, and you work in the area, and you grew up in the area as well, you have a certain celebrity status anyway, even if you are only famous for being the teacher who gets students in trouble—within your own locality you are a little bit famous—so it doesn't encroach on my life all that much.

I have a book coming out next month [*The Woman Who Walked into Doors*] and it'll be riotous for about a month. I'm doing a string of interviews next week, and the whole bandwagon rolls for about five or six weeks, and then it's a bit strange and unusual. Particularly when I'll go touring. I love doing the readings, but it can be odd when you wake up early in the morning at the airport and then you're off somewhere else. It can be a bit hard to keep your bearings. Not when you are in a country as small as Ireland. I was in Scandinavia a year before last—not only was I in a different town a day, but I was in a different country a day. It seemed as if the media all had the impression that they were being sparkling original by having a television interview in a pub called The Dubliner, and I did four different interviews in four different countries in four different pubs, all called The Dubliner. It begins to addle you and you begin to lose all grasp about where you are.

But it's a short spell. You pick up the Irish newspaper and scan it for any reference to yourself, and then you begin reading it. But that's it. An unusual bubble in the normal pattern of the year. If I were given the choice between having my books read or not read by lots of people, then I'd say, "Yeah, please, let's have lots of people read my books, and like them or not like them." But with that comes the inevitable pen name and I guess it's too late now, I suppose, and with that comes fame. But Dublin, and I have only lived here, except for a few places for short spells, is good insofar as they let you have your own life. They won't muscle in on you or stop you or stalk you. I don't think writers get the same horrible attention that rock musicians do. Writers are just writers, whereas rock musicians are expected to be gurus, which is quite ironic if you think about it because if you take away the music you are left with some very shallow lyrics at times, yet they are expected to be the fonts of human wisdom, whereas writers just write novels. So the short answer to your question, it doesn't really encroach on your day-to-day living, which is just as I would like it.

CW: Speaking of people expecting you to be a guru, one of the things I really like about your work is its message of hopefulness, like in *The Commitments* and in *The Snapper*. Oh, did you mean it [Sharon's impregnation, in *The Snapper*] to be a rape?

RD: When I was writing the book, I didn't want to encroach too much. I wanted it to be left up to the reader. Legally, in Ireland, it is not a rape, although I believe that in some states in the States it is a rape. I wouldn't personally consider it a rape. I do believe that he behaved very wrongly in taking advantage of a drunk woman. But, again, does that make it illegal? Where do you step from immorality to illegality? I wanted the circumstances from her memory to be really seedy and awful with this yawning big hole of embarrassment, as much as anything else, with this awful hole and the knowledge inside that must be kept secret. The awfulness is as much the fact that the man is so inelegant—a friend of hers—not the Spanish sailor that she creates. I suspect that it is not the first time she has had sex against the car when she has been drunk. I wanted the circumstances to be left open to interpretation.

Speaking of people reading things that aren't in the book—a few years ago at a reading of *The Van*, a woman starting arguing it was a rape and began to describe the scene and actually she was describing the scene from *Thelma and Louise*. She had mixed the two up. She apologized and we went on. With the film, what was the big issue there—that became apparent when we were in the car park—was the angle of the camera. At one shot, when the camera was above the pair, it looked like he was imposing his will and his physical bulk on her. But when you brought it down to their level, it's not like that at all. I wasn't in London when they did the cuts but they wisely got rid of the high shot. It would be very hard to be humorous after that if you have that sort of picture—a large man taking advantage of this hopelessly drunk girl and then you have the absurdity of it later on. The two don't knit together at all. There's some yawning gap that can't be filled. So it was all about camera angle there.

CW: I thought in the book she didn't remember anything—she was passed out, and then it would have been a rape.

RD: She remembers parts of it. I don't get drunk often, but there have been times I have been and I am aware that things have happened and there are gaps in the evening. By degrees it comes back sometimes. Other times I am not particularly interested because no one phones up and asks me, "How long were you in intensive care?" It's easiest then to take a few Panadol and just smooth things over. But, you see, it's all from her point of view, and it may well be that she's keeping away the seedier side of things, but I don't think she herself thinks it's a rape. If I remember correctly, she halfway wishes it were rape so that she could at least get angry at the thing.

CW: There's a sentence that says something like, "Was it rape? She didn't know."

RD: I think there is a place where she almost wishes she could call it a rape. Of course, that was taken from a male writer's point of view. That was a really tricky point of view for me, just writing that passage, because pregnancy was really an unknown for me, basic biology, and once you read you can use a certain amount of information and imagination to create what it's like. But that particular point—the actual sexual act in the car park—was the really tricky piece and once I got over that, and liked what I'd written, the rest was relatively easy.

CW: I thought, since you dedicated that novel to your wife, that maybe she was pregnant with your first son.

RD: Not at all. I finished *The Van* a couple of months before my first son, Rory, was born. I started *The Snapper* before I'd even met my wife. I started *The Snapper* immediately after *The Commitments*, which I wrote in '86, so I started *The Snapper* late '86. And I met my wife in '87. I was finished in '89, although it was published in '90 in England and Ireland, and a couple of years later in the States. One of the reasons I chose pregnancy was because I knew nothing about it and I wanted to see if I could create a world which had nothing to do with me but which would be convincing. I wrote *The Commitments* very quickly and I didn't think it would be a good idea to fly through another book before I even had the first one published. So it struck me as a particularly good idea to go for an unknown territory so that I'd have to spend a lot of time because I was also writing a play for a theater company here. *The Snapper* took me three years to write—such a short book—it took me longest of any to write.

CW: *The Snapper*—how did you turn such a horrible thing into something so wonderful?

RD: Yes. There were at least two roads one could have gone, the bright and the dark. The dark is another reality. I wasn't trying to say, "This is it, this is how it is," but it is our reality. I think if I had been writing the book in the '50s or '60s or '70s, or in another class group, it would have been darker. All Ireland at the moment—it's particularly healthy, but it's a very unsettling place to be insofar as an awful lot of these stones under which we've kept secrets are being lifted up and these dark and horrible secrets are coming to the surface very very quickly. The reality of child abuse in the Church and what happened to orphans.

I think if I had set the book in the '50s it would have been quite appalling. She would have been sent off to one of these laundries which were run by the nuns and the baby would have been taken from her while she was too weak to know what was going on or to make her own mind up. But the baby would have been gone. These measures were taken to make sure that the mother and child were separated irrevocably. Parent records were falsified. And in some places, like this Golden Bridge Orphanage which has been in the news so much lately, the babies were treated like they were the guilty parties, if guilt really exists, in the most appalling ways. Whereas now, the reality is that in some places in Ireland, one-third of children are being born outside of marriage, and it's not getting smaller, and they are being accepted within the family. It's not a particularly wonderful situation—you've got fifteen-, sixteen-year-old girls being pregnant. I would have thought that they would go back to school or to work or whatever, and it's the mother—the girls' mothers—who are the victims. They should be putting their feet up and listening to the radio for a couple hours in the day. But these women in their '40s and '50s are becoming mothers all over again. So it's not a wonderful situation, but at least in many cases it's warm and accepting, and that's what I wanted to depict in the novel. After the initial shock, and the humiliation or whatever—particularly the eejit across the road—

CW: He was great in the movie.

RD: He's a good actor—particularly that look on his face. Such an unlikely paramour. Once the baby arrives, all these considerations disappear and the baby is loved. It happens. Granted, next door, it may not be as tolerant, but it was a reality. Once you chose to write about one family, you have to concentrate on that family. It's a criticism I hear a lot—why was it so cheerful? But you can't have, "Meanwhile, down the street . . ." It breaks the story up completely. And it's not a sociological tract—it's a story about people. But it was a version of reality. And I know from watching people I know in the same situation. But it's not the big scandal it used to be. It's a pity, and an inconvenience, because it does rob them of their youth. Parenthood should come when you're emotionally ready, not just biologically ready. It robs them of their youth, and it certainly robs their mothers of their middle-age and makes the cramped conditions of their houses even more cramped, but there're love and warmth and affection, which are the most important things for kids growing up.

CW: Well, the first two novels are so upbeat, but the last two . . . *Paddy Clarke's* ending made you want to cry, and the new novel—the snippet I've read—seems pretty grim too.

RD: As I said, when I was writing *The Snapper* I was depicting a reality, and I wrote *The Van* because the father was taking over *The Snapper* and would have given birth to the baby if at all humanly possible—there's another book in him. It's a darker type of book—the storyline parallels *The Commitments*, instead of a band it's a small business enterprise which falls apart at the end. Unlike *The Commitments*, Jimmy Sr. doesn't have his son's energy or resources or education. With the younger Jimmy, unemployment is just something to get out of the way—he's other things to do—he'll survive. He may be knocked about when he gets older, but he's flooding with self-confidence. But the father, once he had his steady job and a couple of quid in his pockets for a few pints, he never has to worry about self-confidence. But it just happens that he is unemployed at the same time in his life that he's slowing down, and he looks back and imagines, "Where were they when I was young?" and he feels like he's missed out, and he feels redundant in every element in his life. It's a darker book by necessity and there's no room for a little sequel at the end. It's just a lot of people in Ireland—unemployment is a reality for the rest of their lives. They missed the modern education system and they're not qualified to do anything else. They missed the reeducation threshold. Basically, the rest of their lives is filling their days. There're hundreds of thousands of people in Ireland like this.

CW: The last one [*The Woman Who Walked into Doors*] is darker too.

RD: There is room for hope, however. This woman has gone through a brutal marriage for seventeen years and the husband is gone. She actively threw him out.

CW: She's an alcoholic.

RD: Yes, she's an alcoholic but she knows she's an alcoholic and quite frankly, she's not ready to do anything about it because she needs it. On the other hand, she's got her independence and she's beginning to gain a certain pride in that. She's creating conditions at home where she's becoming financially independent and she's actively raising her younger children, whereas the older ones—she missed out on them. But the younger ones—she's reading to them, she's taking them to school, she's bringing them home, she's looking at them, and she's determined they will stay in school and that they will get more than the older ones did. She's motivated by guilt to a certain extent but she's also driven by determination. The book is from her point of view—her attempt to sort herself out, her recent past, not her present, and I left it open because it is much better that way. But if you read it, you can see that she is a very funny and very strong woman in many ways. Even though she's been knocked senseless. But you can't help feeling that it's very sad and that she's missed out on a lot, but at the same time that she's going to make a stab at it.

CW: How did you come up with this topic? Was it like *The Snapper,* in which you didn't know anything about wife-beating so you thought . . .

RD: I certainly didn't. I was writing a screenplay for the BBC—an invitation from the BBC to write anything I wanted. There was one guy I was particularly impressed with—a producer from the BBC, Michael Waring—who produced this *Boys From the Black Stuff.* It wouldn't be standard viewing in the States—I don't know if you saw it. It was written by a Liverpool man, Alan Gleasdale. It was broadcast around 1980. I'll never forget it—it was absolutely stunning. And this invitation came from him. And a friend of mine came from London and we decided to work together. I thought I'd write about a family in crisis and I'd decided, for some reason, to have four episodes, and I'd have the story told from four different points of view.

CW: Like Faulkner's *Sound and the Fury.*

RD: I haven't read the book, to tell you the truth. One of many I haven't read. I had to accept about five years ago that I'll never read every book—it's a horrible admission to make. Even if you took the rest of your life off, you could never read them all. I've read some Faulkner, but not that one.

Anyway, I thought I'd take the same episode from different viewpoints, but I dismissed that because I thought it'd have to get a bit tedious by the middle of the second episode and that it would be unbearable by the fourth. So instead, I had about three or four months in the life of this one family; the focus changes in each episode. It started with the father, a man called Charles Spencer, and then it goes to the teenage son, John Paul, then the next episode was Nicola, a slightly older daughter about sixteen, then it finishes up with Paula. Charlo is . . . I was writing the storyline when it dawned on me that one of the ways he would control—and he's a real con- troller—is to hit, and the threat of violence is always there. And that is when it happened—in the first episode, before I'd written the storyline of it—it just dawned on me that this is the type of man he is, and all the other episodes rolled out of that because he was the agent of all the trouble and right up to the fourth and final episode his presence was always there.

When I was writing this last episode—by necessity it was stuck in a couple of months in 1993—and I felt strongly that she had an awful lot that she could say and I had grown very fond of her and very protective of her because she'd been through so much, and I could imagine her sitting down when she had free time—maybe as a result of a writing group, and there are an awful lot of women's writing groups throughout the city—and she would start writing and explore her past. That's where the story grew out of.

By the time the series was shown, it caused a storm here in Ireland— again, one of those stones that has been overturned. I remember the day after the first episode was shown, people were phoning in to the radio sta- tions: "How could she have married him in the first place?" It's a reasonable question on one level, but on another level it's such a stupid question. Everybody goes through different phases of a relationship—the first totally obsessive phase which you cling to and hope to have for the rest of your life. But we all go through that, and things tend to calm down a bit and by the time kids arrive reality beckons in all its glory. It's just a complicated thing. So it was a reasonable question, but an unreasonable one as well. And the book lets her explain to an extent why she fell in love with this man and why he fell in love with her and it made him something less of a monster as well. And again, it goes back to when they met and he does have a kind of a rough charm, although this doesn't justify it by any means. Other people are saying, "Why did he have to be working-class? Upper-class men beat their wives as well." And of course they do, but once you make the choice to choose one family, you can't go, "Meanwhile, down the road this was happening as well"—it's bad art. The book allowed me to give the full woman rather than just a few months of this woman. It confirms the choices you see in the broadcast because it allows her to explain.

CW: So, you say there's hope for Paula Spencer. There's no trend, no downward trend to your works? Nothing has happened to you personally that would cause a more pessimistic view?

RD: Well, it remains to be seen. I don't think so. I have obviously aged—it's been ten years since *The Commitments*, but I don't think that has an impact; one does a lot of living in ten years. I was a teacher for fourteen years. I loved it for a long long time, about ten or eleven of those years; obviously there were times which I hated, around exam time, but generally I loved it. The first couple of years I was hopelessly naïve and I wore these frilly blinders and I saw nothing beyond the wonderfulness of all these kids. But as I calmed down and grew older, then you begin to see malnourishment now and again, to see red eyes of someone who has been up all night, and you begin to wonder why. I am not saying that was the norm—most of the kids were healthy, well-cared-for kids, but you begin to wonder. So I think that is what happens as you begin to grow older. I found that the last ten years have been unbelievable in my life—in most peoples' lives—but so much has happened, not only work-wise, over the past ten years. I got married—if you told me ten years ago that I would have been a father, I would have laughed. I never saw myself as that kind of material—I had no contact whatsoever with young children. The ones I taught were teenagers, and I'd never picked up a young child in me life. So that has a huge impact on you.

Also, a growing awareness—I am very aware of my own luck, my own good luck, and I know that there are a lot of people out there who got my chunk of bad luck. While I'm flourishing, they're not. And I don't know why it can't be evened out somewhat. So as my career began to flourish, I found myself going for darker and darker subjects. I don't think it's a slope; I think it's rather cyclical. While I was writing *The Woman Who Walked into Doors*, I was also writing [the screenplay of] *The Van*, and even though it's dark, it's also very funny. It's hilarious. So I think the two balance each other well. I am working on a screenplay of a book by Liam O'Flaherty called *Famine*, set in the first two years of the Great Potato Famine of 1845 to, according to whichever historian, 1849 or 1851. This is not funny stuff, and it won't be a lighthearted romp through. It's grim, very, very grim. But I just started a novel, the first few pages, which I hope will be funny. But at the same time I have a project in my mind which is dark. So I don't think there was a conscious decision of mine to start off with high optimism and work my way down. I haven't become grimmer—I don't think I have anyway.

Am I happy or content? Happy is hard to sustain twenty-four hours a day. I am content. I feel very lucky. No amount of angst will take that away. I do feel very lucky. There are those who are happy and feel that everyone must be happy.

CW: The last scene in *The Van*, when they drive into the water and Jimmy says, "You can get it tomorrow"—what's going to happen?

RD: You can answer that as well as I can. My interest ends when the book does. I did want to leave an open door so you can keep on walking through it if you want. Maybe they go back with a shovel. I don't know. I don't think it matters because their friendship is over—maybe they'll try to revert to some sort of civility—it'll never be the same again and that's a big loss. Jimmy won't be involved with the van again. But I don't like to imagine too far after that. But they are creations of mine and I suppose I can turn them on and off, but readers will give them flesh, if they like, and are engrossed in the book.

CW: But it seems like you gave Paula Spencer flesh?

RD: Oh yes, but still when you're writing the book it's not driven by the heart all the time. The decision to put one word after another is an intellectual exercise, and is quite manipulative sometimes, because you're working the reader down the page towards some sort of thing. And even though your sympathy is with the character, it can be at times—particularly with the last book—the subject matter can be quite upsetting, now and again. Don't overstress it. But still all the time, you're working with the head—like, "Put a break here and bring it down here so it has a dramatic impact." So, while you're hoping it will be her book, the same time you're working the reader. But if you're working with your head, now and again your heart will catch up and say, "Hey, can I have a look?" So the final book . . . I definitely want it to have an emotional base, but the actual writing is quite a cold exercise.

CW: So, was Maggie behind it all, or was it Bimbo [in *The Van*]?

RD: Again, it's all up to you, but I feel that Jimmy blames Maggie because it's easier than blaming Bimbo. It's clearer in the film, which is in the editing phase now, so it'll be released in September. In the film it's clearer because it's from the film's point of view, not from Jimmy's point of view, and in one scene, after Bimbo has made Jimmy a wage slave, so to speak, he asks Maggie, "Do you think I'm right?" and she says, "Yeah, you are." But it's very obvious that it's his decision. She's involved in the management and that sort of thing, and Jimmy resents it, but what right does he have to resent it? It's understandable because she is bursting in on their territory and he doesn't like it at all, but she has every right to be there. There is one scene where she looks like Lady Macbeth. It's much clearer in the film that she's not to blame. There's one nice scene, which isn't in the book at all, where she and Bimbo are lying in bed, and they are just talking and she says, "You all have been friends for years"—and again, she's being fair. As they are falling asleep, she says, "He doesn't like me—sure he doesn't"; and Bimbo says, "Ah, he does" ' and then she says, "No, no, he doesn't." And then a pause, and she says, "It doesn't matter." And it obviously does matter because she is hurt. The film makes it clearer, and that's a strength of the film, but it wouldn't be a strength of the novel because it would be too cut and dried if she did sit down with needles like Madame Defarge. They are two separate exercises. But it's an easy option—blame her—it's part of his paranoia toward the end.

It's the same with groups too. At the beginning of this year there was a spate of particularly violent murders. And we Irish like to think we are so warm and friendly, and we are. But these murders were very gruesome— three people, four people murdered— and you could tell by the press coverage that they were jumping on blaming it on an outsider. So, one woman murdered grossly in County Kildare, the one right next to this one, and the police jumped to question a man with a French accent. There are also a group of people called the Travellers; they have mysterious origins, dispossessed peasants from a hundred years ago or something, but they are definitely Irish—but they are a separate community altogether. Some of them don't live in fixed homes at all—they travel all the time, hence their name. A small group of them have been involved in violent crime, but the readiness of the community to jump and blame them for any murders. So we do go for the easy answers, and it is much easier for Jimmy to blame Maggie.

CW: Where do your characters come from? Are they composites?

RD: I've never based a character on someone I know. I could never say, "He is that guy." I would never do that. If I did what Irish writers did fifty years ago and emigrate, then it would be easier. It's not an option really. I've never really needed to. As I said, I've grown up and lived in the same general area, and my kids go to the same general school, so it's not a particularly bright thing to do—to invade other's privacy, no matter how interesting that privacy is. There may be snippets of things I know from general observation, but not the characters. Paddy's parents are not my mother and father, for example.

CW: Are you Henno [Paddy's teacher]?

RD: I am not! A different generation and a different style of teaching. But snippets of things. My father's humor comes across now and again in Paddy's father, although he is a distant sort of man. My mother definitely isn't in that book. I basically make them up. But I suppose you can't make things up unless you have some sort of experience. The bulk of it is made up. I've literally never seen anyone beat up someone in a domestic situation. The imagination is often underestimated. I've been to writer's group and heard people say you should write about what you know. In one sense, that's wise, but in a literal sense it's absurd. You've just admitted you're thirty, so you could only write about only a thirty-year-old American woman, and only your particular version of it. You can only see what you've observed and that is not always what happened.

CW: You've done research for your material, haven't you? I noticed in *The Van* you thank those two guys who worked in a chipper.

RD: That was kind of a joke. They are two students of mine who worked in a chipper van on the weekends, and basically I met with them for a couple of hours and brought a notebook with me, and they gave me the inside track on working in a chipper van and I fed them drink and that's that.

CW: Should I be feeding you drink?

RD: No, no, not at this hour. Definitely not. I've never been in a chipper van, no formal research. I did a lot of research on the biology for *The Snapper*, but I did no research whatever, except for that conversation, for *The Van*.

For *Paddy Clarke*, trips up to my parents' attic to remind me of books and what not. It struck me that this was going to be a ten-year-old's point of view anyway, so newspapers and history books really wouldn't help. For *The Woman Who Walked into Doors*, I did a hell of a lot of reading while I was writing—I read a lot about women and violence, women and alcohol, sexual fantasy. And I used very little of it in the strict sense. It was just to make the ice I was walking on thicker as I walked along. The book I am going to start on soon—it's about a very old man who has been around for a long time and he claims to have been bang in the middle of it. So I'll have to do a lot of reading to the extent that it'll take years and years and years to write. But I'm stuck because I can't think of anything else to do.

CW: In *Paddy Clarke*, how do you jump from one section to the next—do they relate? I was going to ask if it was like the Benjy section of *The Sound and the Fury*, but since you've not read it, I guess it doesn't.

RD: You can continue on with your thesis if you wish and just cut out this answer, but basically I just thought it'd be the way a kid's mind would work. It's been a while since I've read the book—four years since I wrote it—so my memory isn't as fresh as yours. I've tried to make links, but indirectly. It may be a question of color or light and something sparks off another memory, and so he goes on to that. I wanted it, particularly the first half, to seem haphazard—winding memories, and by degrees the winding memories become straighter and straighter as the parents' marriage becomes worse and worse. And that's just the way a kid's mind would work.

Also, I wanted to get away from the linear time I used in the previous books, and it just fit the story better. The inspiration for that would be cinematic. As I was writing it I was remembering films like *Amarcord*, Fellini's film—my favorite film—sort of autobiographical, Fellini growing up in the 1930s when Mussolini was at his height. It was seemingly a haphazard year—it goes from clip to clip to clip with no seeming unity. But the unity is there when you see it a second time and you wonder, "Why did I like it so much the first time?" and you see the unity there underneath the surface. There's another film, *My Life as a Dog*, a Swedish film, a beautiful film.

CW: Did you see *Pulp Fiction*? I loved that movie.

RD: Yes, I did. I thought it was fantastic, one of the best in recent years. It was also nice to see John Travolta working.

CW: I was so horrified when *Forrest Gump* won [the Oscars].

RD: I never even saw it, it looked like all flash. I've never seen a movie I liked by Roger Atkinson. He's a real Hollywood animal who works the system. *Forrest Gump* tried to be all things to all people, and when you do that it's nothing to anyone. It obviously worked. I don't think it went down as well in Europe as it did in America.

CW: Okay, now I have to ask the typical question. How much Joyce have you read? I know you said you don't like writers like him because he writes to show off his brain.

RD: Yes, particularly the later Joyce. But I've read everything else, except for *Finnegans Wake*, which I read the first few pages. I haven't read *Stephen Hero*—I've never read that and I don't see the point because I wouldn't want any draft of mine ever to be published. It's a ludicrous exercise. I've read them all, and I think in order.

CW: What about the Spanish sailor, the word "foetus," the red and green hot water bottles, the keyless characters, the *Paddy Clarke* introduction?

RD: Well, I don't think Joyce has a monopoly on the word "foetus"—you have to use some word to describe that thing. The introduction—it's a ten-year-old's point of view and I know that Joyce started off much younger. But I didn't like Stephen, particularly the older Stephen. I thought *Ulysses* was terrific, exhilarating. But what's the point of *Finnegans Wake*? There are so many full-time academics that I don't want to hurt their economy, but I feel like it's a complete waste of time. It's a great pity, because he spent so much time writing that shit that he could have spent writing real books. I've no problem with cleverness or intellectual muscle men, but I just think now and again it becomes gratuitous and you go beyond any sort of reality and you are just wasting your time. And there's a certain snobbery that goes along with it—the inner circle who has read the book and can talk about it while the rest of us are embarrassed to admit we've never read it, or are happy to admit that we've better things to do.

CW: So it's all coincidence?

RD: Actually, I never knew about the Spanish sailor. You're the first to point it out to me. Her inspiration for the Spanish sailor comes from the British film *Letter to Brezhnev*. It was very very popular in Ireland. It's about two women, one unemployed, one who works in a chicken-processing plant—

a very glamorous job—and they are out on the town on a Friday night and one of them robs a wallet from some guy who's getting drunk and they go out and blow the money with two Russian sailors. One of them falls in love with her Russian sailor, and he has to go his separate way and she stays back, and she knows so little about the outside world that she starts writing Brezhnev asking permission to come and visit—Brezhnev is long dead, Gorbachev is actually head at that time—but eventually she visits Russia and marries her Russian sailor. Sharon, in the novel, is a bright woman and knows that there is never a Russian boat on the Liffey, while there are plenty of Spanish about. It's more realistic. The Spanish sailor connection never dawned on me.

CW: What about the red and green hot water bottles and Dante's red— and green-backed brushes?

RD: Well, you know, I've got hot water bottles at home—me kids love them—and they come in red and green. Blue as well, but that's the reality.

CW: What about music—Joyce uses a lot of music in *Ulysses*—and the humor, which is very similar to your work.

RD: Well, I've read the book, so who's to say whether it's not in the back of your mind. But if the influence is there, it's working subconsciously. In this most current book [*The Woman Who Walked into Doors*], I was aware, in the editing stages, of various books—*Black Water*, by Joyce Carol Oates, for example. It's a very short book, but it keeps going back to one episode. One episode is the book. I wanted to do that as well. I wanted Paula to go back to the first time she was hit, and I go back to that four or five times. Joyce Carol Oates's book kept coming back into my head, particularly during the editing. When I was writing *Paddy Clarke*, Richard Ford's *Wildlife* was there. It's about a man in his early forties and he's looking back at a time in his life when he was sixteen and his parents' marriage was falling apart. So that was the spark for that. *The Snapper*'s spark came from [*A*] *Proper Marriage* by Doris Lessing, a description of pregnancy in that book really grabbed me because it got beyond the area below the neck and got into the head—stunning, phenomenal.

So certainly I was aware of some influences, but I was unaware of Joyce. The problem is, it's like a gun is put to your head—"Do you like Joyce?"— and there's no room for "yes *and* no." It has to be "yes *or* no," in journalese. I do resent the academic industry, the summer schools, where all these academics appear for a week in the summer and discuss one writer. Once a reputation is established all the academics want to become experts on this and then you have this huge industry around selected writers to the neglect of other writers. For instance, Shakespeare's the main man. There's a wonderful book by an American, Gary Taylor, called *Reinventing Shakespeare*, which explores the haphazard and political nature of Shakespeare becoming the god of English literature, and it ties into the British Empire and his patronage of the royal family and his depiction of the royal family, and it argues that Marlowe would be just as good a choice as the great playwright, but he's now rather a marginal figure. Everything that Shakespeare wrote is supposed to be superb and people study it and pore over it like it is Karl Marx or the Gospel. It's the same with Joyce—you go out there and you see the T-shirts and the Anna Livia statue, and the statue of Joyce himself. It's right that these people should be remembered, but it's become a huge industry. I suppose every university has its Joycean scholar. Flann O'Brien, I would argue, is just as good as Joyce, but not as many people are aware of him.

CW: Whom do you write for?

RD: At the time I am writing, I write for myself.

CW: Whom do you want to read your books?

RD: Everybody. When I was writing *The Commitments*, being modest, I didn't see beyond Dublin or even a group of friends, but that's when I was putting it together. When I'm writing, I write for myself and I don't care who reads it—in fact, the more strange and exotic the better, and also one would like one's next door neighbors to read it. If I start thinking about people, then there's a small line between people and market, and you start thinking, "Well, will they understand this snatch of dialogue in Wyoming?" Once the book is finished and gone, then I start to wonder, but then it's too late.

CW: Not about critics or the literati?

RD: No. I'm not interested in the critics. The new book . . . I'm excited about the critics. I got people to read it early and the response back was enthusiastic and I'm very happy with the book. No negative criticism will shake me. I'm looking for a mixed reaction, so I can read a variety of criticisms. I won't be losing sleep over the reviews. The critics aren't too influential in my case anymore. They hammered *The Van* and yet it went over very well here. Critics don't seem to have the power of, say, New York theater critics, who can really demolish a play. That doesn't happen here. But with a novel or a play, there are a few key critics and the rest follow their lead. And if you see a big review in a journal, you'll see the key points again and again in other reviews as if fresh. The public seems to ignore the reviews. They liked *The Snapper,* and so they didn't see why they wouldn't like *The Van* as well. So the critics don't really matter at this point. It's a nice position to be in.

But you have to put a check on yourself as well, because there are publishers who will publish any piece of shit I write because it will sell. An absurd example of this: I got a letter from a woman compiling a book of letters from Irish college—it's a college out in the country where you go and just speak Irish, which is a very difficult language. A lot of people go—I went for a month—and she wanted to compile a book with these letters, "If you have any letters left over." So, I didn't have any, and I wrote her back telling her such and wishing her good luck with the project. I got a letter yesterday back from her asking if she could use that letter in her book. Because they couldn't get a real letter, they'd use any bunch of crap to plug my name along the way. They want to use a copy in this book of a letter saying, "No, I don't have a letter." I wrote back saying that if you're ever writing a book of letters saying, "I have no letters of Irish College," then by all means use it, but a book of letters from Irish College should be just that. But it just underlines the point that they'll take any old crap, so I have to be my own critic, and I have to be happy with it and that I am not just deluding myself into thinking that just because I have written a few other books that this one is also good. I have to be careful.

CW: Do you listen to soul music yourself?

RD: I do—not exclusively, obviously, but I do.

CW: Do the songs you use [in *The Commitments*], with their particular lyrics, have any special meaning within the novel itself, for instance in a foreshadowing capacity?

RD: Yes, although my memory isn't as fresh as it was ten years ago when I was writing the book, I did try to integrate the lyrics with the story. I'm not sure if I used the lyrics to predict something that is coming. Pop music will do that for you anyway. If you break down the lyrics, you probably have ten stories, two country-western ones, and three soul. But basically they are the same things, aren't they? Obviously, I'd thousands of songs to choose from, and I chose based on a lot of different reasons. One was the humorous effect—just seeing the Dublin accent written into a song and then changing the lyrics slightly—like in *Night Train* or *It's a Man's World*. They just had humorous possibilities which the others didn't. Any in particular you're talking about that?

CW: None that I care to put under your scrutiny. But I notice you have a lot of James Brown.

RD: Of course—"the godfather of soul" and what not, "the main man of soul," "the godhead." I loved those. When I was reading Gerri Hirshey's book *Nowhere to Run*—a great book—I loved these names, these nicknames that they have to live up to.

CW: Have you seen him live?

RD: Yeah. Last November he came here. He was great. He was late coming, but it was a hell of lot better than not coming at all. It was a great night. It started with Bo Diddley, then Van Morrison played as well. It was a great night.

CW: I've only seen him on various TV specials. Did you meet him?

RD: No, just watched him. The time to have seen him was 1961 or so. He's sixty-odd now. I would have loved to have seen him fall onto his knees—he didn't this time because I don't think he could have gotten up again. But the show was terrific. It was interrupted too often, but once he got into it he was awesome. There were a lot of instrumental breaks—he obviously needs a lot of breaks now—but still, he was pounding away. It was terrific.

CW: What is your writing routine?

RD: Basically, I go from nine—half-nine—when I bring the kids to school, 'til five o'clock when the lady who looks after the kids goes home.

CW: Does your wife work?

RD: My wife's a student. But even if she's around, I stop at five. I gave up teaching because I wanted to write, but I decided I would keep the routine because it fits everybody else's routine. I don't see why I should have to work into the night just because I am a full-time writer. I work roughly nine to five, Monday through Friday. If possible, if I'm working on two things, which I like to do, I tend to try to work on the novel first of all, because if you're working on the novel you get engrossed and if five o'clock came you wouldn't necessarily want to stop in the middle of a sentence. I tend to work on the novel in the first part of the day and the screenplay toward the latter part of the day, because it isn't as engrossing and it's easier to stop. It's not a literary exercise at all. I read then as well—sometimes the newspaper—so it's an hour before I start doing any kind of work. And I pick up the kids and drop into the supermarket, and I bring me kids swimming now and again as well. So it isn't strict at all—I don't put my head down at nine and come up for air at five. That's how I work. We went on holiday for seven weeks last year, and I had to come back to Dublin for two weeks for a rewrite, and in that two weeks I was at home alone, my schedule just went out the window completely—I'd be working late into the night and wake up and start writing. I didn't feel the need for a routine. It's just that the routine fits well into the other elements of my life. It's not the stuff of great literature—I know you're supposed to be a tortured soul and work deep into the night. But that's a lot of crap. I have other little tortured souls to look after.

CW: What is your wife studying?

RD: Business. About which I know very little.

CW: Me too. What's your favorite book?

RD: Tough question—it changes all the time. It changes all the time. There are so many of them. There's At Swim-Two-Birds. There's The World According to Garp, which at whatever age I was when I read it—I think I was nineteen or twenty—it was wonderful. I'd never read anything else like it. Recently, it was Bastard out of Carolina by Dorothy Allison, an American writer. It floored me completely.

CW: Anne Tyler?

RD: Yes, I love her. I guess my favorite by her is Breathing Lessons, but it's not my favorite book. Wise Blood by O'Connor. Ragtime by E. L. Doctorow. A Proper Marriage by Lessing.

CW: Do you read Dickens? Jimmy seems to like him.

RD: I love Dickens. David Copperfield is one of my favorite books. It's no coincidence that I was rereading it when I was writing The Van. I just wanted to remind people how accessible and brilliant Dickens is. I guess now that he is studied at universities and is a classic, he isn't popularly read, but in the nineteenth century, everybody read him. A new installment of Dickens is like a big episode of a soap.

CW: Like 90210?

RD: Oh, is that the Beverly Hills show? No, not like that—British soaps tend to be more down-to-earth. Like *Coronation Street* and *East Enders.* If you have a chance, *Coronation Street* comes on Wednesdays and Fridays, and turn on your TV and catch a snippet of it and you'll see the difference. It's a working-class street, and it's genuine drama, violence, unemployment—all the stuff that is reality. And humorous. I haven't watched in a while because it's on at half-seven, which is a tricky time in a household with two kids, but I imagine it is like a Dickens installment. Somewhere in the twentieth century, they built a wall between popular and high art. It's a great pity. Jimmy discovers Dickens. Dickens is there to be enjoyed by everybody, but rarely is. *David Copperfield* is one of my favorites, *Little Dorrit* as well.

CW: Why is there such an absence of religion in your books?

RD: That's the way it is. There's no religion in me own life, for certain; I've no room for it at all. It's difficult in a country like Ireland because you do have to put your face out and tell it to go away—"Fuck off." You have to be quite blunt to allow yourself your own agnostic space.

There's no car driving as well, because until recently, I wasn't able to drive. Or smoking, because I don't smoke.

CW: Everybody smokes here.

RD: Yes, but far less than they used to. A hell of a lot of kids smoke, particularly young girls. Partly the peer pressure. Just recently have there been the antismoking laws in the restaurants and places, but they're ignored. I personally don't smoke and never have. I would be against introducing antismoking laws in a pub; I agree you shouldn't smoke in restaurants and where there are small children, and I don't want smoking in me own house, but in a pub, it just seems part of it—part of the atmosphere. But in the books there is very little smoking because I don't smoke. I suppose if I did feel the burning need for a gasper now and again, it would be a part of the books.

CW: And drugs—there's a little mention of it in *The Commitments*, marijuana and heroin.

RD: In the new book, one of the kids she suspects is a heroin addict, but he doesn't live in the house so he's not in the book. On his episode [of the TV show] there was substance abuse—he was sniffing glue and drinking alcohol, PH 14. It will be in the new books because it is something I can't ignore. It's a problem in City Centre here, and the problem is city-wide now. It's something I can't ignore. I'd have to go off and do my own research there, because I've never taken heroin in me life. My experience of drugs is very limited—coffee, Guinness, the odd Head-Ex tablet. Literally so. No experience first-hand.

The religion aspect—I wanted to get away from the clichéd view of Ireland. An English critic of *The Snapper* said, "Where was the priest, where was the Church? This is a pregnant girl." And I wanted to say, "Fuck you, pal—what do you know? You live in London." Priests in working-class parts of Dublin are peripheral figures—few people know who they are at all, and they're not particularly welcome when they knock on the door. It's a new picture of Ireland. *Paddy Clarke* is filled with religion—a childish version of it, because it's a different time, the 1960s. Everybody goes to a Catholic school. My older boy goes to a multidenominational school—there are only two on the north side of Dublin, for half a million people. But that's fine because that means they'll be good schools. But the rest are run by the Catholic Church or the Church of Ireland, Anglican. So the religion is still there, but it's more a surface thing. On a Sunday, you'll still see crowds and crowds going to mass, but it's not the deep devotion you might get in the Third World. They'll be chatting in the back of the church. It kind of depresses me when I see all those people in the church. Particularly the kids. What are they going for? They're immortal—they're not, but they should think they are. What are they going there for? When you begin to slow down and there's a rattle in your breathing, then you go off to church to make your peace, not when you're seventeen and you should be avoiding at all costs all that crap. So there's no religion, partly because of my imaginative lack, and also because that's the reality.

One thing in *The Commitments* film which made me uncomfortable was the religious scenes and holy statues and such. The confession scene, very funny lines, but it annoyed me—I didn't write that scene—you know, where he goes in and starts talking about the temptation of women and the soul music and the priest contradicts him. They're playing *When a Man Loves a Woman* by Otis Redding and the priest says, "No, it's by Percy Sledge." It's funny, but it annoyed me. That kid would not have gone to confession. Kids do not go to confession anymore. I don't think it's a sacrament anymore. You don't have to go to confession anymore—you can make your peace with God in your own privacy. Very few people go to confession anymore. None of those kids in the film would have gone near a confession box. But it's in the film and it annoys me.

CW: Do you like your characters? Do you think they live meaningless lives? They get drunk, aren't educated, have meaningless sex, steal, watch too much TV.

RD: What's meaningless about that? That's not meaningless. So why don't they talk about politics? Talking about politics is about as meaningless as talking about sex or talking about football. I don't see any difference in a bunch of kids talking about politics or talking about Manchester United Football. It's just conversation—it's filling gaps. So their lives are not meaningless but are filled with meaning. Their conversation is not deep—so what, whose is? This conversation is not normal—in fact, you're taping it—but we are not having a chat on the bus. But when you do have a chat on the bus, like when I was on my way here today, I stopped and chatted with the caretaker at the local school about the weather, and then later someone stopped me and we talked about a match that was on the telly last night. So these are normal conversations. That's what I wanted to record. In a lot of conversations, it's what they don't say that is more interesting than what they do say. I don't think they lead meaningless lives at all.

CW: Even though Sharon gets drunk all the time?

RD: She's going through a stage in her life. When I was that age, when I stopped being a student and was earning money, one of the things I'd buy with that money is alcohol, and not because I had the burning need for alcohol, but for the sheer pleasure of being with a group of friends and talking all night and getting pleasantly drunk. Getting drunk is incidental, but it was just the whole thing. I don't see any problem with young people getting drunk—I'm not advocating it as a nightly exercise, but there's no point in moralizing and saying that it destroys brain cells because that's just a guarantee that they'll go out and destroy a few more. That's just the wrong approach. When I was a teacher and I had a tutorial and I was trying to get them to talk about smoking—it's very difficult to get fourteen-year-olds to say they are destroying their lungs and health, because, once again, they're immortal, and it's much more important that smoking's cool. Showing them the pictures of the death-rattling lungs and emaciated seventy-year-olds, while it might shock them, they don't see themselves there at all. They are different beings completely.

The books aren't moralistic at all—I've gotten letters from women who are irate that a pregnant woman would smoke, but it happens. Personally, I'd prefer that pregnant women didn't smoke or drink, but I've seen them do both. So what are you supposed to do? Ignore it? A novel is a novel. I'm not a priest or a moralist, and I try to write within reality. I've even had one letter from an American journalist complaining about the ending of *The Van*. I've had a lot of complaints about *The Van*, but one about the ending was a new one on me. She said, "They drive the van into the water and just leave it there?" I said they were going to come back. "We shouldn't leave something like that in our greatest natural resource. They should go back and take it out." Dollymount is a great place to take the kids, but the water is absolutely vile, filthy. Nobody swims in it. It's an outrage. And she was worried about the van—there are a lot more sinister things floating about the water. The van is pristine in all that crap. So people will have objections about everything, so you just shut your ears and go on.

But I don't think they lead meaningless lives at all. Their lives are a different pattern. Jimmy Sr. and Bimbo spend a lot of time sitting on a doorstep and talking about nothing in particular, but the people who are saying their lives are meaningless are sitting in a cafe, talking about the same things, but using different accents and an active vocabulary of about a couple of hundred words, but they may be coming to the same conclusion. They many not have any more depth, but because the setting is right, and they've the right haircuts and are dressed in black, this is depth and that is shallow. I don't see it that way at all.

CW: What are a "dead leg" and "pruning"?

RD: "Pruning" I think is redundant now—I don't think anyone uses it anymore. But what happened to little schoolboys is that other little schoolboys would run up to them and grab their testicles and squeeze. You don't need a diagram. A "dead leg" is when you go up to someone and put your knee there, which numbs the whole leg and you fall over. Absolutely dreadful. It hasn't happened to me since school time. These things would go ripping through the school yard, and you'd have everybody in agony over having dead legs and pruning. There was one phase where you grab the breast of someone and say "whistle." It was absolutely impossible. I guess it only happened in the boys' schools—schools were segregated and I don't think it happened in the girls' schools.

CW: Tell me about *Your Granny's a Hunger Striker.*

RD: It's never been published and it never will. I wrote it over a four-year spell, between 1981–5 or 1982–6. It centers around Dublin, the summer of 1981, with the H Block hunger strikes. A strange time, where you had these men—Sinn Fein, IRA members, in the H Block of Long Kesh in Northern Ireland—who were starving themselves as a protest and they wanted political status as prisoners because they didn't consider themselves standard criminals. They were there as political criminals and wanted political status. They had five demands, none of which I can recall. Thatcher, in her first or second year as Prime Minister, wouldn't give in, and so basically seventeen men died. It was a strange time because a lot of people who should have known better were walking around wearing black arm bands, and you had to decide whether you were against them or for them. It was very hard to remain aloof. It was a very shrill time—a lot of protests. So I wrote this absurd, very snide, undergraduate-type humor story about a group of people who were either by design or accidentally around the H Block campaign in Dublin. It was a very long book, if I remember. I was just glad to be finished. There were some passages which were very very funny, but overall it was dreadful, just dreadful. It'll never be published, not if I can help it. I have all the copies.

CW: Posthumously possibly?

RD: I think there's a way to stop that. I think there is something in me will that forbids its ever being published. Me wife knows anyway. She knows how I feel about it. It was a good exercise, anyway—just getting from the first page to the last is good practice. It's a rehearsal for doing it again, like with *The Commitments,* which only took me six months. Also, I sent a copy off to every publisher I could find, and invariably it came back unopened. So they didn't reject the book—they rejected the notion of some-one sending them a book. So myself and John Sutton published *The Commit-ments* here in Dublin by ourselves, which was a great exercise. But I imagine people wouldn't see any of the other things in the other books in this book—I haven't read it in a long time—but it was a very smart-arsed book if I can remember. But at the time, I thought it was fine. That wasn't easy. But I have no interest in it now. It's hard when I'm touring and people ask me if I wrote anything before *The Commitments*. I have to say, "Yeah, it's called *Your Granny's a Hunger Striker.*" I was doing a reading at a Republican center, where all the paraphernalia of the dead Republican heroes is, and it was going fine, but as I was looking out on the crowd, I know there must have been some active members of the IRA there, and I was just saying, "Don't anyone ask me. Please, please, don't anyone ask me. I need my kneecaps. Don't ask me." I'd have to get in the car after and head for the border.

CW: Why do you write? Is there something burning inside you that needs to be expressed?

RD: No, not initially. That comes later when you are convinced there's a book there. I'm always open to suggestion that there's a book there, or that there just isn't a book there. That hasn't happened yet, but there have been times when it feels like it's happening. Like with *The Snapper*—it took so long. And the last book [*The Woman Who Walked into Doors*]—it was very hard to get her voice, to get to a good level with her, and I was wondering if there was a book. But when you do become convinced there is a book, like with the last one, then it becomes important. I finally really felt the burning, like I really had to get it finished, which I didn't feel about *Paddy Clarke.* I feel it should have been written and I'm glad I wrote it—in an Irish context, it says things that should be said and haven't been said before. So it does become engrossing. Which is good and bad. It makes it easier to get on with the job, less distractions, of course. But it can be a bad thing be-cause it becomes harder to switch off at five o'clock, and particularly when the subject matter is grim. It makes it hard to shake off.

CW: Why is Paddy so violent?

RD: Because little boys are violent. Read *Lord of The Flies*. When the kids don't have any parental guidance, they are little savages. There are two film versions of the book—Peter Brook directed one, and then there's one very bad one, I can't remember who directed or starred in that one—but the very good one by Peter Brook, better known as the theater critic. And he put the kids on the island and just filmed, and his conclusion was that the book was very unrealistic because the kids became savages much, much quicker in reality. The book took too long—he said the little fuckers were on the island for only a couple of hours before they were beating each other on the heads. So kids are very violent. I think also there is a certain amount of curiosity in their cruelty. Cruelty to animals is more curiosity. My own kids—they have rabbits and fish and they love them, but they'll push the rabbit, not to be cruel but to see what would happen if they push the rabbit. Now if you see an adult do that, you've got someone to avoid. But kids are curious. When the kids are cruel to the dog in the back garden, they are just curious to see what will happen. And when they split the rat they want to see what'll come out. The whole thing about skin and what's inside is fascinating to them. Now he's not going to go off mutilating things to see what's inside, but they are just curious.

CW: Veronica in *The Van* has to read *Lord of the Flies*.

RD: Yes, she has to. It's a set text for her course.

CW: Were you reading it too?

RD: In the fourteen years that I taught, I read it dozens of times because it's a set text. The one piece I took from it is the word "stuff." It's a real kids' word. Not so much in the modern context—this stuff and that stuff—but as a word for entrails and what not. So when Piggy is killed and his head smashes on the rock, "stuff" comes out. It's a perfect word to describe what a kid would see. So when Paddy is hitting the rat with the Irish hurling stick, he talks about the stuff that comes out. That's the one conscious thing I took from *Lord of The Flies*. But I really liked the book, because the people I was reading it to, or with, liked it, and that's not a very common experience with a set text. There's little freedom with texts—everyone in Ireland is reading the same thing, and some of it's ridiculous—I was reading *Persuasion* to a bunch of kids who had no interest in reading anything.

CW: Have you seen the movie?

RD: The recent one? Yes, I thought it was OK. I went to *Sense and Sensibility* last night and I thought it was brilliant. I never liked Jane Austen, and I always wondered what if she weren't being ironic at all but being literal? I think the irony, which is always pointed out in notes, you know, wasn't irony at all but snobbery, and snobbery within the snobbery. I think, "Oh God, this is dreadful." And you can imagine teaching this to fifteen-year-olds. But I thought the film lifted the humor, which I found totally absent from the books, and the characters became totally endearing and human, while the story remained. I thought she did a fantastic job. And to make the little kid a character—and little kids are nonexistent in Jane Austen, or at least they never speak—but to make this little kid such a great character, I thought it was a terrific job.

CW: How do you like what they've done to your own movies?

RD: I think they've done a terrific job. I am very happy and increasingly so. I liked *The Commitments*. I wasn't involved in any of the decisions or around for any of the decisions, so when I saw it I was relieved—they could have done anything. I thought Parker would do a good job—I didn't know if it would be my good job—but I was very happy. With *The Snapper*, I was much more involved, and with *The Van*, I was in control from day one and I've seen four or five rough cuts and it looks great. The music is being recorded now—Eric Clapton is doing the music for us. It'll be brilliant and I am dying to see that version.

CW: Why did you have to change the names?

RD: I didn't have to. With *The Snapper*, I did it because I didn't want it to be seen as a sequel. It's not a problem with the book but it is a problem with the film, because if it's a sequel, you have to have the exact same actors, the exact same streets, you'd have to bring the Commitments, at least one or two of them, somewhere along the line since it's the same community. I didn't want that—I thought it'd be a dreadful idea. I just wanted it to be an entirely separate film. Also, *The Commitments* was a big cinematic film whereas *The Snapper* was made for TV. We knew that from the word go that we were employed by the BBC, which caused Stephen Frears to make some cinematic decisions. There are a lot of close-ups and a lot of faces—it was made for the telly and not the big screen. The big screen picture came after. I didn't like it on the big screen—I thought it was grainy. So I changed the names so it would be seen as a fresh new film. And I changed them again in *The Van*—Colm Meany, who is in *The Snapper*, is in it, but aside from that it is an entirely new cast.

CW: He's the guy from *Star Trek?*

RD: Yes.

CW: He's good.

RD: He's great. Again, I wanted it to be fresh. *The Snapper* was promoted in America as "the feel good movie of the year." Now, *The Van,* while it's very funny, is not a feel good movie; the ending is very, very sad, and we are not going to change so it can be billed as "a feel good movie." *The Snapper* had very little music, whereas this one will have much more. It'll be very, very different, so it just made sense to change the names. Also, while I was writing the screenplay, I discovered that the people who had made *The Commitments* had the cinematic rights to the names—but that didn't matter, because I wasn't going to use the same names anyway.

CW: Why Rabbitte? Is there any significance to that name? The thought actually occurred to me that rabbits eat blooms.

RD: You can forget that. Rabbits also eat carrots—they eat a lot of things. I told my kids to go get food for the rabbit, and they came out with a frankfurter sausage and a can of peanuts. It was lovely. Well, names are quite important. They must fit into the flow of things. Get a phone book— there are Rabbittes there—there's a prominent politician called Pat Rabbitte. Rabbitte has a humorous ring to it, but it's also in reality.

CW: There's also a "Paddy Clarke" we found in the phone book.

RD: Yeah. There'd be loads of them, absolutely. Clarke is very common, and Paddy was the most common Irish boy's name.

CW: Tell me about Kilbarrack. We drove through there the other day.

RD: Kilbarrack is about five stops on the north side of the DART. So you get on here at City Centre and you go about five stops—it's about five miles from City Centre. When I was a kid it was bang at the edge of the city. Quite literally, on my side of the road you were in Dublin 5 postal district, and then you crossed the road and you were in County Dublin—you'd left the city. The city limits were right down the middle of the street. There was a farm across the road from us. There was the odd road that had been there for a long time, the people who lived there would have been railway workers for the local train. But gradually as the city grew, the estates grew— early '40s and '50s—and people moved in like my parents, working-class, lower middle class, who were in a position to buy their own houses. In many cases, they were all the same age. It was a great time to grow up—surrounded by all these kids—a lot of freedom as well. As I grew up, the city cooperations bought out the farms, and the private developers bought out the other farms, and it gradually grew more inner-city. People who moved into it would have been more solidly working-class—from the inner-city. Dublin had the worst slums of any city in Europe. These awful tenements—decayed Georgian houses—had in some places eighty people living in them. The norm was that a family lived in one room. It was the Dublin of Sean O'Casey. So these were all demolished in the '50s, '60s, '70s, and these people moved out into the suburbs, into Kilbarrack and into other areas of the Ring of Dublin. So this working-class, traditionally blue-collar, manual workers, had never worked, but was being bracketed as working-class. It's much trickier now than it used to be. Middle-class traditionally was white collar. Me own father . . .

CW: He was a printer?

RD: Yes. So he would have been blue collar, since he had ink under his fingernails. Then he became a teacher of printing, and so he took off his blue collar and put on a white one. I think he was earning roughly the same money—actually, I think he took a dive in pay for a while. Then he coordinated the training of printing teaching, so he was then a civil servant. His father was a tram driver. So his background was definitely working-class, whereas my mother's background was more middle-class—her father was a civil servant, a state employee. And she stayed in school until she was eighteen, which was quite unusual for a girl, whereas my father left when he was fifteen. So their backgrounds were definitely different. So a lot of Irish people are in this gray zone between working- and middle-class.

Also, I started my secondary education in 1971, and it was free. My parents had to buy books and pay for transport, but it was free. Up until 1968, it wasn't free. The state might have put some money into it, but it wasn't free at all; I think there was a fee of some sort. So that meant a closed door to a lot of people—whereas people of my generation, there was a new door opened up. I think my parents would have sent me to secondary anyway—they could have afforded it—but what I am saying is that it became the norm to go to high school; everybody went. I was part of that generation that benefited from free secondary education. Education facilitated the move for me from working-class to middle-class.

CW: And then college.

RD: Yes, I went to college. There were fees for college. If you lived at home, like I did, you'd really want to be on the bread line to get any kind of grants or anything. When I was in college, it was measured by family income—and my mother was working, my father was working, my two sisters lived at home and were working, so I didn't get any kind of grants because family income was way too high. I worked during the summers. Now, there are no fees for college, which I don't think is a particularly clever move because when you go into primary schools, the neglect is horrendous. I think a lot of primary schools, although they all get the same amount of money from the state, it's the parental money which gives it the edge. If you're in a working-class area, where there's 60–70 percent unemployment, where there's not that much surface money, so if there's any money to be spent, it shouldn't be spent on third-level education, it should be spent at the bottom, in primary education, if they genuinely want to even things out and make everything the same for everybody.

In my own case, I've grown up with a foot in each class. It's a very useful position, especially socially. People who have grown up solidly working class seem to be hopelessly lost in a different version of reality. Whereas being from the gray area, you seem to be a little more street-wise. You tend to have more sympathy with things. You don't give out about tax as much, because you know that tax goes to people who need it, and so what if a few waste it? Not all of it is wasted. Whereas those from all middle class tend to see it as their money. It's a useful position to be in, especially as a novelist.

CW: Did your brothers go to college too?

RD: I have one brother and two sisters. No, he didn't.

CW: Are you Darren [Rabbitte]? He's going to college, isn't he?

RD: Not at all. A different generation. He'd be typical in an unusual context for a working-class kid going to college. My sisters didn't go because they didn't get the exam results wanted to go. They went off and did commercial courses—typing and such; one does computers now, but she got her training in the bank where she works. I don't think my brother wanted to go. Actually, I was the only one who probably was academically able to go. I was the only one who was interested.

CW: Did you always want to be a writer?

RD: Yes and no. I always wanted to be a professional footballer, but was never good enough. And I always wanted to be a professional rock musician.

CW: I wanted to be Madonna.

RD: Oh yes—and you probably will want to be all your life. But you know you will never be her, but that doesn't stop you from dreaming. Wanting to be a writer is much the same. As a teacher, I found myself with a lot of free time and not needing to fill it with getting another job to make more money. It's an easier path than learning how to play the guitar. I already know how to write—I learned years and years ago. All you need is a pencil and paper—you don't need money. I suppose there was a little ambition in the back of me head—I'd read an awful lot at the time, and somewhere along the line I figured I'd try to see if I could do it.

CW: Did you take courses?

RD: No. They were and are quite rare here. I think writing courses are quite common in America, but there are only a couple in Ireland.

CW: Yes, they are. . . .

Has your family changed since you've become famous?

RD: No. My parents are very happy that it's happened—very proud. My mother likes to go to all the "launching parties" and she'll be very excited about this new book.

CW: I've talked to a few older women here, and they think your books are too filled with profanity. Does she?

RD: My mother will admit that people do use it, but she doesn't like it herself. She's more open about it, as is my father. I think she liked the films more than the books. And she really admires the new one—she read it in a day, and called me very quickly. She didn't know the world was like that, and she found it quite shocking, but she admired it. They don't agree with me on religion and politics, and even if they don't like the subject matter, they like the idea that I'm doing it. They're very happy with it all. I get a lot of encouragement from them all. Of course, they've changed over ten years.

CW: What about politics? There aren't any politics in your novels?

RD: Belfast, if the traffic is with you, is only two hours away, but it seems like a different country. When the violence starts, we close down psychologically to an extent. It becomes a place very far away again. If you were a writer in Toronto, would your book be a lesser book because it didn't contain anything about Quebec? It's the difference between politics with a little "p" or a big "P." But a book about a woman in a violent marriage is a political book. A book about two unemployed men is a political book. This *Family* series brought domestic violence to the forefront, to the top of the political agenda, with a small "p," for a few months.

I've very little interest in party politics. I don't think that's what politics is about. The only way to get politicians to do any thing is to force, and to probe, and to make them see it is worth their while—if they don't do it, they'll lose votes, and if they do, they'll get exposure, which is what they crave. That's what real politics is. I'd defend the need for a democratic structure—this idea that you have one group on one side of the room and another on the other side, and they get up and debate like teenagers, and they say "Hear, hear." I find, when you watch the BBC, it's particularly dreadful—all these men, "Yah, yah." Something about the English politicians—you want to kill them. Whereas in Ireland, it's more rural and they're screaming and shouting at each other, and you say, "Jesus, they're big kids." But it's better than anything else—I don't want Hitler or Stalin. So give me democracy, but I don't want to be engrossed in it. It's all so much appearance and media. I find American politics fascinating. All the candidates [in presidential elections] were confirming their status as outsiders, and Pat Buchanan has been writing speeches for political farts for years, and has never moved outside of Washington in his life.

CW: You follow American politics?

RD: To an extent. You can't but. I read up on it. I was fortunate to be in America during the last Republican convention when Bush and Quayle were elected, and I found it fascinating and disturbing. I think you can take it to an extreme, if you elect dogcatchers and the such. I do find American politics interesting. For black reasons, I was hoping that Lamar Alexander would last a bit longer—with his plaid shirt and his wife Holly, is it? And his kids. Just the name—Holly and Lamar Alexander, with his plaid shirt; an ex-Secretary of Education, and he was an outsider, a man of the soil. Ah, Jesus. It is disturbing to say that the only way to establish your standing is to say you're an outsider. The government is not necessarily the enemy, but they make it seem so. Until recently, about four years ago, the use of the word "liberal" . . . When they use the word "liberal" it's to sneer at chinless guys who guaranteed anything—in context of the British Liberal party, which isn't around anymore, all chinless wonders which were never for or against anything—they'd never definitely say "yes" or "no." But in American politics, "liberal" is almost evil, sinister, perverse. It's fascinating how one word can mean one thing and the exact same word something different. So I do follow it some—the razzmatazz of it all.

CW: I didn't realize how stupid it all was until I married my husband, who is in politics. He's in it as little as possible.

RD: What I found so horrible is the abuse and use of the family. I've got four politicians in my constituency—and they all send me Christmas cards. I don't want a Christmas card from them, and the majority of the people are like me. I vote for them not on their image but on what they stand for. But they're trying to push an image. You get them playing in the snow. It snows here very rarely, like once every four years, so they must be on the lookout for it—"Here's some snow—get the photographer." They're rolling around in the snow with the wife and kids—they use the children and wives as part of the package. Ugh.

CW: Being the wife of a politician, I am always nervous I am going to do something that'll cost him a vote. Like eat a grape in the grocery market before they've weighed it or something.

RD: "Wife of politician caught robbing."

CW: One last question—what about language? Your "unprecedented use of the Irish vernacular"? And in one interview you discussed how the Irish have a particular relationship to language because of the storytellers and the English coming in and such.

RD: Yes. I've always wanted to bring the books down closer and closer to the characters—to get myself, the narrator, out of it as much as I can. And one of the ways to do this is to use the language that the characters actually speak, to use the vernacular, and not ignoring the grammar, the formality of it, to bend it, to twist it, so you get a sense that you are hearing it, not reading it. That you are listening to the characters. You get in really close to the characters. I think it's a stronger achievement, in the context of my books, especially my latest book, because it gets you smack in the middle of it. You can't ignore this woman—it's not an option—you're in this woman's life. That's why I do it, because it fits the book. Probably not the next one—it'll be a bit different.

CW: The one about the famine?

RD: No, the old man one. I don't know what it'll be like, but it won't be similar. I've never had a problem with being a fan of rock music, of popular music. Of course, you can't say fan—"I'm a fan of Mozart"—you can't use that word. But I don't see why you can't be both. I don't see why I can't read Salman Rushdie's new work and Elmore Leonard's new work. I don't see any real difference, except that one's more self-consciously literary than the other. They're both good literature. And yet, if I go buy Rushdie's book in Waterstone's around the corner, it'll be in "Literature," whereas the other will be under "Crime." I don't like these divisions. When I was a teenager, you'd go for a band because it would give you a certain status, a certain depth, which wasn't necessarily the case, but it just seemed so. So I've never liked the division between the high and the low, between the literary and the popular.

One of the big issues about my books is whether they're literary or not. They were on the list for books to be taught in schools, but they're off the list now because the Minister of Education decided they weren't literary. It's utter drivel. I'm quite happy they're off because I'm not quite comfortable for them to be taught in an exam situation. But the idea that they are less literary because they use the vernacular—I don't agree. The decision to use the vernacular is a literary decision. The decision to use the word "fuck" is a literary decision. It's a decision of rhythm. It's not even a decision—it's a habit. Whereas in the context of writing the books, it's a literary decision to use these words. To use images from television instead of books, to use advertising jingles and such—it's a literary decision. I've tried to surround the characters with their own world. So that's where the language, the images, the music, and the rest come from—the same reasoning. I try to get down to the characters.

CW: What do you do in your spare time, besides take your kids swimming? What's your other son's name, by the way?

RD: Jack. My free time . . . Lately, I clean the kitchen, make dinner . . .

CW: Me too!

RD: I'm interested in football, as a fan. I read a lot, go to the movies.

CW: So, like in *The Van*, you're into soccer.

RD: Yes, the whole country is. I spend a lot of time going out to eat, quite a lot. I enjoy books, I enjoy going to pubs—once or twice a week I'll meet a couple of friends in a pub and we'll just talk and such. We go on holiday quite often, quite close generally, just fill the car and drive for an hour and a half. Last year we went to France. I do what most people in Ireland my age do. I probably read more than the average person, and I probably go to movies more than the average person, but much the same. I'd rather go to the movie than wait for the video. I usually make the effort.

CW: Did you see Kenneth Branagh's *Henry V*?

RD: Yes. I liked it, although as a play it doesn't do much for me. Behind all that glory is a lot of bloodshed and human misery, and Ireland's had its fair share of all human misery. I'm not anti-British or anything. I can see how in wartime it would go down a bomb and quite rightly so, like in 1940 in the Battle of Britain—quite stirring stuff, but I am not convinced that it has a place. I don't think we should ban it or anything, but it didn't do anything for me in 1991. Life is more complicated than the world of *Henry V*. I prefer *Henry IV*.

CW: I think that's everything.

RD: Well, if when you go back, you find you have omitted anything, write me and I'll get back as quickly as possible to you.

CW: Thank you so much. This has been so nice of you. It was wonderful to meet you.

A Star Called Henry

Roddy Doyle's latest novel, *A Star Called Henry*, is paradoxically a marked departure from and a continuation of his previous work. Although the departures from his traditional work are noteworthy, the savvy reader can easily discern the Doyle trademark.

Henry Smart, the narrator/protagonist of the novel, is, by his own account, an extraordinarily handsome young man who plays a significant role in the Irish rebellion, first as one of the rebels cordoned in the GPO during the Easter Uprising and later as an IRA gunman. Henry tells the reader about the first twenty years of his life, beginning with the incredible poverty of his childhood—he survives on the streets by stealing, begging, even baiting and catching rats. The novel then jumps nine years to the Easter 1916 Uprising, during which the fourteen-year-old Henry, out of self-interest rather than nationalism, joins the forces garrisoned in Dublin's GPO. This particular section shows how the banality of days of inaction can quickly change into the surrealism of massive bloodshed. Henry manages to escape imprisonment and survives for a few months by being a stevedore by day and a paramour by night. He falls in with the IRA and enjoys the notoriety his presence at the Easter Uprising engenders. Because of his blind loyalty and amorality, he rises through the ranks and becomes a gunman, one of "Collins's anointed" (208): in Henry's own words, Collins "would give me a name and I'd deliver a dead man" (240).

During this time he also weds Miss O'Shea (Henry purposefully never learns her first name), of whom he had been enamored since before the Easter Uprising. As the killings continue, he inevitably is captured, beaten, and imprisoned. After his eventual escape, he realizes that he is only a pawn in the IRA's hands, "sprawling on a pin / . . . pinned and wriggling on the wall." When, because of his growing disenchantment with the organization and weariness of the lifestyle, he attempts to "unpin" himself, his own name is put on the list of those to be eliminated. The novel ends in 1922 with his wife in jail because of her own seditious activity and the twenty-year-old Henry on the run.

Anyone who is familiar with Doyle's work cannot fail to see his stamp all over this novel. The setting of the novel is primarily the lower-class sections of Dublin, although Henry Smart is far poorer than any of Doyle's other characters. The vibrant language, which gallops along at its own breakneck pace, is also vintage Doyle. The thoroughly convincing narrative tone is reminiscent of Doyle's last two novels, *Paddy Clarke Ha Ha Ha* and *The Woman Who Walked into Doors*, in which Doyle succeeds in capturing the voices of two other marginalized characters. Also interesting about these three narrators is the hint of unreliability in all their voices: Paddy, because his age prevents him from fully understanding what is going on in his parents' disintegrating marriage; Paula, because her wretched marriage and alcoholism cause her to question her interpretation of large chunks of her history; and Henry, because his machismo and bravado suggest exaggeration and self-aggrandizement. Doyle himself says that Henry "is a very old man who has been around for a long time and he *claims* to have been bang in the middle of it" [my italics]. Finally, this novel, in typical Doyle fashion, upsets traditional Irish values: the typical family life that Doyle razes and rebuilds in all his novels, especially the Barrytown trilogy, is again reconfigured. The bond between Miss O'Shea and Henry is a real one, despite the fact that all they seem to do together is have sex and murderously harass English sympathizers. The role of the typical Irishman during the revolution is also exploded, as Doyle depicts the average citizen concerned more with his own welfare than with nationalist pride.

Despite the similarities, the departures from his previous work are startling. This is his first historical novel and his most typically Irish. A word of advice to those not inculcated in Irish history: although Doyle does a good job of making his novel accessible to most readers, beware of becoming slightly confused with the names, places, and factions during the revolutionary period. The novel does not contain the uproarious humor present with the Rabbittes, nor even the understated humor found with either Paddy or Paula. This book is grim, and Doyle shows us a seedier, harsher Ireland than he has previously presented. The novel moves more quickly than his previous work, as it encompasses both rural and urban Ireland during twenty violent years. Finally (and I hesitate to include this for fear of the label "prude"), this book is much more sexually graphic than his previous work—as much as Jimmy Rabbitte Sr. talks about "rides," he rarely gets one; the handsome Henry does not have that problem.

A Star Called Henry is a remarkable book, if only for the amount of research Doyle has done. It is, however, remarkable for much more: for yet another memorable narrator about which we care, despite his murderous and profligate tendencies; for the characterization of rebellion-ravaged Dublin, which seems a different creature than Barrytown; and for showing us yet another side of the multifaceted Doyle, who has given us the confusion and expectation of an pregnant teenager, the loneliness and feelings of inadequacies of both a ten-year-old boy and a middle-aged man, the difficulties of a woman struggling to emerge from her alcoholic and abused haze, and now the remembrances of a man-boy during a terrifying period of Irish history.

References

Adams, Tim. 1996. "Hot Roddy." Book review of *The Snapper*, by Roddy Doyle. *Observer* (London), 7 Apr., 16.

Allison, Dorothy. 1992. *Bastard Out of Carolina*. New York: Dutton.

Appelo, Tim. 1992. "Down the Rabbitte Hole." Book review of *The Van*, by Roddy Doyle. *New York Times Book Review*, 20 Sept., 3–15.

Barnacle, Hugo. 1990. "Burrowed Laughs." Book review of *The Snapper*, by Roddy Doyle. *Independent* (London), 10 June, 33.

Battersby, Eileen. 1993. "Not Bord Failte's Ireland." *Irish Times* (Dublin), 20 May, 10.

Bell, Robert H. 1991. *Jocoserious Joyce—The Fate of Folly in Ulysses*. Ithaca, N.Y.: Cornell Univ. Press.

Bowen, Zack. 1974. *Musical Allusions in the Works of James Joyce*. Albany: State Univ. of New York Press.

———. 1989. *Ulysses as a Comic Novel*. Syracuse, N.Y.: Syracuse Univ. Press.

Bowman, Donna. 1997. "*The Van*." Movie review. *Nashville Scene*, 15 Sept., 61.

Bradshaw, Nick. 1994. "Doyle's Dubliners." *Details*, Feb., 128–30.

Chodorow, Nancy. 1979. "Mothering, Male Dominance, and Capitalism." In *Capitalist Patriarch and the Case for Socialist Feminism*, edited by Zillah Eisenstein, 83–106. New York: Monthly Review Press.

Christgau, Robert. 1989. "Citizen's Band." Book review of *The Commitments*, by Roddy Doyle. *Village Voice*, 18 July, 60–61.

Christon, Lawrence. 1994. "Doyle Talks the Talk." *Los Angeles Times*, 23 Mar., F9.

Davies, Hunter. 1993. "What I Did in the School Hols." *You Magazine*, 23 May, 20–24.

Deane, Seamus. 1994. *A Short History of Irish Literature*. Notre Dame, Ind.: Univ. of Notre Dame Press.

Dodd, Stephen. 1993. "What's on the Boil for Roddy Doyle?" *Independent* (London), 2 May.

Donoghue, Denis. 1994. "Another Country." *New York Review of Books,* 3 Feb., 3–6.

Doyle, Roddy. 1989. *The Commitments.* New York: Vintage.

———. 1990. *The Snapper.* London: Secker & Warburg.

———. 1991. *The Van.* London: Secker & Warburg.

———. 1994. *Brownbread and War.* With an introduction by the author. New York: Penguin.

———. 1994. *Paddy Clarke Ha Ha Ha.* New York: Viking Penguin.

———. 1996. *The Woman Who Walked into Doors.* London: Jonathan Cape.

Eaton, Andrew. 1990. "A Dubliner Who Doesn't Write for Mother." *The Sunday Correspondent,* 19 Aug., 1.

Eisenstein, Zillah. 1979. "Developing a Theory of Capitalist Patriarchy." In *Capitalist Patriarchy and the Case for Socialist Feminism,* edited by Zillah Eisenstein, 5–40. New York: Monthly Review Press.

Elliott, George. 1959. Afterword to *Adventures of Huckleberry Finn,* by Mark Twain. 284–88. New York: Penguin.

Estes, Clarissa. 1996. *Women Who Run With the Wolves.* New York: Ballantine.

Fay, Liam. 1993. "Never Mind the Bollix!" *Hot Press,* 20 May, 4–8.

———. 1996. "What's the Story?" *Hot Press,* 3 Apr., 18–20.

Fitzgerald, Penelope. 1991. "Fried Nappy." Book review of *The Van. London Review of Books,* 12 Sept., 16.

Flanagan, Mary. 1994. "Enter Laughing." Book review of *Paddy Clarke Ha Ha Ha. New York Times Book Review,* 2 Jan., 3–21.

Foster, Aisling. 1996. "More Than Just an Accidental Talent." Book review of *The Woman Who Walked into Doors. The Times* (London), 11 Apr., 36.

Galligan, Edward L. 1984. *The Comic Vision in Literature.* Athens: Univ. of Georgia Press.

Giffin, Glenn. 1995. "Roddy Doyle's Dublin not on the Tour." *Denver Post,* 8 Jan., F12.

Gordon, Mary. 1996. "The Good Mother." Book review of *The Woman Who Walked into Doors. New York Times Book Review,* 28 Apr., 7.

Gowrie, Grey. 1996. "The Novelist Who Is Walking to Greatness." Book review of *The Woman Who Walked into Doors. Daily Telegraph* (London), 13 Apr., A6.

Grawe, Paul. 1983. *Comedy in Space, Time, and the Imagination.* Chicago: Nelson-Hall.

Harding, Louette. 1996. "Roddy Doyle: Writer with a Gender Agenda." *You Magazine*, 14 Apr., 10–11.

Hartsock, Nancy. 1979. "Feminist Theory and the Development of Revolutionary Strategy." In *Capitalist Patriarchy and the Case for Socialist Feminism*, edited by Zillah Eisenstein, 56–82. New York: Monthly Review Press.

Heaney, Seamus. 1990. *Selected Poems: 1966–87*. New York: Noonday.

Heller, Zoe. 1993. "Sticking With the Masses." *The Independent on Sunday* (London), 6 June, 2–4.

Hewson, Paul. 1988. "Migrant Minds: The White Nigger." In *Across the Frontiers. Ireland in the 1990s*, edited by Richard Kearney, 188–91. Dublin: Wolfhound.

Hirshey, Gerri. 1984. *Nowhere to Run: The Story of Soul Music*. New York: Times Books.

Joyce, James. 1965. *A Portrait of the Artist as a Young Man*. New York: Viking.

———. 1986. *Ulysses*. Edited by Hans Gabler. New York: Vintage Books.

Kearney, Richard, ed. 1988. *Across the Frontiers. Ireland in the 1990s*. Dublin: Wolfhound.

Kiberd, Declan. 1994. "Darling of the Brits. Not." *Irish Literary Supplement*, Spring, 23–24.

Kotre, John. 1995. "Using Your Memories to Improve Your Future," interview by Judith Stone. *Glamour*, Sept., 168.

Lacey, Colin. 1996. "Roddy Doyle: Ruffling Feathers After a Booker." *Publishers Weekly*, 25 Mar, 55–57.

Lane, Anthony. 1994. "Dubliners." Book review of *Paddy Clarke Ha Ha Ha. The New Yorker*, 24 Jan., 91–94.

Lewis, Paul. 1989. *Comic Effects: Interdisciplinary Approaches to Humor in Literature*. Albany: State Univ. of New York Press.

Mantel, Hillary. 1993. "International Books of the Year." Book review of *Paddy Clarke Ha Ha Ha. Times Literary Supplement* (London), 3 Dec., 12.

McFarlane, Noel. 1991. "Raucous Days in Barrytown." Book review of *The Van. Irish Times Limited* (Dublin), 10 Aug.

McGuinness, Gerry. 1996. *The Commitments: The Story of How and Where This Film Was Made in Ireland*. Dublin: GLI.

Mulkerns, Helena. 1994. "The Reluctant Celebrity." *Irish Echo*, 26 Jan.–1 Feb., 21–24.

Nolan, Philip. 1991. "The real creative forces behind *The Van* are the people the novel is based on." Book review of *The Van. Irish Times: Evening Press* (Dublin), 7 Aug.

O'Connor, Paulette. 1993. "Roddy Doyle Is Laughin'." *Irish Press*, 29 May, 2C.

O'Hagan, Andrew. 1993. "Eating Jesus." Book review of *Paddy Clarke Ha Ha Ha*. *London Review of Books*, 8 July, 17.

Olson, Elder. 1968. *The Theory of Comedy*. Bloomington: Indiana Univ. Press.

O'Toole, Fintan. 1987. "See It and Disbelieve It." Theater review of *Brownbread*. *The Sunday Tribune: Arts* (Dublin), 20 Sept., 18.

———. 1991. "The Sound of Suburbs." *Irish Times* (Dublin), 12 Aug.

———. 1993. "A Comic Opera of Childhood." Book review of *Paddy Clarke Ha Ha Ha*. *The European*, 17–20 June, 21.

———. 1994. "Life after Charlo." *The Irish Times* (Dublin), 28 May, 12.

———. 1996. "Roddy the Realist." *Irish Times Supplement* (Dublin), 24 Apr., 10.

Palmer, Jerry. 1994. *Taking Humor Seriously*. New York: Routledge.

Plato. 1987. *Gorgias*. Translated by Donald Zeyl. Indianapolis: Hackett.

Richter, Stacey. 1997. "'The Van' Stinks Hook, Line and Sinker" *Tucson Weekly*, 18 Aug., http://www.weeklywire.comww/08–18–97/tw_cin.html

Riedel, Johannes. 1975. *Soul Music Black and White: The Influence of Black Music on the Churches*. Minneapolis: Augsburg.

Rose, Cynthia. 1990. *Living in America. The Soul Saga of James Brown*. London: Serpent's Tail.

Schaeffer, Neil. 1981. *The Art of Laughter*. New York: Columbia Univ. Press.

Shepherd, Allen. 1994. "Never the Same Again." Book review of *Paddy Clarke Ha Ha Ha*. *New England Review* 16 (Spring): 163–67.

Shone, Tom. 1993. "What It's Like to Be Ten—Brilliant." Book review of *Paddy Clarke Ha Ha Ha*. *The Spectator* (London), 12 June, 48.

Slater, Christine. 1996. "Inside the Skin of One of Life's Survivors." Book review of *The Woman Who Walked into Doors*. *Toronto Star*, 6 Apr., D4.

Toibin, Colm. 1995. "Dublin's Epiphany." *The New Yorker*, 3 Apr., 45–53.

Turbide, Diane. 1993. "Dublin Soul." *MacCall's*, 30 Aug., 50.

Turner, Jenny. 1996. "Perils of Being Paula." Book review of *The Woman Who Walked into Doors*. *The Guardian* (London), 12 Apr., 2.

Twain, Mark. 1959. *Adventures of Huckleberry Finn*. New York: Penguin.

Tyler, Anne. 1988. *Breathing Lessons*. New York: Berkley Books.

Waters, Maureen. 1984. *The Comic Irishman*. Albany: State Univ. of New York Press.

Welty, Eudora. 1957. *Place in Fiction*. New York: House of Books.

Index

abortion, 15, 81

abuse. *See* spousal abuse

Academy Award nomination, 34

African traditions, 49

Aidan (fict.), 99, 108

alcoholism, 118, 154–55

Alexander, Lamar, 180–81

alienation, 68–70, 86

allegory, 81

"All You Need Is Love" (song), 55

Amacord (Fellini film), 161

anxiety, 90–92

artistic nature, 101–3

Atkinson, Roger, 162

At Swim-Two-Birds (O'Brien), 102, 167

audience. *See* readers

Austin, Jane, 174–75

authorial commentary, 9–10

autobiographical content, 27, 41

Ballymun, 6

Barrytown: autobiographical aspect of,
27; description of, 10–12; *Paddy Clarke
Ha Ha Ha* and, 98, 99–100; religion
and, 14–16; Sharon and, 63, 70

Barrytown trilogy, (Doyle): distinctive
qualities of, 143; filming of, 34–36;

overview of, 4; publication of, xiii;
significance of family in, 17. *See also
Commitments, The; Snapper, The; Van, The*

Bastard Out of Carolina (Allison), 131, 167

Battersby, Eileen, 3

BBC: miniseries by, xiii, 1–2, 32–33; *The
Snapper* and, xii, 34–35, 175

Becker, Ernest, 76–77

Beckett, Samuel, 7

Billy (fict.), 60

Bimbo (fict.): and chipper van, 4, 84–85;
Jimmy Sr. and, 93–96, 144, 159; life
of, 171; redundancy of, 92; Richter on,
36

black history, 45, 46–47

Black Water (Oates), 7, 163

Bloom, Molly (fict.), 64

Booker Prize: Doyle's reaction to, 25; for
Paddy Clarke Ha Ha Ha, 1; *The Van* and,
xii, 32, 83

books-on-tape, 1

Boys from the Black Stuff (Gleasdale film),
155

Branagh, Kenneth, 183

Breathing Lessons (Tyler), 53, 167

British Academy of Film and Television
Arts (BAFTA), 34

Brook, Peter, 110, 173–74

Brown, James, 48–50, 166
Brownbread (Doyle play), xi, xii, 2, 31–32
Brownbread and War (Doyle), xii
Bugsy Malone (Parker film), 33
Burgess, Anthony, 3
Burgess, George (fict.), 63, 76, 80
Burgess, Jackie (fict.), 77–78
Burgess, Yvonne (fict.), 65, 77

Cannes Film Festival, xii, 33, 34, 35
capitalism, 95
Carmel (fict.), 117, 137–38
Carver, Raymond, 3
Casey, Eamonn (bishop of Galway), 15
casting, 175–76
Catholic Church, 38
celebrity, 40–41
"Chain Gang" (song), 51, 53
characterization: humor and, 78–79; in
    Paddy Clarke Ha Ha Ha, 99–107; in *The
    Snapper*, 64; in *A Star Called Henry*, 186;
    in *The Woman Who Walked into Doors*,
    117–36
characters: basis for, 11–12, 28, 160; in
    Brownbread, 31; in *The Commitments*, 43,
    56–57, 59–60, 60–61; community
    and, 10–11; comparison of, 129–30;
    criticism of, 16; development of,
    182–83; dialogue and, 12; in Doyle's
    works, 142; Doyle on, 170; humor
    and, 20, 77; Irish persona of, 23; in
    Paddy Clarke Ha Ha Ha, 115; place and,
    10; purpose of, 37–38; qualities of,
    142–44; reality and, 11–12; in *The
    Snapper*, 62; speech of, 7–9; in *The Van*,
    83, 97; in *War*, 31–32; in *The Woman
    Who Walked into Doors*, 127. *See also
    specific characters*
Chekhov, Anton, 12

Clapton, Eric, 175
Clarke, Mr. and Mrs. (fict.), 110–12
Clarke, Paddy (fict.): characterization of,
    99; community and, 11; compared to
    Dedalus, 101–3; compared to Jimmy
    Sr., 96; compared to Paula, 120–21;
    death and, 107–9; family and, 17;
    fascination with words of, 101–3;
    Huck Finn and, 103–7; humor of, 144;
    perception of, 107; perspective of,
    5–6; poetic/artistic nature of, 101–3;
    religion and, 14, 113; sustaining
    qualities of, 142–43; tragedy of, 21;
    voice of, 185
Clarke, Mr. and Mrs. (fict.), 110–12
Clement, Dick, 33–34
Clery's Clock, 51
comedy: *The Commitments* as, 43–44;
    definition of, 18; in Doyle's works,
    143; hero of, 64–68; humor and,
    18–20; identity and, 18–19; plot of,
    67–68
comic heroine, 62–68
comic spirit, 89–90, 97
Commitments, The (Doyle): components of,
    142; criticism of, 43; Doyle on, 154;
    drugs and, 168; emphasis of, 59–60;
    focus of, 59–60; humor in, 56–60,
    143; music in, 42–56, 165–66;
    optimism in, 96; overview of, 4–5; plot
    of, 42–43; publication of, xi–xii, 2,
    30–31, 42, 172–73; reality in, 144;
    significance of family in, 17; social
    vision of, 21, 59–60; writing of, xi,
    30–31, 152
Commitments, The (film): awards of, 34;
    Doyle on, 175; production of, 33, 175;
    religion in, 169–70; soundtrack of, 45
community: effect on characters, 10–11;
    Jimmy Sr. and, 11, 86; Paddy and, 11;

relationships of, 70; Sharon and, 63, 68, 70; significance of, 16–18
contraceptives, 15
Coronation Street, 168
criticism: of characters, 16; of *The Commitments*, 43; for exclusion of religion/politics, 16; for lack of description, 3–4; of *Paddy Clarke Ha Ha Ha*, 5–6; of *The Snapper*, 169; for use of profanity, 8–9; of *The Van* film, 36. *See also* reviews
critics, 3, 33, 164
cruelty, 109–10, 114–15, 173–74

Dangerous Liaisons (Frears film), 35
dashes, 9
David Copperfield (Dickens), 86, 167–68
dead leg, 171–72
Deadly Films, xiii, 35–36
Dean (fict.), 60
death, 107–9
death threat, 40–41
Deco (fict.): African immersion of, 49; betrayal of, 55; character of, 43, 56–57, 60; in exercise in unity, 50–52; relationship with band, 54; role of, 59, 61
Dedalus, Stephen (fict.), 3–4
democracy, 180–81
Denise (fict.), 138
depression, 90–92
Derek (fict.), 42, 60
description, 3–4, 9, 98
dialogue: characters and, 12; in *The Commitments*, 57; in *Paddy Clarke Ha Ha Ha*, 98; in *The Snapper*, 62; in *The Van*, 97
Dickens, Charles, 9–10, 86, 167–68
Diddley, Bo, 166

divorce, 107
divorce referendum, xi, xiii, 15, 38–39, 111–12
Doctorow, E. L., 7, 167
Doyle, Belinda Moller, xii, 40, 152, 167
Doyle, Ita, 27–28, 177–78, 179
Doyle, Jack, xii, 40, 183
Doyle, Kate, xiii, 40
Doyle, Roddy: ambitions of, 179; appeal of, 23–24; availability of, 2; biography of, 25–41; birth of, xi; childhood of, 26–28; critics and, 33, 164; education of, xi, 28–29, 177–78; fame and, 40–41, 150–52; family of, 27–28, 40, 152, 177–80; favorite books of, 167; film making of, xiii, 33–37; interview with, 149–83; maturity as novelist, 62, 98; pastimes of, 183; perspective of, 25–26; politics of, 38; on pregnancy, 152–54; reasons for writing, 173, 179; religion and, 39–40, 168–70; success of, 142; teaching experience of, xi, 29–30, 157, 170–71, 174–75; works about, 149; writing career of, 29–30; writing routine of, 166–67
Doyle, Rory (elder), 27–28, 177–78, 179
Doyle, Rory (younger), xii, 40, 152
drugs, 168–69
Dublin, 14–16, 42–43, 46–48, 49, 176–77, 185. *See also* Barrytown

East Enders (soap opera), 168
Easter 1916 Uprising, 184
economic oppression, 46
education, 28, 177–78
emasculation, 88
endorsements, 38
Evita (Parker film), 33

Fagan, Joey the Lips (fict.): character of, 43, 56; music and, 55; as parent figure, 61; religion and, 58–59; struggles of, 60

fame: Booker Prize and, 32; *The Commitments* and, 61; Doyle's view of, 149–50; family and, 40–41, 179–80; style and, 142

Fame (Parker film), 33

family: of Doyle, 27–28, 40, 152, 177–80; in Doyle's works, 16–18, 61, 142; humor and, 18, 20; significance of, 16–18. *See also* relationships

Family, The (Doyle miniseries) : airing of, xiii; basis for, 40; politics and, 13; as precursor, 6–7, 116; reception of, 32–33, 156–57; scripting of, 33; social viewpoint of, 39; violence and, 6–7, 180; writing/production of, 1–2, 155–56

Famine (O'Flaherty), 37, 145, 157–58

Fellini, Frederico, 161

feminism, 130–36

films: Barrytown trilogy, 1–2; *The Commitments*, xii, 33–34; directed by Frears, 35; directed by Parker, 33; Doyle on, 175–76; influence on Doyle, 161–62; *The Snapper*, xii, 34–35, 62; *The Van*, xiii, 35–36

Finn, Huck (fict.), 103–7, 112–14

Finnegans Wake (Joyce), 162

first-person narrative, 106–7, 116–19, 119–20, 143

focus: of *The Commitments*, 59–60; of *Famine*, 145; increasing seriousness of, 144–45; of *Paddy Clarke Ha Ha Ha*, 145; of *The Snapper*, 62; of *A Star Called Henry*, 145; of *The Van*, 83; of *The Woman Who Walked into Doors*, 140–41

Ford, Richard, 3, 163

Forrest Gump (Atkinson film), 162

Fox Searchlight, xiii

Francis (fict.), 99

Franklin, Aretha, 50

Franklin, Dan, xii, xiii, 31, 40

Frears, Stephen, 2, 4, 35–36, 175

Friel, Brian, 8

Gaelic oral tradition, 7–8, 181–83

Gleasdale, Alan, 155

Golden Bridge Orphanage, 153

Gorgias (Plato), 132

GPO, 184

Great Potato Famine, 157–58

Grifters, The (Frears film), 35

H Block hunger strikes, 172

Henry IV (Branagh film), 183

Henry V (Branagh film), 183

Hewson, Paul (pseud. Bono), 46

history: of blacks in America, 45, 46–47; development and, 137; influence on Barrytown, 12–13; of Ireland, 12–12, 47, 186; in *A Star Called Henry*, 185

homosexuality, 15

hope: in Doyle's works, 20–22; Jimmy Sr. and, 96; Paddy and, 115; Paula and, 140–41, 157

humor: comedy and, 18–20; in *The Commitments*, 43–44, 56–60, 166; definition of, 19; in Doyle's works, 142; family support and, 18, 20; in names, 176; in *Paddy Clarke Ha Ha Ha*, 109–10; in *The Snapper*, 62, 74–82; in *A Star Called Henry*, 186; in *The Van*, 89–90, 92, 97; in *The Woman Who Walked into Doors*, 128

identity: comedy and, 18–19;
    development of, 132; Jimmy's loss of,
    89–90; of Mrs. O'Leary, 118, 123, 137;
    patriarchal society and, 130–36;
    search for, 46, 118–20; sex and,
    132–33; stage names and, 49
"I Heard It" (song), 55
"I'll Feel a Whole Lot Better" (song),
    54
Imelda (fict.), 43, 56, 59, 61
impregnation scene, 74, 76, 83, 150–52
independence, 137
influences, 161–63
injustices, 20
intellectual curiosity, 121
IRA, 38, 172, 184–85
Ireland: attitudes in, 23; divorce
    referendum in, 111–12; education in,
    28–29, 177–78; history of, 12–13, 47,
    186; social/economic oppression in,
    46; unemployment in, 84
Irish Potato Famine, 37
Irish rebellion, 184
irony, 174–75
Irving, John, 7
isolation, 127–28, 136
"It's a Man's Man's Man's World," 55–56
It's a Man's World (film), 166

James (fict.), 59, 61
Jonathan Cape Publishers, xiii
Joyce, James: lack of influence on Doyle,
    7, 162, 163–64; Molly Bloom's credo,
    64; music and, 43–44; Stephen
    Dedalus's longing, 100–103

Kevin (fict.), 99, 102
Kilbarrack, xi, 26, 176–77

King Farouk Publishing, xi, 30–31
"Knock on Wood" (song), 55

La Frenais, Ian, 33–34
landlady (fict.), 138–39, 140
language: Doyle on, 181–83; Doyle's
    fascination with, 7–8; oral tradition
    and, 47; Paddy and, 101–3; as social
    power, 46–47; in *A Star Called Henry*,
    185; in *The Van*, 97; vocabulary used,
    3–4
Larry (fict.), 36
Lavin, Mary, 113
Leavy, Charles (fict.), 100, 108, 110
Leonard, Elmore, 2–3, 7, 182
Lessing, Doris, 62, 163, 167
Letter to Brezhnev, 162–63
Liam (fict.), 99, 108
literary divisions, 2–3, 182–83
literary influences, 7
Little Dorritt (Dickens), 168
Lord of the Flies (Golding), 110, 173–74
lyrics, 44, 50, 51–56

Maggie (fict.), 84, 92–93, 159
Marlowe, Stephen, 164
Mary Reilly (Frears film), 35
maturity/maturation: of Doyle's work, 98,
    143, 145–46; of Huck/Paddy, 105–6;
    humor and, 78–79
McEvoy, Ian (fict.), 99, 102
Meany, Colm, 175–76
memories, 116–19, 136–40
Mercier, Paul, xi–xii, 31–32
metaphor, 130–36
Mickah (fict.), 58, 60, 61
Miramax Films, xii
Mississippi Burning (Parker film), 33

money, 85–87, 92

Moran, Ira (fict.), 53

Morrison, Toni, 10

Morrison, Van, 166

movies. *See* films

multilayered works, 107–14

music: in *The Commitments*, 42–56, 165–66; Doyle's preferences, 40; source of, 182–83

My Beautiful Laundrette (Frears film), 35

Myles, Lynda, 35–36

My Life as a Dog (film), 161

"My Vocation" (Lavin), 113

names: changed for films, 175–76; choice of stage names, 49; humor/reality of, 176

narration, 106–7, 185

Natalie (fict.), 56

Night Train (film), 166

"Night Train" (song), 51–52

1916 Easter Uprising, 12

novels, 167. *See also Commitments, The; Paddy Clarke Ha Ha Ha; Snapper, The; Star Called Henry, A; Van, The; Woman Who Walked into Doors, The*

Nowhere to Run: The Story of Soul Music (Hirshey), 45, 166

Oates, Joyce Carol, 7, 163

O'Brien, Flann, 7, 102, 164

O'Carroll, Brendan, 4

O'Casey, Sean, 177

O'Connor, Flannery, 167

O'Farrell, Bickies (fict.), 131

O'Flaherty, Liam, 157–58

O'Leary, Derek (fict.), 123

O'Leary family (fict.), 118

O'Shea, Miss (fict.), 184

Olympia Theatre, xi–xii, 31

optimism: Jimmy's loss of, 89–90; of *The Snapper*, 74–77; throughout Doyle's work, 144; of *The Van*, 83

oral tradition, 7–8, 181–83

Outspan (fict.): character of, 57; role of, 42, 61; song for, 57; struggles of, 60

Paddy Clarke Ha Ha Ha (Doyle): Booker Prize for, xii, 1, 25, 32; characterization in, 99–107; components of, 142; criticism of, 5–6; distinctive qualities of, 143; focus of, 145; hope in, 20; introduction for, 162; mood of, 114–15; multilayered aspects of, 107–14; narrative tone of, 185; overview of, 5–6, 98–115; publication of, xii–xiii; religion and, 14, 169; research for, 103, 161; setting of, xi, 98; significance of, 115; social vision of, 21; spark for, 163; structure of, 98–99, 161; title of, 100; translations of, 1; violence in, 173–74; writing of, 173

Parker, Alan, 33, 175

Passion Machine, xi–xii, 31–32

paternity issue, 63, 66, 71, 78, 80

patriarchal society, 130–36

Penguin Books, Ltd., xii

perception, 103–4, 107

perspective, 25–28, 30

Persuasion (Austin), 174

pessimism, 22–23, 157

place, 10–11

plays, xi–xii, 2, 31–32

plots: of *Brownbread*, 31; of *The Commitments*, 42–43; of *The Snapper*, 62–64; of *A Star Called Henry*, 184; of *The Van*, 83–85; of

War, 31–32; of *The Woman Who Walked into Doors*, 119
poetic/artistic nature, 101–3
politics: abuse in, 13; in *The Commitments*, 45, 48; criticisms for lack of, 13; divorce referendum, 111–12; of Doyle, 38; in Doyle's works, 142; Doyle on, 170, 179–81; spousal abuse, 118, 130–36; unemployment, 95
popularity, 1–2, 32–33, 61
Portrait of the Artist as a Young Man (Joyce), 100–103
poverty, 32, 184
pregnancy: choice of as topic, 152–54; graphic details of, 66–67; maturity and, 69–70; optimism and, 74–76; in *A Proper Marriage*, 163; theme of *The Snapper*, 62–64
premature adulthood, 105–6
profanity, 3–4, 8–9, 13, 43
Proper Marriage, A (Lessing), 62, 163, 167
pruning, 171–72
pub, 86
publicity, 40
Pulp Fiction (film), 161
Puzo, Mario, 9

Rabbitte, 176
Rabbitte, Darren (fict.), 87; in *The Commitments*, 42; in *The Van*, 83–84, 86–87, 93, 96
Rabbitte, Georgina (fict.), 14, 71, 79, 83
Rabbitte, Jimmy, Jr. (fict.): character of, 42, 56–57; family and, 17; motivation of, 21; as parent figure, 61; politics and, 13; role of, 59; in *The Snapper*, 75; solutions of, 60; spotlight on, 4; sustaining qualities of, 142; in *The Van*, 83, 87, 96

Rabbitte, Jimmy, Sr. (fict.): alienation of, 86; Bimbo and, 144; comedy role of, 75; in *The Commitments*, 42; community and, 11, 86; compared to Paula, 129–30; decline of, 21; family and, 17; humor of, 77–78, 79–80; life of, 171; maturation of, 73; politics and, 13; relationships of, 69, 70–71; religion and, 14; Sharon and, 63–64, 67–68; in *The Snapper*, 4, 62, 71–73; sustaining qualities of, 143; tragedy of, 20; in *The Van*, 4, 83–97
Rabbitte, Leslie (fict.), 77, 84
Rabbitte, Linda (fict.), 42, 84, 93
Rabbitte, Sharon (fict.): as comic heroine, 62–68; in *The Commitments*, 42; community and, 11, 63, 68; compared to Paula, 129; drinking of, 170; family and, 17; humor of, 21, 77–78, 79; as individualized character, 68–71; maturation of, 69–71; politics and, 13; role of, 4, 73; sustaining qualities of, 142–43; tragedy of, 20; in *The Van*, 84, 87, 93, 96
Rabbitte, Tracy (fict.), 42, 84, 93
Rabbitte, Veronica (fict.): in *The Commitments*, 42; reading of, 174; significance as family member, 17; in *The Snapper*, 75, 77; in *The Van*, 83, 87–88, 93, 96
Ragtime (Doctorow), 167
rape, 74–77, 150–52
readers, 33, 61, 75, 164
reality: basis of characters, 11–12; Doyle's depiction of, 144, 152–54, 163, 171; of names, 176; prominence of, 22; religion and, 169; in soaps, 168
redundancy, 83–92, 144, 154. *See also* unemployment
Reinventing Shakespeare (Taylor), 164

relationships: in *The Commitments*, 61; in communities, 70; in *The Family*, 156; humor and, 77–78, 79; of Jimmy Sr. and Bimbo, 93–96; in *Paddy Clarke Ha Ha Ha*, 99–100, 110–12, 114–15; in Rabbitte family, 71–74, 92–93; slave/master form, 135–36; in *The Snapper*, 68–69, 79; in *A Star Called Henry*, 185; in *The Van*, 86–88, 92–93, 96; in *The Woman Who Walked into Doors*, 118, 123–27, 124–27, 137–39

religion: Catholic politics, 38–39; in *The Commitments* film, 34; criticisms for lack of, 14–16; in Doyle's works, 142; Doyle on, 168, 169; Doyles and, 179; humor and, 58–59; in *Paddy Clarke Ha Ha Ha*, 106, 112–14; in *The Snapper*, 81; soul music and, 50

research, 103, 129, 160–61

resiliency, 140, 142–43

reviews: of *The Commitments*, 30–31; of Doyle's work, 1; of *The Family*, 32; of plays, 32; of *A Star Called Henry*, 164; of *The Van* film, 36; of *The Van*, 32, 83. *See also* criticism

revolution, 145

rhythm, 50

Rushdie, Salman, 2, 182

screenplays, 36–37, 157–58, 167

Secker & Warburg Ltd., xii

self-esteem: abuse and, 136; Jimmy Sr. and, 84–89, 92–93; Paula and, 123–26, 126–28

self-hatred, 131

Sense and Sensibility (Austin), 174

setting: of the Barrytown trilogy, 10–12; of *The Commitments*, 42; of *Paddy Clarke Ha Ha Ha*, 98; of *A Star Called Henry*,

185; of *The Van*, 83; of *The Woman Who Walked into Doors*, 6

sex, 186

sexual power, 132–33

SFX Centre, xi–xii, 31–32

Shakespeare, William, 164

Sicilian, The (Puzo), 9

Sinn Fein, 172

slang, 8–9

slapstick situation comedy, 57–58. *See also* comedy

Sloper, Jillsey (fict.), 128

Smart, Henry (fict.), 184, 185

smoking, 168, 171

Snapper, The (Doyle): allegory of, 81; as comedy, 143; components of, 142; criticism of, 169; Doyle on, 150–52; as entertainment, 2; film of, xii; focus of, 62; hope in, 20, 96; overview of, 4–5, 62–83; plot of, 62–64; publication of, xii; reception of, 40–41, 165; religion in, 14; research for, 160–61; social vision of, 21; spark for, 163; writing of, xi, 32, 154, 173

Snapper, The (film), 34–35, 62, 151, 175–76

soaps, 168

soccer, 183

social oppression, 46

social realism, 143–44, 145

social vision, 20–23, 44, 59–60

soul music, 42–53, 165. *See also* music

Sound and Fury, The (Faulkner), 98, 155

Spanish sailor (fict.), 63, 65–66, 162–63

Spencer, Charlo (fict.): character of, 6–7, 116; courtship of, 123–24, 128–29; in *The Family*, 156; patriarchal society and, 134–36; Paula and, 117–18, 126–27; violence of, 125–26

Spencer, Jack (fict.), 127, 140–41, 156

Spencer, Leanne (fict.), 127

Spencer, Nicola (fict.), 118, 126, 127, 156

Spencer, Paula (fict.): alcoholism of, 154–55; Charlo and, 117–18; compared to Jimmy Sr., 96; courtship of, 123–24, 128–29; creation of, 116; Doyle on, 158; in *The Family,* 156; family and, 17–18; as four characters, 120–26; patriarchal society and, 130–36; role of, 6–7; salvation of, 126–28; search for identity, 118–20; sustaining qualities of, 143; tragedy of, 20–22; voice of, 185

spousal abuse: choice of as topic, 155; Doyle on, 180; emotional aspects, 130–36; identity and, 123–26; self-esteem and, 136; in *The Woman Who Walked into Doors,* 118

St. Fintain's Christian Brothers School, 28

Star Called Henry, A (Doyle): focus of, 145; language in, 182, 185; overview of, 7, 33, 184–86; reception of, 1; release of, xiii; research for, 161; setting of, 185

Stephen Hero (Joyce), 162

storytelling, 33, 47, 181–83

structure: of *Paddy Clarke Ha Ha Ha,* 5–6, 161; of *The Woman Who Walked into Doors,* 6–7

style, 2–4, 56–57, 106

style indirect libre, 106

success: in commerce, 1–2; of *The Commitments,* 61; Doyle's reaction to, 32, 35; future of, 145; international fame, 142. *See also* fame

superstitions, 104–5

Sutton, John, 30–31, 173

Synge, John Millington, 5–6

Taylor, Gary, 164

teaching experience, xii, 29–30, 157, 170–71, 174–75

teen drunkenness, 170–71

television miniseries: airing of, xiii; miniseries for, 6–7, 39, 116, 155; ratings of, 32–33; violence in, 180

Thatcherism, 95, 172

trademarks, 43–44

tragedy, 83, 96

transformation, 126–28

transitional work, 96

translations, 1

Translations (Friel), 8

Travelers, 159–60

trends, 20–23, 144–45, 154–58

truth, 136–40

Twain, Mark, 103–7

20th Century Fox Film Corporation, xii

Tyler, Anne, 3, 7, 53, 167

Ulysses (Joyce), 162, 163

unemployment, 84–92, 154, 180. *See also* redundancy

unity, 50–52, 54, 78–80

University College, xi, 29

validation, 137

Van, The (Doyle): Booker Prize short list for, 1; closing scene of, 158; components of, 142; criticism of, 165, 171; focus of, 83; hope in, 20; importance of, 97; overview of, 4–5, 83–97; plot of, 83–85; politics in, 13; publication of, xii; reality in, 144; research for, 160; setting of, 83; significance of family in, 17; social

Van, The (cont.)
vision of, 21; as transitional work,
143–44; writing of, xii, 32, 152, 154
Van, The (film): approach to, 35–36;
casting of, 175; Doyle on, 159–60;
name changes for, 175–76; US
promotion of, 176
verbal power, 46–47
vignettes, 98
Viking Penguin Books, xii–xiii
Viking Press, Inc., xiii
Vintage Contemporaries, xii
violence: children and, 109–10, 173–74;
Doyle on, 159–60, 180; self-esteem
and, 136; spousal abuse, 32, 118,
123–26, 130–36
Vlach, Michael, 46
voice: difficulty with, 173; in Doyle's
works, 142; of Paula, 119; unreliability
of, 185; of women, 134

"Walking in the Rain" (song), 56
War (Doyle play), xii, 2
Waring, Michael, 155
Wesley, Fred, 48, 49
"What Becomes of the Broken-Hearted"
(song), 50–51
wife beating. *See* spousal abuse
Wildlife (Ford), 163
William Heinemann Ltd., xii, 31, 42
Williams-Jones, Pearl, 50

Willis, Ellen, 134
Wise Blood (O'Connor), 167
Woman Who Walked into Doors, The (Doyle):
basis of, 33; characterization in,
117–36; complexity of, 144;
components of, 142; distinctive
qualities of, 143; focus of, 140–41;
hope in, 154, 157; message of,
140–41; metaphor of, 130–36;
narrative tone of, 185; overview of,
6–7, 116–41; plot of, 119; precursor
to, 116; publication of, xiii; reception
of, 1, 116; research for, 161; setting of,
6; significance of family in, 17–18;
social vision of, 21–22; structure of,
117–19; teachers in, 28; truth vs.
memory in, 136–40; writing of,
173
words: *dead leg*, 162; *foetus*, 162; *fuck*, 182;
Paddy and, 101–3; power of, 46–47;
pruning, 162; *slut*, 133; *stuff*, 174; use of
liberal, 181
World According to Garp, The (Irving), 128,
167
writing: Doyle's routine for, 166–67;
Doyle on, 158, 160, 164; reasons for,
173, 179; styles of, 3

Yeats, William Butler, 7
Your Granny Is a Hunger Striker (Doyle), xi,
30, 172–73